Bastard Culture!

How User Participation
Transforms Cultural Production

Mirko Tobias Schäfer

Amsterdam University Press

MediaMatters is a series published by Amsterdam University Press on current debates about media technology and practices. International scholars critically analyse and theorize the materiality and performativity, as well as spatial practices of screen media in contributions that engage with today's digital media culture.
For more information about the series, please visit: www.aup.nl

The open-access-publication of this book is made possible by a grant from the Research Institute for History and Culture (OGC).
The research is made possible by the Department of Media and Culture Studies (MCW) and the Research Institute for History and Culture (OGC) at Utrecht University.

Cover illustration: Axel Swoboda
Cover design: Suzan Beijer, Amersfoort
Lay out: Philos, Almere

ISBN   978 90 8964 256 1
e-ISBN   978 90 4851 315 4
NUR   670

Bastard Culture!

Table of Contents

Acknowledgements

I am indebted to many people who in one way or another contributed to realizing this work. I must pay tribute to the people at the Department for Media Studies (MCW), and at the Research Institute for Culture and History (OGC) at Utrecht University for supporting not only my research, but also for providing me with an open-minded, friendly, and intellectually stimulating environment.

I want to thank my colleagues at the New Media & Digital Culture (NMDC). At countless occasions I benefited from their knowledge and wisdom. I thank Frank Kessler and Joost Raessens for their efforts in overseeing this venture and guiding my often unorganised thoughts into direction of a more solid argument. I am also very grateful for the helpful comments and remarks I have received numerous times from Marianne van den Boomen, Bernhard Rieder, William Uricchio, and Imar de Vries. I am also indebted to my research students Lisette van Blokland, Jaap Kok, Vlad Micu, Pascal Rancuret, and Javier Sancho Rodriguez for numerous interviews with members from the homebrew and console gaming scene, as well as for their hands-on investigation of homebrew software and modded game consoles. My thanks also to Steph Harmon for her careful editing and the staff at Amsterdam University Press, especially Inge van der Bijl for smoothly managing this project, and Jeroen Sondervan for his indefatigable support and prospective view on copyrights and publishing in the digital age.

Many people have been important, at one stage or the other by giving feedback and commenting on concepts and/or unfinished chapters and half-baked ideas: Aibopet, Florian Cramer, Andreas Leo Findeisen, Frank Hartmann, Patrick Kranzlmüller, Franz Lehner, Koen Leurs, Geert Lovink, Dennis Jaromil Rojo, Douglas Rushkoff, Tanja Sihvonen, Kim de Vries. I also thank Jesse Darlin, Ralf Futselaar, Pepita Hesselberth, Jim Hurley, Boris May, Nancy Mauro-Flude, Audrey Samson, Peter Steinberger, Axel Swoboda, Nanna Verhoeff, and Florian Waldvogel, and of course my family for their support. Finally my gratitude goes to Eva Stegeman.

Introduction
Yet Another Media Revolution

The desktop revolution has brought the tools that only professionals have had into the hands of the public. God knows what will happen now (Marvin Minsky, Time 1983).

In 1983, Time magazine nominated the PC as the 'Machine of the Year'. The edition's title, 'The Computer Moves In', announced the Information Age's entry into our living rooms. On the cover, a man sits alienated in front of his new roommate. What he plans to do with the computer or what the machine might do to him is not quite clear. In January 2007, a computer was again displayed on the Time cover, but this time the computer screen is a mirror reflecting the 'Person of the Year': 'Yes, You. You Control the Information Age. Welcome to Your World'. The cover is a symbol of the emancipation of the computer user from the alienated user of 1983 to the 'hero of the Information Age' in 2007.

The attention devoted to the computer in 1983 marks an important milestone in the emergence of what has become known as the 'information society'. What started as a secret technology for military research – an accounting machine in scientific laboratories and corporate companies, advanced technology initially unthinkable as a mass-produced consumer good – suddenly entered the lives and homes of common users as the microcomputer.

With this microcomputer, users had a high-tech device at their disposal, a machine which was able to execute every task provided in a symbolic language the machine can understand. Over the past two decades, the computer has developed into an everyday medium. Due to easy-to-use interfaces and the Internet, which has increased the reach and use of computers globally, computer use has become common everyday practice. The 24-year interval between the two editions of Time magazine bridges the gap between the introduction of the computer into the consumer sphere and the emergence of a new global cultural practice. Several trends during this time span ultimately shaped the contemporary cultural practice of computer use:

1. The computer developed into a medium for work, leisure and entertainment
2. The Internet became the primary means to connect computers, thereby constituting a world-wide information infrastructure
3. The emergence of the World Wide Web (WWW) which, with its graphical user interfaces and hypertext structures, made networked computers a useful tool for common users and consequently became a mass medium by 1995
4. Most recently, in concert with the above, broad-band Internet connections

and related services enabled users to publish, organize and share large quantities of data online.

The result we are witnessing today, emphasized in the above-mentioned edition of *Time* magazine, is referred to as 'participatory culture', which describes the new role users have assumed in the context of cultural production.[1] But the new media practice didn't immediately manifest itself on such a large scale. Despite the attention the microcomputer received in the 1980s, it remained a tool used primarily in offices or as a gadget for enthusiastic early adopters often referred to as 'nerds', who developed an understanding of the computer and its applications that very much shaped the way personal computers are perceived today. The machine initially developed for solving complex and repetitive arithmetic problems thus developed into a common office device, and subsequently into an everyday medium for consumers who can use it for practically anything that can be formulated as an algorithmic process, from filing tax returns to organizing holiday pictures. The Internet and its successful application, the World Wide Web (WWW), have been crucial in this development.[2] The WWW has enabled large media audiences to recognize the computer as a handy tool for communication, entertainment and leisure activities. Software like web browsers, which embed networking in a graphical user interface, and attractive services such as web-based e-mail, chat programs, online communities, and Internet forums have increased the computer's appeal to a large group of consumers. The Internet has diffused aspects of the computer so that not only machines but also people have become globally connected, and the networked computer is now a commonly used medium in Western industrialized countries.[3]

Participation has become a key concept used to frame the emerging media practice. It considers the transformation of former audiences into active participants and agents of cultural production on the Internet. Popular media acclaimed the new possibilities for consumers to actively create and produce media content. Users became explicitly active participants in the cultural production thanks to the latest WWW developments. The buzzword 'Web 2.0', coined by publisher Tim O'Reilly in 2005, actually described a set of web technologies, often abbreviated as AJAX for 'asynchronous Java and XML', that facilitate easy publishing and content sharing, as well as the establishment of social networks. Web 2.0 applications have been attracting a multitude of users, pushing the trend towards socialization and the creation of 'user-generated content' (UGC). In 2010, about 73 percent of American teenagers and young adults online use social networking sites (SNSs) such as Facebook or MySpace (Lenhardt et al. 2010). As early as 2006, every third American Internet user had participated in categorizing or organizing online content by adding meta-data (Rainie 2007). These figures seem to confirm the perception of the increased capability of users to participate in cultural production.

However, the enthusiasm about user activities is, as I will argue, somewhat premature and rather unbalanced, because it often neglects the fact that underlying power structures are not necessarily reconfigured. Although the new media practice challenges some established business models, it does not necessarily make the industries exploiting those models disappear. In the cultural industries, traditional companies not only adapt and attempt to change business models accordingly or develop new ways of earning revenues; it is also evident that new enterprises emerge and gain control over cultural production and intellectual property in a manner very similar to the monopolistic media corporations of the 20th century. The powerful 'culture industry' is therefore not overturned by an alleged revolution of users. It is undeniable that there are fundamental transformations of user-producer relations, markets and politics unfolding. This book describes the consequences of user participation as an extension of the cultural industries. The interactions between users and corporations, and the connectivity between markets and media practices, are inherently intertwined and constitute something I have brashly dubbed 'bastard culture' to indicate how the most heterogeneous participants and practices are blended together.

Users were granted new possibilities for cultural production that were previously inaccessible to consumers of industrially produced goods and mass media: media content could be produced, published and distributed by amateurs on a global scale at negligible cost. Internet users could maintain weblogs[4], publish photos, edit videos, engage in online communities, exchange music files on a global scale and cooperate in editing encyclopedic knowledge and software programming. Chapter 1 analyses how these activities are tied to a rhetoric of progress which promised social progress through technological advancement. In order to promote these new technologies, they have been deliberately put forward as enabling technologies capable of empowering passive consumers and disadvantaged citizens around the globe to let them actively participate in media productions and market activities.

The Internet has therefore also become a platform for discussion and political debate. The online encyclopaedia Wikipedia and the open-source operating system GNU/Linux can be seen as a collective production of knowledge and artefacts. Fan culture communities collect, store and distribute media texts produced by the traditional culture industry and add their own productions and comments to these shared archives.[5] Beyond the production channels of conventional industries, users create their own media texts, for example fictional texts, videos, radio programs, music, software and the like, and distribute them on the Internet. The *netlabel scene* or the computer demoscene can be seen as exemplary of cultural production taking place outside of the confines of the media industry while not necessarily being related to its products at all (e.g. Tasajärvi 2004; Timmers 2005; Reunanen 2010). Chapter 2 explains how these user activities constitute an extension of the cultural industries into the realm of users and reveals a twofold meaning of user participation as explicit and implicit participation.

The technological qualities of computers, the Internet and software are crucial constituents for the emerging participatory culture. Software is as modifiable as any product, that is, it can be changed, extended, and used in different contexts, but software has special qualities which especially encourage its modification and distribution. Furthermore, the technical design of computers, the Internet and software reveals social values and either stimulates or represses various media practices. These technological qualities are analysed in chapter 3.

An extensive set of case studies in chapter 4 shows how participatory culture unfolds heterogeneously between a multitude of users, various corporations, communities and organizations, and different mindsets and social contexts. User activities are clearly distinguished as explicit and implicit participation. The explicit participation becomes most easily recognizable in the deliberate and conscious appropriation of products on the fringes of the cultural industries.[6] User communities meet online and engage collectively in software development projects. This has an effect on all software-based products, since users can suit them to their needs. A Microsoft Xbox becomes a Linux computer.[7] Nintendo's Game Boy gets turned into a music instrument,[8] and Sony's robot dog AIBO learns how to dance.[9] Users change software-based consumer goods by altering their original design. Software design and user appropriation reveal processes of interaction between the many participants in contemporary media practice: the often accidental collaboration or the many conflicts caused by user activities lead to the collisions of old business models with new practices. While old business models struggle with the explicit participation of users, new business models thrive on their implicit participation. Here, user activities are embedded into the software design of web applications benefiting from what users do with and on those platforms. Simply through using platforms such as Flickr, YouTube or Facebook, or services such as Google and Amazon, users create value and often actively contribute to the improvement of services and information management.

Chapter 5 revolves around the different consequences of the new technologies and media practices for markets and politics. How do companies deal with the new challenges emerging from participating users? The possible dynamics of user-producer relations are analysed in terms of confrontation, implementation and integration. These dynamics raise debates on the regulation and legalization of emerging computer applications and user activities, and in turn, this regulation and legalization shape society's perception of these technologies.

The availability of computers and the Internet expands the traditional culture industry into the domain of users, who actively participate in the cultural production, either by appropriating products from the commercial domain or by creating their own. However, while user activities constitute a significant loss of control for certain sectors of traditional media industries – especially in the area of distribution – the larger cultural industries benefit from user-driven innovation through the appropriation of corporate design. Furthermore, the media industry is undergoing a shift from creating content to providing platforms for user-driven social interactions and user-generated content. In these extended cultural industries, participation unfolds not only in the co-creation of media content and software-based products, but also in the development and defence of distinctive media practices that represent a socio-political understanding of new technologies.

The aim of this book is to reveal the constituents of the emerging participatory culture and provide an analysis that is not blurred by either utopian or cultural pessimistic assumptions. I will briefly map the discourses shaping the public understanding of participation and show to what extent it affects the perception and development of technology. Analysing the role of technology reveals discursive elements inscribed into technical design and how it can either repress or stimulate certain media practices. These practices are then analysed in case studies, which clarify to what extent users actually participate in design development, and to what extent companies, users, and technology are interconnected.

As a consequence of these new media practices, different dynamics are unfolding that are either aimed at confronting user activities and preventing them from challenging established business models, or attempt to implement them into new revenue models, or to integrate the new practices in socio-political responsible ways into technological design and its various uses.

Don't believe the hype!

Participation is part of a discourse that advocates social progress through technological development as well as aims to create expectations and understanding for technology. This discourse is related to the struggle against exclusion from political decision-making processes, as well as exclusion from ownership of the means of production and the creation of media content. The promise of social progress and a reconfiguration of power through participation is embedded in technological development and postulated anew with each 'media revolution' (Daniels 2002; Flichy 2007; Turner 2006). Many user activities seem to confirm the expectation raised by references to participation in popular discourse, and many design decisions are directly affected by the claim for and promise of broad access to information and information technologies. This discourse constructed a moral framing of participation which developed blind spots with regard to analysing different levels of use and design. There is an intellectual short cut that far too readily perceives increased user activity as a fundamental shift in power structures within the cultural industries. In consequence, many accounts of user participation romanticize user activities and overestimate the user's capacity of action. Contrary to this, the aim of this book is to step outside the morally biased perception of participation. Defining participatory culture merely within a morally determined framework, and associating participation only with positive connotations, is highly problematic. Proponents of such a perspective neglect to acknowledge the roots of what is in fact a long tradition of claiming participation and expecting social progress through technological development, and become uncritical of the meta discourse of participation.

They also develop a blind spot for another shift taking place within cultural production: the transformation of media corporations from content producers to platform providers for user-created content. One may ask to what extent the many user activities that were first described as a process of emancipation have been integrated into new business models and are subsequently subject to corporate control. In addition, participatory culture cannot be reduced to user activity alone. Machine processes and software routines contribute to production as well, and actively engage with users. The hybrid quality features of information systems assign participatory agency to software design and generate many of the unfolding activities as the result of collective interactions between machines and users. Consequently, another often-marginalized aspect is the role of technology itself. The specific qualities of the technology stimulate or repress certain uses and thus influence the way technologies are used and implemented by consumers in society. These features affect both design and user appropriation. Technology cannot be treated as a neutral black box. When examining technology, it becomes evident that engineering culture as well as a specific socio-political mindset is inherent in its design. Socio-political debates, regulations and the promise of participation can be translated into design decisions.

What has been called 'participatory culture' is actually a complex discourse consisting of the following factors:

a. a rhetoric that advocates social progress through technological advancement
b. a cultural critique demanding the reconfiguration of power relations
c. the qualities of related technologies, and
d. how these qualities are used for design and user appropriation
e. the socio-political dynamics related to using the technologies

This book examines the constitutional aspects of contemporary media practice as they unfold and provides an analysis of participatory culture. In tracing the many aspects involved in the construction of current media practice, my research will identify and analyse the constituents of a participatory culture, thus providing a comprehensive understanding of the complex relations involved in the development of online cultural production. This research will also analyse the constituents of contemporary media practice, framed as a participatory culture, by exploring the relationship between material aspects of technology and the social use, the unfolding debates and the dissent that exists with respect to the use and implementation of new media practices. In order to address the question for the various constituents of a participatory culture as a whole, the following sub-themes will be treated in five individual chapters:

1. Participation as the promise of new media
2. New practices of participation and how to analyse them

3. How technological design affects user participation in digital culture
4. How users appropriate software-based products, develop new media practices and innovate design
5. How new media practices and user participation transform markets and business models in the cultural industries

In the conclusion, questions are raised as to how contemporary media practice can be integrated into socio-political regulation, and whether it will be possible to connect it to a participatory democracy.

This book focuses on specific qualities of technology, designers, users and social perceptions of technology and its use. Rather than adhering strictly to one established approach, the theoretical framework I've used consists of aspects from different approaches.

Analysing participatory culture

The enthusiasm about user participation resembles a veil behind which the actual constituents of participatory activities in cultural production are hidden. Participatory culture is not achieved simply by employing new technologies and should not be reduced to its symptoms, that is, users taking part in the processes of production and distribution. Rather, the phenomenon unfolds on different levels: the promise of participation that constitutes a rhetoric of progress employed for promoting computer technology and the Internet. Claiming participation is an inherent element of scholarly commentary on media practices. Here, media and media practices are rated according to their alleged potential of empowering consumers and enabling political activism. Somewhat hastily, this discourse considered the emerging media practices as fulfilling this promise. But the question of participation also unfolds on the level of technology's basic features. Therefore, technology cannot be perceived as being either neutral or socially and culturally determining with regard to its use and effect. Technology also has to be acknowledged as being discursive, or at least as something which represents the ongoing discourse on participation. In analysing technology, socio-political debates, values and social programmes are revealed in its design. Analysing participation therefore requires an analytical approach that considers discourses, media practices and technological design. Within these domains, participation will be revealed as a legend, as a political claim, as an actual media practice and as a design solution that either stimulates and even channels certain uses or represses various practices.

Looking at participation in terms of 'media dispositives' means that the various aspects, both discursive and non-discursive, human or non-human, would be related to each other by power structures, knowledge about technology and its design and appropriation, the discursive representation of socio-political issues, and the transformations taking place through the interaction and relation of all participants. According to Foucault, a 'dispositif' consists of 'discourses, institutions, architectural forms, regulatory decisions, laws, administrative measures, scientific statements, philosophical, moral and philanthropic propositions – in short, the said as much as the unsaid' (Foucault 1980:194-195).[10] In spite of the differences, one can say that a dispositif describes formations of various participants. Foucault employed it in order to analyse medical, legal and socio-political discourses, for example, as well as the formation of power relations in and through such discourse. The concept has been further developed into a dynamic set of interacting connections (Deleuze 1992) and more broadly defined as a concept of 'in-between' formulated by Peeters and Charlier (1999, cit. in Kessler 2006:4).

The use of theoretical tools such as the concept of the dispositif as it has been coined in media studies helps to avoid merely focusing on hermeneutic readings of media content and also takes economical, institutional and social contexts into consideration.[11] In the context of this study, the notion of the dispositif is also open to elements such as participation, playfulness and even sensual experiences in the analysis of any given media dispositif. It offers the possibility of understanding the 'in-between' as the capacity of action, the transformations and transactions between the various aspects of 'the said and the unsaid.' Looking at participation in its various forms in the domain of digital media in light of the dispositif means to describe a variety of formations of different relations between three domains, namely the domain of discourses (popular, scholarly, bureaucratic, legal...), technology (basic features and design) and people and social use (what users actually do with the new technologies).

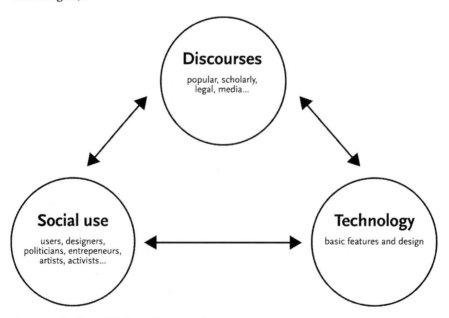

Figure 1. The dispositif of participatory culture.

Discourses, technology and social use are all interrelated and transform the meaning of participation itself, as well as the meaning of related technologies, their socio-political framing and their legal regulation (see fig. 1). As figure 1 shows, discourses, technologies and social use (actions) reciprocally affect each other. This perspective represents a macro level, however. When zooming in on the dispositif of participation, as I do in the case studies in chapter 4, the macro level reveals a set of relations and interactions that can be understood as actor-networks. In order to further analyse these relations, I employ terminology derived from actor-network theory (ANT) (Latour 2005). Developed by Madeline Akrich, Michel Callon, Bruno Latour and John Law, ANT offers a different understanding of technology as well as a practical terminology and a set of methods that have to be considered when researching the use of artefacts. For ANT, Latour points out, neither the social nor society are given assumptions (2005:37), rather they have to be 'reassembled' in the translations an actor-network reveals. One example of an assumed stable factor explaining online cultural phenomena is the metaphor of the 'community', which is often used as the equivalent for the social constellation of family, friends or neighbourhood communities in real life in order to describe social interaction and the construction of meaning in virtual life (e.g. Rheingold 1993; Turkle 1997; Jenkins 2002; Benkler 2006). In light of information systems, which are used by a large number of people who often do not communicate with each other, the term 'community' is no longer sufficient to explain online cultural production.

Another important aspect drawn from ANT is the consideration of non-human actors and their agency as active contributors to the constitution of participatory culture. While analysing how users appropriated the Xbox, the proprietary Microsoft software development kit appeared as a crucial non-human actor. Following the traces of the Xbox software development kit (XDK), which was initially issued only to licensed partners of Microsoft but eventually leaked out to a broader public, reveals an entire actor-network of appropriation. Mapping the various actors relates the hacking of game consoles directly to the design development at Microsoft and to an emerging and lucrative grey market for modified computer chips for the Microsoft Xbox. This actor-network, in other words, consists of a variety of actors, such as Microsoft, the software development kit, various hacker teams, manifold websites of the console gaming community, producers and distributors of modified chips.

One explicit assumption made by ANT is the increasingly evanescent distinction between culture and technology (e.g. Akrich 1992; Latour 1991; 1992), which affirms the heterogeneity of our *Lebenswelt*, and the hybrid alliances established within that world. It recognizes relations, labeled as networks, consisting of human and non-human actors and does not significantly differentiate between the two during an initial analysis. In following and tracing actors, non-human actors are handled in the same way as human ones and vice versa. The aspects, human and non-human actors, involved in the failing of a large military aviation project are analysed by Callon and Law (1992). Using the example of a science project in the Amazon forest, Latour explains the interrelating chains constructing scientific artefacts, established by methods, tools, categorization and mapping (Latour 1999). ANT describes all related aspects as 'actors', whether human or non-human, and tries to flesh out their relations by monitoring their 'traces'.

In this book I map various actor-networks in the appropriation of electronic consumer goods. Naturally, the scope of such a network is limited, and the mapping does not represent all possible actors and interactions. I deliberately limit it to selected key actors that appear to be crucial in constituting the heterogeneous and hybrid nature of participatory culture as analysed in the chosen cases. A larger scope of social interactions and collective production unfolds in socio-technical ecosystems. Here, users interact not only with each other on web applications, they also interact with the software design and the underlying structure of databases and information management systems. The term socio-technical ecosystem is derived from the concept of a 'socio-technical system', used in management studies and organizational development to describe the interaction of people and technology in workplaces (e.g. Berg 1997; Monarch et al. 1997). Socio-technical ecosystems describe an environment based on information technology that facilitates and cultivates the performance of a great number of users. Design and user activities are mutually intertwined and dependent in order to improve the overall system. The term socio-technical ecosystem aims to emphasize its hybrid character and increasingly complex system-wide performance. The photo-sharing website Flickr constitutes such a socio-technical ecosystem. A system-wide plurality of users is actively engaging in Flickr, but behind the graphical user interfaces on the Flickr servers, information management systems react to user activity. Socio-technical ecosystems can easily be incorporated into other systems. Flickr is connected to the Yahoo search engine and influences search requests for images by delivering results, matching the Yahoo user's search request with keywords generated by Flickr users when uploading their photos. Like actor-networks, socio-technical ecosystems are also subject to the overall dispositif of participation. It can be an actor-within-an-actor-network, while at the same time consisting of actor-networks itself.

Employing the concept of dispositif, mapping participants as actor-networks and describing web applications and their users as socio-technical ecosystems, I provide an analytical framework to cover complexity and dynamic interconnections of the different constituents of participatory culture. Tracing the constituents of participatory culture can best be compared with an undercover detective's work analysing a syndicate. In that respect, it recalls McLuhan's notion of the 'suspended judgement', which is described as 'the technique of starting with the thing to be discovered and working back, step by step, as on an assembly line, to the point at which it is necessary to start in order to reach the desired object' (McLuhan 1964:69). This research therefore disavows a hasty enthusiasm for users being turned into heroes. Instead, I start by following the different lines along which participatory culture unfolds, beginning with discussions about participation regarding its material foundations to actual media practice and its effect on established ways of cultural production. By examining the meaning of technology, the discourse represents socio-political debates, expectations and attempts for regulation and implementing technology into society itself. As philosopher of technology Andrew Feenberg says, 'Technologies of course do have a casual aspect, but they also have a symbolic aspect that is determining for their use and evolution' (1999:84). Technologies have a function as well as a meaning, and if the meaning is lacking, the technology is liable to become inoperable as well. The social relations, ideology, desires and political claims can be found in the artefact's design (see e.g. Latour 1991). The actual social use of software, software-based products and Internet technologies will be analysed according to three procedures that shape technology: affordance, design and appropriation. These are terms which differentiate specific aspects in technology development according to the actors involved.

Affordance describes the specificity of technology. Donald Norman introduced the term affordance to describe the very aspects that channel consumers' use (1998). Affordances delineate the fundamental properties that determine how an object could be used (1998:9). He uses a chair as an example of how the design suggests one sits on it. Norman refers in general to the design of objects, which he calls 'everyday things', but exceeds that meaning by assigning a material aspect to the concept of affordance. He uses terminology from psychology to refer to the material aspects of an object and the stuff of which it is made. He gives the example of British Railways experiencing acts of vandalism in their shelters. The glass panels were smashed and the plywood-panelled shelters were defaced by graffiti. Norman blames the psychology of materials, since glass, besides providing transparency to look through, can also be broken, and flat, smooth surfaces can be used not only for building a shelter but are also appropriate for being written on (1998:9). This material aspect, called affordance, determines the design in the first place, before it affects the appropriation by users. Material aspects have to be considered when analysing the way users might use, change, and modify the designed object. Affordance describes two characteristics, the material aspects, or the specificity of an object or a technology, and the affordance imposed on it through the design.

Design describes the creation and shaping of artefacts. Design creates its own affordances but is also subject to the affordances of the materials utilized. The design process usually involves an evaluation of the specific features of materials used for a designated object, and an evaluation of the user's appropriation to be incorporated into a next level of development. However, software affords many more opportunities for appropriation than other artefacts, which opens a multitude of possible modifications. Furthermore, the process of design is influenced by the engineer's specific social context and socio-political mindset.

Appropriation means that users integrate technology into their everyday practices, adapting and sometimes transforming its original design. It covers the use, the modification, the reuse and further development of artefacts in ways often unforeseen by the original designers (Dix 2007). Reacting to the initial design of an artefact and changing it according to other needs has been described as a common consumer and user activity (Pacey 1983). The material aspects of Internet culture and the effective possibilities for collaboration have only aggravated this practice on a global scale. Appropriation is related to affordance, because the material characteristics and the design choices affect the act of appropriation. Design and the specific material qualities form the basis for use and appropriation.

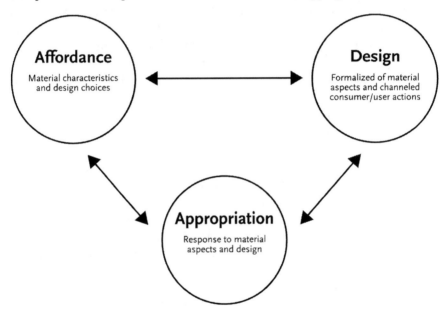

Figure 2. Affordance, appropriation and design.

As shown in figure 2, affordance, appropriation and design are interdependent. Affordance exists in both, namely the specific material features used for design, and in the design process, which also constitutes affordance. Design is the formalization of anticipated user activities through the use of certain materials or technologies and the shaping of these into artefacts that constitute the designated affordances. The challenge for design is to employ material characteristics accordingly. A prototypical example of contradictory design will be presented in the case of the Microsoft Xbox, a game console that actually had the typical characteristics of a personal computer but was limited, due to its design, to the functionality of a game console. Users hacked and modified the game console in ways unintended by the vendor. Microsoft learned from these acts of user appropriation and formalized several aspects into the design of the next game console, the Xbox 360, aiming to include several forms of game console use and attempting to exclude others that

BASTARD CULTURE!

were more efficient than the older design. The labour of user communities, their innovations and their way of using a device were then formalized into new design decisions and therefore implemented in further developments. During all stages of development, the involved participants can be professional designers employed by a company, individual users, a collective of enthusiastic students, or a user community, a team of hackers and so on; all of these participants are users and producers.

Tracing participation

Tracing the relations and activities that take place can be achieved by following as many actors as possible and examining the media texts and artefacts produced within various formations of the dispositif of participation. The various actors explored in each case are subject to the general formations of discourses, individual people, communities, and technologies as outlined in the dispositif. Actual media practices and software designs are revisited in relation to the promise and claim of participation, and its socio-political implications. Technically, this research was conducted through an explorative analysis, starting with the media attention for participation and agenda setting for new technologies, to the hidden connections between various participants and the agency of material aspects that so often are easily overlooked. At a practical level, this research proceeded by analysing the popular discourse with respect to cultural references (metaphors, associations, images) that are employed to promote new media. As for the appropriation of technology, examples were chosen in order to analyse how users actually alter software-based products. The research was conducted through interviews, analysis of design and appropriation processes, examination of the ways specific appropriations were represented in the media, and the initial definition of the original designers and the legal departments of the companies involved.

As a consequence of new technologies and practices, a whole range of new sources needs to be examined when analysing media culture. Conventional media and cultural studies analyse media texts such as film, television, radio, comic books, music and the like in order to formulate a critique of media production or inherent ideology, or to describe consumer culture. Students of the Internet also focus on all digital media texts such as audio, film, graphics, graphical user interfaces – the visual surface of new media as well as on different kinds of texts, namely software programs, hardware configuration, and technical protocols, which define the configuration and regulation of information infrastructures that can be analysed and interpreted, such as conventional media texts. Political statements, policies, corporate white papers, artwork, advertising and even metaphors enrich the considered resources, revealing ideological connotations and the framing of technology. Since the debate on participation is highly informed by the socio-political claims of the recent 'media revolution', a close look was taken at the representation of ideological aspects. This included the ways in which promoters of the new media framed technology as well as their choice of cultural references, images, associations and metaphors to describe technology in speeches, advertising, business talks or policies. Requests for comments (RFC), a database representing developers' discussions on the development and the implementation of Internet technologies, defines technical standards and outlines a procedure for collective decision-making and consensus. This practice has been employed by other collaborative projects as well. End user license agreement (EULA) or terms of service (TOS) documents, found in most online services and software-based products, make up important aspects of the quality, definition and legal regulation of current media objects. These texts regulate content ownership, whether provided by a company or a user, and they regulate the further use, compensation, and liability of involved parties. Application programming interfaces (APIs), provided by designers of information management systems, channel the further third-party use of data stored in an information system's database. The APIs were developed to be powerful gatekeepers of information flow and regulate to a large extent how open a system is and what data and functions can be embedded or shared.[12] The documentation of software applications, their interfaces for user feedback or user participation, their provided information in the form of frequently asked questions (FAQs), user forums and so on are another set of important texts to consider. Other texts include the comments and the communication between developers and producers with their consumers. Thanks to the popularity of blogging, countless corporate blogs inundated the Web by publishing development diaries, in the tradition of the legendary computer games company iD Software. The Xbox development team maintains a weblog, as do the programmers of Microsoft's Internet Explorer.[13] The search engine giant Google maintains several blogs to communicate with its developing community and its users. Corporate policy, and its corporate view on technology regulation, market trends and Internet governance are communicated in a Google Public Policy Blog.[14]

Along with established producers, users and third parties who further develop the original devices, or modify or change the use of original devices publish their documentation, comments and even ideological communication in weblogs and user forums. Users evaluate and discuss hardware such as game consoles, in modified and non-modified forms, from a perspective of experienced users and from a perspective of media practice claiming their cultural freedom to appropriate the original design. All of these different texts refer to the process of designing and appropriating software and software-based products. They were not only important to this research for gathering crucial information about these processes themselves, but also appear to be important actors transforming, changing and influencing design, appropriation and public perception. Finally, interviews with people affiliated with specific communities, companies or working individually, and thus loosely associated with a scene or group, helped me to gain insight into the work processes and understand social and aesthetic codes. Many informal talks took place over the past years at festivals and conferences with different members of various communities.[15]

Chapter 1

Promoting Utopia/Selling Technology

We will create a civilization of the mind in Cyberspace. May it be more humane and fair than the world your governments have made before (Perry Barlow, 'Declaration of Independence of Cyberspace', 1996).

New technologies spread by word of mouth. Legends, myths and narratives accompany a new technology while it is still in development and announce it to a broader audience in society, to its potential users. Many stories have been told of imagining futures drafting possible trends in the use and development of technology (Barbrook 2005). The attempt to bring technology to perfection and to create a utopia through engineering has been recognized as an important agent of change (e.g. Peters 1999; Daniels 2002; De Vries 2008). Whether a positive or negative utopia is depicted depends on which terminology, images, and associations are chosen to imagine and present the new media. In view of participation, a negative utopia manifests itself as the dark side of the tempting promise for social progress, as the potential abuse of technology for repression. However, popular discourse rarely touches upon this. Rather, it promotes a positive utopia. The new media, the Internet, the personal computer, but also the mobile phone and wireless communication entered popular discourse in tandem with a rhetoric of promise which envisioned a brighter future. Jan van Dijk points out four examples where technological design is related in popular discourse to utopian notions of participation and social progress: The notion of teledemocracy in the 1980s, virtual communities and the new economy in the 1990s, and most recently the Web 2.0 (2006). Here, metaphors, associations and images create a certain imago of technology. They are part of a rhetoric of progress that can be recognized in the representations of new media in popular discourse. Referring to past media revolutions or a culturally constituted imagination of technological progress, they are often familiar and thus comprehensible for audiences and easily employable for promoters. Science fiction texts from Jules Verne to William Gibson, alternative concepts of society from Thomas Morus to 1960s counter-culture, and images from Fritz Lang's *Metropolis* to the Wachowskis' *The Matrix* contribute to this and are representative of the current debates. McLuhan described our limitation for perceiving the future only in terms of past developments, as if we looked 'at the present through a rear-view mirror' (1967:74). A rich cultural repertoire of images, associations and narratives informs the present rhetoric of progress that accompanies information technology.

The framing of new technologies occurs in two types of discourse: a popular discourse, aimed at a broad audience, which introduces and promotes new technologies on a large scale, and a scholarly discourse, which examines their social use. However, both discourses tend to cross over, due to a lack of specialized scholarly discourse on the topic and the need to create attention for both the emerging media and its academic framing. A key example is Nicholas Negroponte's book *Being Digital*. Despite being written by a respected scholar, it targets a broad audience and hardly meets the need for scholarly reflection and analysis, instead promoting a utopian future of digital media and their impact on society (1996).

Promoting and building information technology has unfolded simultaneously. With respect to the 'second coming' of the Internet in the form of Web 2.0, the imagination and promotion of this technology's prosperous future and its beneficial use can be seen as inseparably linked to the technology's own development.[1] Therefore, promoting the Internet revolution while still in progress required the creation of a suitable language, a rhetoric that made an Internet future comprehensible to a large audience, and that mediated things that seem so natural today.

The first time an interested public could have a glance at the new information infrastructure and its potential effects was the 1991 special edition of *Scientific American* entitled 'Communications, Computers, Networks', featuring articles by Al Gore, Nicholas Negroponte, Vint Cerf, Mitch Kapor, and Alan Kay. The range of occupations and the different backgrounds already indicate the broad nature of agenda setting. In this special issue, a scholar (Negroponte), a politician (Gore), a computer scientist (Kay), a programmer and activist (Kapor), and an Internet pioneer (Cerf) cover a wide field of topics and potential applications of an electronic information infrastructure. Alan Kay portrays possibilities of using computer networks for teaching children and how these technologies could enable and stimulate kids to teach themselves, and Mark Weiser sketches a future of ubiquitous computing, in which the computer of the 21st century is a pervasive technology accessible from many different tools in all kinds of situations. While Al Gore introduces the 'information superhighway', Mitch Kapor, co-founder of the Electronic Frontier Foundation (EEF), claims civil rights for the concerned citizens of Cyberspace.[2] In 1994, the Superhighway Summit held at UCLA's Center for Communication Policy demonstrated the Clinton/Gore administration's efforts to set communication technology on the national agenda. In his speech, Al Gore outlined the main regulations that were being established by the governing administration for dealing with the 'Information Superhighway', emphasizing the role of entrepreneurs and free market principles.[3] Along with the popularization of information technology in special interest and mainstream media, politicians already saw the implementation of an information infrastructure on their horizon and started to conceive regulations accordingly.[4]

In communication theory, the concept of agenda setting is used to describe the effects of mass media on the dissemination of political ideas, and the shaping of public perception of individual politicians and their policies. The term describes how issues come to the awareness of a broader audience and how the mass media actively drive the process of generating attention and decision-making (Shaw,

McCombs 1977). As political concepts are framed and put forward in society's discourses, so technology is framed in various ways and becomes a part of the discussed agenda. In these discourses, new media have successfully been established as empowering technologies that fundamentally enable participation. Although the mass media are crucial for communicating current trends in technology development and creating the necessary attention for the demand and adoption of technology, they are not the only factors in agenda setting.[5] Many different actors play a part in the framing of technology. Advertisements, manifestos and policies constitute a rhetoric of progress and formulate a promise of participation. Here metaphors, images and associations are used to create a picture of what the Internet or the World Wide Web will be for citizens and consumers.

But the challenge is to imagine and mediate a subject that is often even unclear to its own promoters and completely unknown to most of the audience. When the Internet and the WWW became a subject of mainstream media around 1995, journalists reverted to an entire vocabulary and cultural pool of associations that had already shaped and described computer technology and information networks.[6] Early metaphors affecting the perception of media include the computational metaphor, which is a linguistic and semantic transformation from the concept of human accountant to an electronic calculator.[7] The humanization of the machine, which overemphasizes the labour involved in processing accounting tasks and which was formerly conducted by humans, was an attempt to coin the metaphor of the 'electronic brain' (Hally 2005:85, 101). The term World Wide Web itself is a metaphor, using the picture of a web wrapped around the globe. The network metaphor was also influential and became synonymous for the changes taking place in a society perceived as an organization of networks (Castells 1996-2000). Of the many metaphors used to describe communication and information technologies, two were successfully employed and embedded in popular discourse: Information highway, coined by the Clinton/Gore administration, and Cyberspace, popularized by science fiction writer William Gibson. Cyberspace denotes a blend of cybernetics and space which identifies that element of space which creates information machines and communicational feedback, 'a consensual hallucination experienced daily by billions of legitimate operators, in every nation, by children being taught mathematical concepts. [...] A graphic representation of data abstracted from the banks of every computer in the human system. Unthinkable complexity' (Gibson 1984:51).

Perceiving information technology as a new space allows promoters of this metaphor to portray users as citizens cultivating, inhabiting and developing it. As Wendy Chun emphasizes, cyberspace proved to be a powerful metaphor in promising a new space in which to realize utopian concepts (Chun 2006:28).

The metaphors 'hyperspace', a space above the familiar real-world space, or 'augmented reality', a reality enhanced by ubiquitous information services, creating an 'infosphere', were popular alternative terms. The Information highway recalls nationally organized transport sectors, controlled and hierarchical structures and bureaucratic regulation. This last metaphor has been criticized for its limited capability of imagining the use and shape of future technology and for being too narrow by virtue of its relation to bureaucratic organizations (Dyson et al. 1994). In their text *A Magna Charta of the Knowledge Age*, Dyson, Gilder, Keyworth, and Toffler analyse the cyberspace and information highway metaphors, finding the latter inappropriate for facing the new material challenges of online social and political organization, whereas the cyberspace metaphor typifies a spatial perception of a new world rather than an understanding of new highways that would be maintained and administered by bureaucrats (Dyson et al. 1994). The function of these metaphors is clear, and what Bruce Sterling acknowledges for cyberspace is true for the information highway metaphor as well:

> The word 'cyberspace' is a sleek container for all kinds of suspicious techie marvels – notions with radically different premises – and considerable commercial promise. People – some of them, millionaire entrepreneurs – are in technophilic ecstasy, boldly comparing 'cyberspace' to the telephone, the automobile, the Wright flyer, the personal computer (Sterling 1990:54).

The 'Information Superhighway' was yet another sleek container, though it had a bureaucratic tint, a state-mediated project but in favour of a free market economy and commercial application. Metaphors are not neutral or passive, since the choice for or against a metaphor entails important design and regulation decisions. The metaphor of the information highway explicitly invited associations of neo-liberal market organization and the entrepreneurs as the pioneering actors to build, shape and exploit the new information infrastructure:

> We are on the verge of a revolution that is just as profound as the change in the economy that came with the industrial revolution. Soon electronic networks will allow people to transcend the barriers of time and distance and take advantage of global markets and business opportunities not even imaginable today, opening up a new world of economic possibility and progress (Gore 1997).[8]

This rhetoric is used by many different people, organizations, and institutions to describe and label the technology and its use in a society-wide debate. A bard such as John Perry Barlow dreamt of a new and better world, politicians such as Al Gore promised a fast ride on information highways that would lead from the industrial age into the rosy future of the information age. A computer pioneer and activist such as Mitch Kapor recognized the need for socio-political representation and citizen rights on the electronic frontier, while business leaders such as Bill Gates anticipated 'business at the speed of thought'. The way media and technologies have been presented reveal an expectation of socio-political progress through technological development. The various participants from the worlds of business, journalism, politics, activism and art provide a rhetoric that addresses and communicates new technologies. Their statements and the way they present technology have a profound effect on developers and designers attempting to devise solutions that fulfil the proclaimed promises. Those concepts were addressed by prominent spokespersons who quickly became identified with the new media and the new economy, and who were sometimes referred to as the 'digerati' (Brockmann 1996). Fred Turner convincingly shows how counterculture and business converged during the early development of personal computers. Young entrepreneurs and activists teamed up to produce tools for a 'new frontier', entering virgin social and technological territory (Turner 2006). Coming from the most divergent fields related to computer and information technologies, these diverse groups of scholars and writers, entrepreneurs and publishers, activists and politicians, programmers and engineers very much dominated the debate on the implementation of the global information infrastructure.[9] The media appearances and publications of opinion leaders and prominent techno-advocates contributed to the semantic constitution of associations and metaphors for describing, perceiving, and experiencing technology. A plethora of texts was produced by these advocates describing what the Internet and the information revolution was about and which changes society would undergo during the transformation to an information society.[10] The second coming of the Internet as Web 2.0 has a similar dynamic. A flying circus of the usual suspects spread the gospel about the next new thing.

Technology is expected to solve many social problems and abolish many obstacles created by social interaction and power structures. Drawing on psychoanalytical theory, French sociologist Patrice Flichy conceived the concept of the 'imaginaire' to describe the 'collective imagination of technology' (Flichy 1999; 2007). This technological imaginary is constructed by the expectations and projections for cultural and social advancement and manifests itself as an immaterial aspect of technology. It pervades the discourse on technology, whether in popular texts, journalists' articles, the work of artists, debates at conferences and board meetings, and the slick presentation of marketing professionals. It finds expression in the policies of political administrations as well as in the manifestos of activists. The promising rhetoric used to promote the new media in the 1990s represents a technological imaginary that refers to the ideal of egalitarian access to means of information and the freedom to communicate beyond all geographical, political and educational boundaries.

The new technologies have been promoted in the mass media and have stimulated the creation of many new special-interest media, the most popular probably being chief editor Kevin Kelly's Wired magazine, which features and supports many of the key players in popular discourse and the computer and software businesses.[11] In Wired, the amalgam of counterculture and business found a medium with roots in Stewart Brand's hippie magazines The Whole Earth Catalog and The Whole Earth

Review. Later dubbed the 'Californian ideology' (Barbrook, Cameron 1995), *Wired*'s philosophy attempted to link counterculture politics with the polished new economy entrepreneurship, along with a libertarian, evolutionary, Darwinesque philosophy spiced up with a new communalist ideal (Turner 2006: 195). As Turner has pointed out, concepts of social utopia, the free flow of information, the ideal of access to resources and the sharing of information were developed within the counterculture of the 1960s and merged with an emerging entrepreneurship largely rooted in the hobbyist communities of computers and electronics. These counterculture entrepreneurs believed computers should be personal tools, useful for one and all, thereby enabling the advent of the common user. Though this target group eventually proved to be a source of profit, it was initially chosen for ideological reasons: to relinquish the means of production to the people.

Participation and socio-political progress are some of the new technologies' recurring promises. They propel creative talent and act as alluring arguments for the introduction and diffusion of new technologies (Daniels 2002). The development of the computer into a mass medium was highly driven by the desire to enable future users to develop better ways of achieving labour objectives (Engelbart 1962; Licklider 1965; Papert 1980), but also by the idealistic desire to achieve social progress and egalitarian access and participation (Nelson 1974; Kay 1972). The graphical user interfaces (GUIs) so common in today's computers have been developed very much from a perspective of allowing users to participate in the creation and use of knowledge (e.g. Nelson 1974/1987; Kay; Goldberg 1977/2003).[12] During the development of the Internet, developers were already implementing their expectations for socio-political change into the basic design of the technology, where 'initial choices were profoundly marked by the representations of these actors who dreamed of a communicating, free, universal and non-hierarchized network' (Flichy 2002:201). The counterculture of the 1960s recognized the potential in computer technology and information networks for realizing many of their ideals of social progress, freedom of information, access to education, and a means of conquering both social injustices and geographical disadvantages (Turner 2006). This utopian vision gave important meaning to the new media, and contributed to the 'imago' that was communicated in countless advertisements, manifestos, policies and media coverage in the emerging new market in the 1990s. The promise of participation was crucial to the discourse inherent in the implementation of the Internet and the World Wide Web, and it is also inherent in the developers' culture and the many design decisions they make while constructing these technologies. It was used for promoting the new technology and explaining alleged beneficial effects to large audiences. The technological imaginary is therefore represented in the way opinion leaders communicate about new media to their audiences and in the way engineers design technology. Obviously, reality does not uphold the promises of the technological imaginary, but it has been convincingly argued that the formulation of utopia alone is crucial for developing and designing technology (Daniels

2002:31). Although the socio-political expectations have not been met yet, the present need for them is an important agent for change and development.

The idea of increasing possibilities for participation has been formulated from different perspectives and is a key aspect of the new technologies' promise for social improvement and the abolishment of inequality. References to past media revolutions and images of social uses of technology were marshalled to create an imago for the technologies to come. However, the way participation is conceived takes on a variety of guises.

During the first era in which new technologies and the Internet were promoted, from the early 1990s to the decline of the new economy in 2001, participation was defined as access and connectivity. Participation was presented as a major opportunity for citizens, entrepreneurs, and consumers to improve socio-political reality, business opportunities, and media consumption through connectivity. Accessing information online or using computers for self-education, connecting to overseas business partners, and plugging into remote markets were popular themes in imagining the uses of technology. Participation was a major rhetorical trope in promoting the information revolution. It became a great legend of information and computer technology, highly visible not only in political policies and artists' visionary accounts, but also in companies' corporate communications. The often almost evangelical impetus discernible in corporate media campaigns for the Internet and computer technology is closely related to the cultural heritage of the counterculture and libertarian entrepreneurship (Brockmann 1996; Castells 2001:37-38; Turner 2006). It became a popular narrative, thriving on the tempting promise that changing the world for the better and making money aren't mutually exclusive. In the following phase, characterized generally by the label Web 2.0, the connotations attached to the idea of participation shift: now collaboration and social interaction have become its core elements, thus bringing forth a slightly different type of discourse. This shift can be clearly recognized in two campaigns promoting the IT company Cisco Systems.

1.1   Cisco Systems: empowering the Internet generation

The glorious future described in Al Gore's promising words was represented in the advertisements, business talks, white papers, and publications of IT companies and their spokespersons. The network metaphor was used to describe a new step in globalization, the creation of a worldwide information infrastructure that would abolish the disadvantages of local bondage and physical barriers. The promise for participation became a key motive in promoting information technologies. Prime examples are Cisco Systems' campaigns from the mid-1990s and the recent Web 2.0-related campaign exemplifying the framing of new technologies as social progress.[13] Cisco Systems is a perfect example, among the enormously prospering

IT companies, of how to build the physical network, the Internet, and simultaneously establish it as an enabling technology, potentially empowering every user.[14] Their advertisement campaigns represent the technological imaginary and demonstrate how metaphors and associations can construct a technology's imago. Moreover, Cisco Systems found ways to speak of the Internet to a broad public in a comprehensible language and chose pictures that imagined a possible future. Although this was the key message of Cisco's communications, both campaigns – the 1998 campaign and the Web 2.0-related campaign of 2005 – emphasized participation differently.[15] In the first one, the idea of connectivity and access appears in various forms: developing nations were to gain access to the global electronic marketplace, which in a neo-liberal ideology would be a fair and democratic institution, where the best producers could distribute the best products for the best prices. The Internet promised connection to remote marketplaces, overcoming geographical distances, and access to knowledge resources through online learning. Cisco Systems emphasized the aspect of access and the possibility of actively participating in the new information space, which was mainly characterized as a marketplace and a knowledge space for learning and education, but also as a network to play in. The advertisements reveal metaphors and signifiers that refer to the official vision of the 'information highway' as endorsed by the Clinton/Gore administration. Several key themes can be identified in Cisco's advertisements:

1. Access and participation due to new technologies
2. The development of new business opportunities
3. The global connection of markets and people

In the advertised world of Cisco Systems, social and geographical disadvantages can be compensated by technology.[16] The first major campaign, 'Empowering the Internet Generation', was launched in 1998; TV spots were used to promote the Internet and its endless possibilities. The title already indicates an evolutionary progress, a new generation adapted to technology (the Internet) and the prospect of socio-political change (empowerment). The TV spots consist of fragments of a monologue spoken by people from different nations with different accents. Each utters a short fragment of the monologue, which in turn makes up a narrative of the fast diffusion of the Internet:

> There are over 800,000 jobs openings. For Internet specialists. Right now. Three million more in the next five years. By the time I am eighteen over a billion jobs will require Internet skills.

The monologue connects the images of speakers from different nationalities in their different locations. In the following sequence, another series of different speakers poses a question to the camera: 'Are you ready?' The spot continues:

Virtually all Internet traffic travels across the systems of one company. The same one sponsoring thousands of networking academies. Cisco Systems. Empowering the Internet generation.[17]

According to this advertisement, Cisco is not only building the hardware and software for the Internet, Cisco is also enabling people to learn how to use the Internet and is connecting virtually everybody on the planet, thereby diminishing access barriers to education, markets, and social communities.[18] The message was widely disseminated and reached consumers far beyond Cisco Systems' actual target group. The early Cisco campaigns emphasized participation in terms of diminishing geographical distance and providing access to information; the more recent campaigns emphasize potential collaboration, but even more the possibility of being together while geographically far apart. They promote a notion of generating meaning through sharing special moments, leading to creativity and contributions to collaborative works. The 'Empowering the Internet Generation' campaign presented participation as access to education and business opportunities through connectivity, but the 'Human Network' campaign shows participation in a global society as contributing to a collective knowledge resource, communicating and collaborating over far distances, and maintaining a state of perpetual contact, thereby enabling the sharing of special moments and emotions and achieving common objectives. Many popular user activities familiar from Web 2.0 applications are featured in the 'Human Network' advertisement. A child's voice-over comments on a series of scenes where maps are rewritten as Google Maps, books are edited like the editing of a Wikipedia article, and home videos are published. Again a new world is promised, one created by the enabling technology and the enthusiastic participation of its users:

> Welcome to a place where books rewrite themselves, [...] welcome to a place where a wedding is captured and recaptured, again and again, where home video is experienced everywhere at once, where a library travels across the world, where businesses are born, countries are transformed, and we are more powerful together than we ever could have been apart. Welcome to the human network.

In Cisco commercials, connectivity describes people extinguishing time zones and space, enabling unhindered access to the sharing of ideas, playful interaction and communication from anywhere, at any time. Most important is the emphasis on the empowering and enabling quality of information networks with respect to participating in economical and educational progress. The images, associations, and metaphors Cisco uses in the campaigns fit into the rhetoric used in the popular discourse on the Internet and simultaneously complement it and resemble those used by other IT companies (Goldman, Papson, Kersey 1998/2003; Cock, Fitchett, Farr 2001). Presented as both a revolution and techno-Darwinist evolution, the globalization, deterritorialization, social use, and user activities displayed in the campaigns constitute the public perception of information technology.

The advertisements reveal a 'technological imaginary', an imagination of social and economical progress, that is projected onto technical design. Translating the promise of participation into pictures of children, students, and business people prospering from the global information infrastructure was supposed to explain why every individual should acquire Internet skills, and why each company should alter their business accordingly. The campaigns confronted an audience already aware of the new technologies due to agenda setting in popular discourse. At this point, Cisco Systems attempted to inextricably associate its name with the Internet and its socio-political agenda, promoting both the Internet and the company. While creating a standard vision of common users and citizens and small-sized businesses to meet the common interest in technological development and its effects, Cisco Systems comprehensibly translated current developments in information technology. Cisco Systems itself participated significantly in shaping the information age by:

a. developing crucial backbone technology
b. establishing a business model which can be seen as a prime example for the next new economy
c. promoting the Internet to the public and pushing an imago of the technology

A surprising aspect of the Cisco Systems campaigns is that they focused on a broad audience far beyond their usual target group. The large scale of the campaigns, as well as the 'Empowering the Internet Generation' slogan, and its most recent successor, 'The Human Network', more resemble a wake-up call for the promotion of the Internet and its social use as such than simply an advertisement for Cisco Systems' products. In order to sell their Internet-related products, Cisco, as well as other IT companies, were forced to first explain what the Internet precisely was and what it was good for. During the 1990s, innovative information and communication technology companies developed a rhetoric that identified the Internet as a global marketplace and described the transformation from the industrial age to the information age as necessary evolution, irresistible revolution, and a process of speed (Cock, Fitchett, Farr 2001).[19] They participated in constructing narratives of a technological revolution, and their advertisement represented a 'technological imaginary', in so far that information technology promised economic prosperity, social improvement and global democratization. However, the promotion of participation, social progress, and global democratization in such campaigns stands in stark contrast to allegations that IT companies such as Cisco Systems, Yahoo, Microsoft, and Google are providing the means for and are actively participating in surveillance, censorship, and repression in undemocratic countries.[20]

1.2   Web 2.0: celebrating collaboration

Web 2.0 is, of course, a piece of jargon, nobody even knows what it means. If Web 2.0 for you is blogs and wikis, then that is people to people. But that was what the Web was supposed to be all along (Tim Berners-Lee, 2006).

With the advent of Web 2.0, the narrative of participation shifted from emphasizing access to emphasizing collaboration and collective action. A large user base already provided with the means of accessing the Internet appears to be a precondition for the tremendous success of the Web 2.0. The unfolding diffusion of the Internet and the World Wide Web required companies and public administrators first to build the necessary infrastructure and to promote the new technologies. Another phase, often labelled as 'the second coming of the Web', builds upon the existing infrastructures and large audiences familiar with basic features and media practices as well as a large number of skilled users who can actually participate in developing applications further. Many media practices enabled by Web 2.0 applications were developed earlier, but easy-to-use interfaces in popular applications have led to an amazing increase of user-generated content. Two different kinds of content can be distinguished here, user-created data and user-created (or user-provided) media content, such as images, films, sound or text. Tracking user activities as well as storing the personal data they provide in the process of signing up for a service fills a database that is employed for improving the information processing related to the platform's services as well as for targeting adverts. The success of a Web 2.0 platform depends on a large group of users providing data and media content (O'Reilly, Battelle 2009). On the surface, user activities and their cultural production appear as an unexplainable conjoined interaction of a plurality of individuals. Unsurprisingly, references are made to the phenomenon of emergence (e.g. Morowitz 2002; Johnson 2002) and the incomprehensibly well-organized actions of bees, ants or human crowds (e.g. Surowiecki 2005, Shirky 2008). In *Wealth of Networks*, Yochai Benkler implicitly speaks of an invisible hand conducting the dynamic processes leading to a concerted effort of cultural production (2006). With an often unexpressed reference to Pierre Lévy, the term 'collective intelligence' is used to label the phenomenon of large numbers of users interacting and collectively contributing to information management and content creation. O'Reilly speaks of 'harnessing the collective intelligence of users' but emphasizes the role of software design as the prime facilitator (O'Reilly, Batelle 2009). However, the popular discourse was successful in shaping an image of the Web 2.0 as a friendly, caring and democratizing way of simply using technologies in order to stimulate creativity. Symptomatic is Clay Shirky's mantra that 'communication tools don't get socially interesting until they get technologically boring' (Shirky 2008). Shirky rightly assumes that when communication technologies are easy to use and it's easier for a user to participate in media production, then more users will participate. However, he completely neglects that easy-to-use design often comes at the price of proprietary lock-in and, therefore, limited opportunities for appropriation. The history of radio teaches us that the potential for interactive communication through radio was consequently prevented, leaving the user with nothing more than a simple control panel for receiving a limited choice of broadcasting stations. Technology is not acknowledged as a prime facilitator that channels user activities so that companies can generate revenues from their actions. Technology is presented instead as a neutral means for enabling users to get in touch with their community and to benefit from collective achievements. The intelligence in the back end and the subtle ways of directing user activities through the graphic design of the front end is unacknowledged, while the emancipatory use of software is overly emphasized. Technology companies in particular explicitly point out the beneficial effects of collective production and the heart-warming community feeling, literally constituting a global village. The above-mentioned advertisement 'The Human Network' by Cisco Systems is exemplary in emphasizing this new participation as a collective and community-constituting aspect of the Web 2.0, where we allegedly 'are more powerful together than we ever could have been apart'. In a 2009 series of commercials launched by the former monopolist of telephone services in the Netherlands, KPN, the use of the mobile phone as a 'tactical medium' is pointed out in different situations. In one, children playing hide-and-seek simply dial the phones of their hidden mates; in another, an elderly woman on a night out with her husband checks the online ratings of a restaurant he suggests and then advises him to pick another one. These situations portray the 'Generation KPN', a generation not defined by age but by how technology is used and information is shared. Similarly, the German branch of Vodafone coined the term 'Generation Upload', which, in contrast to the 'passive downloader', spreads creativity, engages with expanding social networks and turns unconventional ideas into successful business opportunities. The claim of Vodafone's 200-million-euro campaign entitled 'Whatever you start, it can shake the world, this is your moment. Vodafone' introduces Vodafone as partner of Generation Upload, providing the means for empowerment, while the community stimulates the creativity. In a series of advertisements with allegedly well-known German bloggers and self-proclaimed Web 2.0 'celebrities', publishing online, producing amateur art or sharing aspects of daily life with the community are presented as core aspects of the emerging media practice. An accompanying spot in the campaign features various users covering the David Bowie song 'Heroes' while doing all kinds of things supposedly worth recording and sharing with others. Becoming a hero is easy, at least in the legends, the popular discourse tells us. John Blossom opens his book, entitled *Content Nation. Surviving and Thriving as Social Media Changes Our Work, Our Lives and Our Future*, with the lines:

> This is a story about you – one of billions of publishers in the world today. Sent an email lately? You're a publisher. Posted a photo, a video, a comment, or a vote

on a Web site? You're a publisher. Keyed in a text message to friends on your cell phone? You're a publisher (Blossom, 2009:2).

Three aspects are noteworthy about the popular framing of 'social media':

a. claiming that users belong to a community; drawn from the notion of collective intelligence and peer-based production, the 'social' in 'social media' receives a positive connotation as a community experience, and it is perceived as a social phenomenon rather than a commercial one.
b. claiming mediated communication equals publishing; simply using technology that mediates communication and facilitates interaction is presented as turning users into content producers replacing established media production.
c. claiming that these practices are specific features of the Web 2.0 and distinctive from earlier media practices online.

Quite different from the emphasis on access during the earlier wave of popular discourse on the World Wide Web, the recent commentary on the Web 2.0 constitutes a 'rhetoric of community', emphasizing aspects of togetherness, equality, collective production and democratic decision-making. Turning users into media producers is only one part of what the 'social web' promises, the other is changing the world for the better through collective efforts facilitated by 'social media' (e.g. Leadbeater 2008; Shirky 2010). While earlier discourse framed social progress as an effect of technological advancement, the rhetoric of community frames social progress as a collective effort achieved by using advanced technologies properly. In his programmatic text *We-Think. The Power of Mass Creativity*, Charles Leadbeater dreams of a way to amplify the collective intelligence of the plurality of users who then, in a joint effort – provided technology is used 'wisely' – could 'spread democracy, promote freedom, alleviate inequality and allow us to be creative together, en mass' (2008:6). The 'social media' acquired through this repetitive positive connotation of 'social' a public understanding that goes beyond the original denotation of social interaction and organisation. The phenomenon of social interactions and its socio-political implications is blurred by the overly positive perception of users interacting online. Actual events in which Web 2.0 applications were used, such as the Obama Campaign in 2008, or the response to the Iran elections of 2009, helped to create a strong belief in the revolutionary potential of media technology. However, this image is mostly shaped by not telling the entire story and therefore creating media myths. The Obama campaign team was indeed the first to employ online media significantly, but the amount it spent on advertising in broadcasting media – mainly television – was ten times higher than on online media, and quadrupled that of its competitor, McCain. Although the Internet increasingly became an important source of campaign information and related news, especially among young Americans, television still remained the dominant medium overall.[21] In case of the Iranian rebellion following the election, it cannot be emphasized enough that, despite the concerted actions of Internet users, the very same technology actually helped the Iranian authorities to trace protesters. It remains unclear to what extent the activities in social networks actually exposed protesters, but it is undeniable that Western companies, such as Nokia Siemens, provided telecommunication equipment suited for efficiently suppressing dissent. As Evgeny Morozov puts it, Internet technologies can be an effective means of control: 'Contrary to the utopian rhetoric of social media enthusiasts, the Internet often makes the jump from deliberation to participation even more difficult' (Morozov 2010a). He refers to the successful infiltration of dissidents in Belarus by authorities. Gathering information from social networks, the authorities could easily identify members, interfere with planned demonstrations and approach dissidents individually to either scare them off or arrest them (Morozov 2010b).[22] Apart from this, the statistics on the use of Internet and social media do not indicate a large number of users being actively involved in revolutionary upheaval but rather e-mailing, using search engines, watching videos, shopping online, updating their profile on social networking sites and interacting with peers (PEW Trend Data Online Activities; Lenhart et al. 2010). Furthermore, it appears that only a small minority of Web 2.0 platform users contribute actively by producing media content, while a large majority simply consumes it (e.g. Prieur et al. 2009). Web 2.0 platforms established themselves successfully as community-driven platforms committed to public weal. And while enthusiastic promoters celebrate these platforms' potential to empower passive consumers, entrepreneurs have long realized that the 'social media' users are not only yet another audience for advertising, but also a crowd of helping hands in distributing the commercial messages. A plethora of marketing-oriented books promises to provide strategies on how to employ social networks for commercial success and how to boost a company's image by appearing friendlier and more committed to customers communicating through 'social media'.[23]

Recently, some critical voices are pointing out problematic aspects about Web 2.0 platforms (e.g. Lanier 2006 and 2010; Keen 2007; Zimmer 2008, Scholz 2008; Petersen 2008; Mueller 2009; Schäfer 2009). The oft-quoted account of Andrew Keen is ultimately a culture-pessimistic rant against the emergence of amateur producers and an arbitrary fear of users putting professional producers out of business, eventually destroying the quality and reliability of media content (Keen 2007). Despite the urgent questions Keen is bringing up, his speculative and poorly supported approach is not very helpful in formulating critique.

Critical perspectives can be divided into three accounts. The free labour account draws from the post-Marxist critique of labour in media consumption (Andrejevic 2002; Terranova 2004; Virno 2004). The critique aims at the unacknowledged implementation of user-generated content for commercial ends (e.g. Scholz 2007a, 2007b, 2008; Petersen 2008). A joint effort in revisiting participatory culture as

38

unpaid labour for corporate companies has been initiated by Trebor Scholz on the mailing list of the Institute for Distributed Creativity and a conference with the programmatic title 'The Internet as Playground and Factory' (Scholz 2009). Another branch of critique emphasizes the violation of privacy in online services (e.g. Zimmer 2007, 2008; Fuchs 2009) and the power structures facilitating means of control and regulation (e.g. Galloway 2004; Chun 2006; Deibert et al. 2008; Zittrain 2008). A third thread of criticism considers Web 2.0 platforms as emerging public spheres (Münker 2009) and the new socio-political quality of user-producer relations in governing software applications and their users (Uricchio 2004a; Kow and Nardi 2010). This is exceedingly important to consider, since Web 2.0 platforms are indeed becoming something similar to traditional third places where conversations take place as much on private issues as on socio-political concerns. In expanding the traditional private and public spaces and increasing the possibilities for socio-political organization and debate, the actual social quality of online media is revealed. The function and role online platforms will occupy in daily social life are still subject to negotiations between various stakeholders ranging from common users to corporate producers and public administrations. These debates result from the technological qualities of new media as well as from media practices that are eventually transforming social interaction, markets and politics. Drawn from a deep-rooted idealism for participatory societies, democratic decision processes and freedom of expression, expectations are formulated for the potential use and regulation of these new technologies. Traditionally, this claim for participation finds its expression in culture critique and the humanities.

Chapter 2
Claiming Participation

2.1   New media, new participation?

Unlike traditional media, the Net is not just a spectacle for passive consumption but also a participatory activity (Richard Barbrook 1997).

Participation has been perceived as a key concept to democratization and the balancing of inequalities in society, dating back to the civil revolutions and rebellions of the 18th century and the structural transformation of the public sphere (Habermas 1962/1990). After political participation had been primarily claimed by those who already had economic power, the bourgeoisie-participation was formulated in the more contentious terms of class struggle, calling for access to means of production. The rising mass production of consumer goods and the increasing prominence of mass media witnessed participation claiming access to media production and its means of distribution. Socio-political critiques aimed at the media and its ownership structures criticized its inherent ideology. The legacy of the civil claim to participation is very much embedded in current media practice and the understanding of participatory culture.

The many recent publications on participation emphasize clearly that consumers are increasingly accessing the apparatus of production, not only by adopting, consuming or modifying industrial goods but also by establishing an amateur culture on a global scale; consumers are expanding their own skills and increasing their technological capital, improving opportunities for social organization, and focusing on gaining political influence (e.g. Bruns 2006; Jenkins 2002, 2006b; Leadbeater and Miller 2004; Raessens 2005, Uricchio 2004a; Benkler 2006; Lessig 2008; Shirky 2008; Schäfer 2009). The significant shift emerging from these accounts is that audiences are turning from interpreting to actually producing media texts. The participation of mass media audiences as examined by Stuart Hall, John Fiske, and others was limited to reading media texts and engaging with them simply through interpretation (Hall 1980; Fiske 1995). Critiques frequently took the form of reviews, an activity that in itself was conducted in a highly professional manner. Consequently, the diffusion of the Internet and the WWW as mainstream technologies was accompanied by a discourse of critique as well. Especially the Nettime mailing list, founded in 1995 by Pit Schultz and Geert Lovink, and the

Next5Minutes conferences in the 1990s formulated a critical commentary referred to as 'netcritique'.[1] This discourse blended with activism and media art and employed the new technologies as 'tactical media' (Lovink 2003a). Frank Hartmann perceives netcritique as a specifically European approach to the US-dominated commercialization of the Internet (2000:318-21). In a way, netcritique was an attempt to extend intellectual critique directly into the sphere of activism by literally turning words into actions, something that is very possible to achieve with software.

The new technologies allow common users not only to produce, alter, and distribute media texts, but also to develop or modify software, the production means of the digital age. This feature is also emphasized by Joost Raessens, who argues that the emerging participatory culture is different from 'culture participation'. As opposed to taking part in a surrounding culture, participatory culture requires 'a more active attitude' (Raessens 2005:383). Indeed, he points out that interpretation and intellectual deconstruction of media content are extended into action in interactive media. Instead of writing a review or critique, digital cultural critics attempt to modify the program.[2] This is the very political meaning of Richard Stallman's oft-quoted slogan that software should be free, 'free as in free speech' (Stallman 2002; Wynants 2005:72). The possibilities of reacting to media texts have multiplied. Interpretation in the digital age can be expressed in an act of construction. Deconstruction of media texts is possible through an act of construction, hence the production of new and alternative texts or the modification of existing ones. In the wake of the World Wide Web and its recent label Web 2.0, the traditional claim for participation in media production in order to participate in socio-political decision-making has been formulated again (Carpentier, Cleen 2008).

Our understanding of participation has been very much shaped through the practices users developed in employing media technology for social interaction and political activism (see also Carpentier, Cleen 2008:3) In view of the social interactions and productivity unfolding among computer and Internet users, the concept of participation as a promise and a critical practice returns prominently into culture studies discourse.[3] While participation has been employed in popular discourse as a promise for promoting new technologies, in scholarly discourse it serves as an explanation for an emerging cultural phenomenon, and is modelled into the key metaphor for explaining contemporary media practice. A plethora of work describing various kinds of user participation has appeared over the last years, often picking up Alvin Toffler's terminology of the 'prosumer' (Toffler 1980) or coining new terms like 'produser' (e.g. Bruns 2006, 2007, 2008), user-generated content, DIY culture, peer-to-peer, and enthusiastically celebrating 'the former audience' (Gilmore 2006:136).[4] Dubbed by Henry Jenkins as 'participatory culture', it formulates a concept of social interactions of users in order to produce media texts and commentary on politics and corporate media productions collectively and in large-scale collaboration (Jenkins et al. 2006). Audiences do not seem to be restricted to the position of a 'critical reader' anymore, and instead can rely on new worldwide connected social structures, communication, and distribution channels, facilitated by the Internet, through which they collectively can produce media texts and influence established producers (Jenkins 2006b:246). Jenkins accurately emphasized that amateur culture is not new but, due to the Internet, it has been pushed to a different scale (2002). Common user-driven amateur and fan culture is now shifting from being marginalized in the media industry to being a crucial aspect in generating and distributing media texts. This participatory culture is defined by Jenkins as a new mode for cultural production:

1. with relatively low barriers to artistic expression and civic engagement
2. with strong support for creating and sharing one's creations with others
3. with some type of informal mentorship whereby what is known by the most experienced is passed along to novices
4. where members believe that their contributions matter
5. where members feel some degree of social connection with one another (at the least, they care what other people think about what they have created). Not every member must contribute, but all must believe they are free to contribute when ready and that what they contribute will be appropriately valued (Jenkins et al. 2006:7).

The first point in Jenkins's definition refers to technological aspects of the emerging media practice, the fact that production means are easily available and costs are low. The four other aspects are related to a certain social practice, which read rather like rules of conduct. Participation would be therefore limited to areas where people follow these rules, as happens in communities that are often defining directives to guide how their members interact with one another. An ideological connotation is inherent to this definition, presuming participatory culture unfolds on a socially 'cosy' matrix. Jenkins emphasizes the community aspects, the mutual understanding and genuine interest in each other's productions, collaboration and support. Such an understanding of participation confines user activities to communities and intrinsic motivation in achieving collectively defined objectives. This understanding might be valid for the fan communities upon which Jenkins' research draws, but there are other user activities unfolding in the extensions of the cultural industries that revolve around different dynamics, and do not show tightly knit social relations or community identity.[5]

Jenkins touches upon two important issues in his definition, namely the creation of artefacts and the distribution of knowledge among users. Participatory culture is often presented as taking place in an area of conflict. In his notion of 'convergence culture', Jenkins argues that top-down approaches typical of the culture industry converge with bottom-up activities of users (2006b:18). Jenkins refers to several examples where the activities of users collide with the business interests of media companies. A supposedly critical stance on the part of users is seen in the creation and distribution of media texts, and in particular satirical ones, criticizing politicians. Jenkins emphasizes the often entertaining form this takes, using methods and motives initially provided by the media industry (2006b:206).[6] The use of 'photoshop for democracy', as Jenkins describes the critical media productions, is most evident in the many film posters that have been photoshopped in such a way that the original icons in popular film posters, such as James Bond, the Lord of the Rings, Harry Potter and others, are replaced with members of the Bush administration 'starring' as evil rogues.[7] The many forms of appropriation of corporate media texts from popular culture have supported the idea of consumers consequently turning into producers. Drawing from popular media texts, fan communities develop different modes for framing the original texts. Slash fiction employs characters from popular films or TV series, such as Harry Potter or Star Trek, in erotic, often homosexual short stories (Jenkins 1992; Green, Jenkins and Jenkins 1998). Satiric Star Wars films made by fans are another example of how media reception also takes place as the construction of new media texts. However, it should not be forgotten that this form of participation represents only a fraction of the target audience in comparison with book, merchandising and box office sales. Stating that amateur culture will replace corporate media production is one of the persistent claims of the overly optimistic and hasty assessments of media use.

Jenkins confined his research primarily to fan culture, where he defines user participation as the appropriation of media content initially produced by established production channels of the media industry. Jenkins's work, as well as that of others, provides a valuable insight into the activities of fans who employ the Internet and computer technology to accumulate material revolving around commercial media content. This is not sufficient, however, for analysing all the other domains where these new media practices emerge, nor how they are, or are not, related to established culture industries. It often neglects independent productions created completely outside the realm of media corporations and their related markets. Participation doesn't take place only in relation to existing media productions, nor is it necessarily opposed or in conflict with them.

Henry Jenkins's understanding of participation primarily deals with intrinsically motivated actions exercised in social formations which share a high degree of interaction, common objectives, and interests. It is a form of production that can be best described as explicit participation. It requires explicit action to participate in a community and consciously produce media texts and artefacts. However, new information management systems, as employed in popular Web 2.0 applications, reveal an implicit participation, which exists below the threshold of explicit participation and goes beyond mere participation in a surrounding culture: social interaction and user activities are channelled and controlled by design. On what one might call a rather subliminal level, users are participating – often without any form of acknowledgement from the companies offering such services – in shaping and expanding the information infrastructure. By analysing implicit participation, one can highlight the crucial role software design plays in channelling user activities on corporate platforms, and assigning agency in participation to information technology as well, rather than confining it to user activities.

Axel Brun's concept of 'produsage' (Bruns 2008) marks a step towards understanding participation as a heterogeneous and hybrid practice. Produsage describes to what extent all participants at different stages of online cultural production can act as users and producers. Bruns emphasizes the role of software in facilitating these collaborative processes.[8] Although Bruns puts the community's role in the production process into perspective and rejects a collectivist thought process (2008:327), he still provides an understanding of social formation. He calls the latter 'produsage communities'; these communities produce and use artefacts-activities that are sometimes also referred to as 'user-led content creation' (2008:3). Bruns correctly recognizes opportunities for media corporations to implement user activities in their business model, a strategy he labels 'harvesting the hive'.[9] The resulting socio-political dynamics are often inadequately analysed and, instead, framed in terms of the 'good' or 'bad' effects of participatory culture and the technologies it employs, that is, the Web 2.0 applications. These applications are labelled 'social software'; this label is problematic because, in this case, 'social' has an overly positive connotation, something along the lines of: 'nice people are collaborating nicely with each other in order to create nice things'. A constant problem with the discourse about Web 2.0 and participatory culture is the ultimately rather myopic idea that participation by many users somehow equals democracy. Biased by taking these kinds of intellectual shortcuts, the discourse becomes stymied by moral musings on participatory culture, without thoroughly examining the socio-political dynamics or the ambiguous nature of technology.

What is often embraced as something that opens up technologies for users so they can be used as genuine media practices simultaneously makes room for new strategies for the culture industry. Frequent misunderstandings in the discourse on participation are the following:

1. thinking social progress is inherent to user participation
2. assuming that participation is only explicit, community-based and primarily intrinsically motivated
3. neglecting the fact that participating in cultural production does not mean participating in power structures or benefiting from generated revenues
4. neglecting how media practices in user participation are implemented into software design

Two crucial aspects deserve further attention in order to develop an analysis of participatory culture: firstly, the heterogeneous user activities emerging in different areas of an extended culture industry which do not appear to be homogeneous with regard to a socio-political mindset – the motivation for participation – and forms of social organization. They are not confined to areas affected by the culture industry, but can intertwine with it in a great variety of forms. Secondly, a distinction has to be made between implicit and explicit participation in order to differentiate to what extent user activities and software design affect cultural production.

2.2   Domains of user participation

The following section attempts to structurally map the various activities of users that are often simply summarized as user-generated content, collective production, fan culture, user-led creation, DIY culture, convergence or word combinations with the prefix 'social'. Labour executed by Internet users can be mapped according to the following three categories: accumulation, archiving (or organizing), and construction. These three domains are not mutually exclusive and overlap to a certain extent. The logic of electronic distribution and the copying of files applies to all of them. As will be discussed later, recent software design for information management systems channels these user activities and proposes interfaces and functions that stimulate and regulate them.

Accumulation describes all activities that revolve around popular media content and products, for the most part initially developed by corporate companies. Fans expand these artefacts not only by contributing to discussions and debates, but also by creating related media texts. Jenkins's major contributions cover that field extensively (Jenkins 1992; Green, Jenkins, Jenkins 1998; Jenkins 2006a, 2006b; Jenkins et al. 2006). An example of fan culture would be the platform Theforce.net, a popular website for *Star Wars* fans, along with discussion forums, news sections, material collections on films and a section on related events such as conventions and fan meetings; the website also hosts a section containing fan productions. The fans don't just watch *Star Wars*, they produce their own versions, and some of these fan films are sophisticated productions.[10] They range from two-minute animated short clips to feature-length films that take advantage of a variety of editing and animation tools. Tutorials teach other enthusiasts how to create special effects, while another section is used for sharing the spaceship models used in animation sequences. In 'Google Idols', Internet users mimic the Endemol programme *Idols* and perform popular songs in front of their web cams (Marwick 2007). Websites like Classicgaming.com or The Oldskool PC revolve around industrial products that are not available on the market anymore, like old computers and old computer games. Using emulators, these applications can be executed on current platforms. This activity shows an overlap between accumulation and archiving by maintaining the cultural heritage and providing access to out-of-date technologies with emulators.[11] The domain of accumulation works according to the principles of 'remixing', combining, changing and adapting texts that have been already produced. Many of these activities could be covered by fair use rights, but are often subject to the restricting Digital Millennium Copyright Act and cause 'cease and desist' letters to be written. This domain thus has considerable potential for confrontations between users and copyright-holding companies.[12]

Archiving/organizing takes place on several levels. On an active and intrinsic level, users store artefacts, build online data collections and reorganize cultural resources and knowledge bases. Prime examples would be platforms such as the Internet Archive, the Gutenberg Project or Scene.org. The latter is a platform initially used by members of the 'demoscene', a culture rooted in the early computer subcultures of illegal copying and cracking of copyright protection systems, but today primarily focused on the creation of sophisticated real-time animations. Scene.org serves as the main distribution platform and archive for their productions, as well as for the netlabel community, which is in need of a distribution platform as well, since traffic costs can still be incurred.[13] The *Netlabel Catalogue* is a wiki-based system for documenting and organizing the multitude of netlabels according to genre and linking them to individual websites. The Gutenberg Project provides access to texts that are already in the public domain, as does the Internet Archive for audio, film and text files. The original purpose of the Internet Archive was to save as many websites as possible over an indefinite period. Users participate by uploading files to the Internet Archive. A whole array of film documents from conventional archives have been stored online. Another example of archiving work is the multitude of fan sites that organize links to related content or the many weblogs and web forums that share content originally produced by corporate companies. This ranges from pornography communities, mostly organized around a 'category' or 'fetish', who share related links and files to BitTorrent sites providing links to audio and film files that are often distributed violating copyright infringement laws. Services offering web space to store large files, such as Rapidshare, Flyupload, Bandango, and the like are frequently used to distribute copyright-protected files. Communities focused on sharing those files use web forums to provide commentary post links to online stored files. This area is often affected by the copyright holder's attempts to shut sites down or have content removed. If files are removed due to copyright claims, they frequently are reposted very soon. Figure 3 indicates an overlapping area in the domains of construction and archiving that is frequently affected by copyright laws. Here the media practice of appropriating, accumulating, and distributing artefacts collides with the commercial interests of the original designers and copyright holders. The affordances of new technologies, in other words, collide with business models developed in the age of mechanical reproduction.

Construction is production occurring outside established culture industries. It describes the emergence of new distribution and production means that are not institutionalized and not necessarily controlled by an owner, but rather generally at the user's disposal. It describes the production of new content and new technologies, as opposed to media that comment on or relate directly to popular media productions. A prime example would be software production, the netlabel scene and the demoscene, contexts where production often takes place independently from corporate companies. In the field of web design, many developers collaborate in informal and non-monetary-based networks on a global scale to produce resources and production means that are exploited at a local level in 'creative industries'. Frameworks for building web applications such as Django, written in the collaboratively developed programming language Python, are designed according to open-source principles by a community of programmers and web designers who are actually collaborating to build the necessary tools for their daily business of programming web applications. Deeply rooted in Internet media practices, these designers are aware of the need for cooperation.

Another overlap between the cultural industries and consumers has to be mentioned. In the field of modification of software-based artefacts, computer games, game consoles, hand-held devices and so on, consumer goods are exchanged by users. The 'homebrew software scene' is developing applications for industrial devices like the Xbox or the Playstation Portable. In the field of software production, many official ties between companies and developing communities are discernible. For companies, a major advantage of users appropriating software is that the products become more useful, an aspect which the computer game industry stimulates by providing tools for editing game levels, among other things (Nieborg 2005). It is interesting to note that the construction of artefacts leads to the establishment of structures for archiving and distribution. For homebrew software, such a platform is the download server Xbins, which provides hundreds of unofficial Xbox applications.[14] A popular platform for distributing open-source software is the website Sourceforge.net, which hosts over 155,000 software projects and offers an infrastructure for development, project organization, and representation.[15] Within the domain of construction, traditional copyrights and the various copyleft licenses and other open-source and free licenses can be applied. Software is often released under copyleft licenses, assuring that the knowledge and its further development remains within the cultural resource.[16] Music, demos, and other texts are often distributed under open content licenses, such as Creative Commons licenses, protecting fair use rights as well as the right of the copyright holder to control the exploitation.[17] In that respect, user activities don't just contribute to already existing material, as the domain of accumulation indicates, they also create new resources that are consequently expanded. Furthermore, user activities in the area of archiving don't simply provide access to those resources, they start transforming cultural heritage through digitalization and make old resources available.

The three areas of accumulation, archiving, and construction certainly overlap, especially in light of Web 2.0 applications, where all three areas are often inseparably connected. While accumulation, archiving and construction indicate user activities extending cultural production from the established industries into the domain of users, the emergence of 'social media' or 'Web 2.0' applications demonstrate the ability of media industries to employ these user activities commercially. As I will explain in chapter 5, user practices that have been developed during the past decade are here successfully implemented and integrated into web applications and even business models.

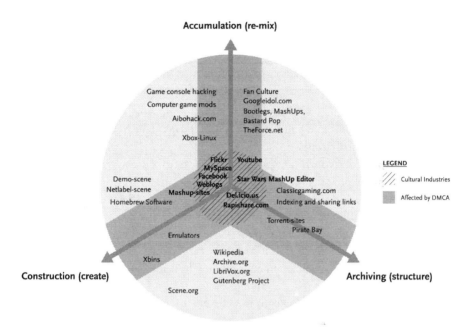

Figure 3. Accumulation, archiving, and construction and overlaps.

Figure 3 shows the three areas and the overlapping user activities in the extended culture industries. Wherever user activities affect copyright and intellectual property of established producers, confrontations emerge often involving lawsuits, PR campaigns and lobbying for law enforcement. The Digital Millennium Copyright Act aims at preventing users from challenging existing business. Figure 3 indicates DMCA-affected areas of user participation. In its center the area is indicated where accumulation, archiving and construction become an inherent aspect of commercial Web 2.0 applications. A more complex level of archiving and organization is the dynamic and complex interaction of a plurality of users and information technology in 'social media' applications. While users automatically engage in structuring the World Wide Web by creating hyperlinks, which affect Google search results, they can participate more actively by creating meta-data, or tags. This is information added to stored data, such as photos, hyperlinks or articles on weblogs. The design of many recent information management systems – often recognized as typical Web 2.0 applications – stimulates users to provide these meta-data implicitly. As outlined in detail in section 4.2, design channels user actions in a way that encourages their participation in expanding a system-wide database, adding meta-data, and thereby structuring stored information semantically. Platforms for user-generated content employ these techniques for their system-wide information management system. In that respect, Web 2.0 applications create a blurring of recognized user activities, because users can accumulate, archive, and organize media content on these platforms as well as create, add, and archive their own productions.

It also provides the possibility for cultural industries to shift from content creator to platform provider for user-generated content, and hence effectively extend their production mode into the sphere of consumers.

As shown in figure 3, accumulation, archiving, and construction describe the main areas of user activities, which can certainly overlap. YouTube is a prime example of a platform combining all domains. YouTube provides traffic and web space for storing and distributing videos. Due to the sheer scale of traffic, YouTube itself is an industrial player, functioning as an infrastructure for users. Many of the videos revolve around popular media content or archive snippets from TV shows, such as the most embarrassing moments during the singing contest *Idols*, the Eurovision Song Contest, and homemade videos of those who desperately wish to appear in those shows. But YouTube is also an example of a new communication channel with non-professional commentaries on contemporary issues, the videos of which are stored on YouTube, as well as many homemade films, such as screencasts by software developers who take advantage of YouTube's free distribution system. Examples of DIY culture are the many how-to and tutorial videos that provide information on how to use software or how to replace a broken iPod battery. Flickr shows how construction and archiving can completely merge and how explicit and implicit participation in cultural production interact. Users store their homemade pictures, and just by adding a title to a picture, they already contribute to a system-wide database of information that shapes ways of navigating through the stored content. MySpace and Flickr, simply by virtue of their scale, are industrial infrastructures used for creating personal profiles. Often these profiles refer to popular culture by featuring pop songs or references to other icons of popular culture. MySpace, like Facebook and Xing, are services for organizing and archiving nodes in individual social networks. These systems are a means for the organization and distribution of information among their users. Activities performed on the above-mentioned web platforms are often summarized as user-generated content (but not the implicit participation, which is mostly neglected) published and distributed through a platform provided by a commercial enterprise.

Participation in cultural production is evident in the domains of accumulation, archiving, and construction. Many practices of users unfold in a complex dynamic with the cultural industries; they may develop through accidental or deliberate collaborations, or in competition, or completely outside of established production channels. Production outside the established cultural industries can be incorporated into the modes of production. The alleged shift from corporate cultural production to user-led production, however, is an extension of the cultural industries into the sphere of users. It also constitutes a domain for new markets and business opportunities, as well as new resources for the cultural industries' production processes. The overlapping areas of the three domains of participation can be best analysed by distinguishing explicit and implicit participation as two different, but not mutually exclusive, modes of user activities.

2.3   Explicit and implicit participation

Participatory culture is co-constituted by the material aspects of computer technology, software, and the Internet. Often these aspects have been treated as mere 'black boxes' and were reduced to 'enabling technologies' without further examination. Participation was therefore only understood as explicit participation. It has been described as a conscious practice of competent consumers. In information management systems, however, participation rather unfolds implicitly, and many users are actually not aware that they contribute to an application simply through using it. Therefore, it is necessary to distinguish between explicit and implicit participation.

Explicit participation is driven by motivation, either intrinsic or extrinsic. Reasons to participate are as diverse as the skills and abilities of those who do. Reducing these activities to critical activism, anti-hegemonic attitudes or altruistic motives is not sufficient. Explicit participation is heterogeneous and concerns users who range from unskilled novices to professional programmers and come from the most diverse contexts, such as paid labour, leisure, or unpaid voluntary work, and it is heterogeneous in terms of the methods used, too.

Implicit participation is channeled by design, by means of easy-to-use interfaces, and the automation of user activity processes. In contrast to explicit participation, it does not necessarily require a conscious activity of cultural production, nor does it require users to choose from different methods in problem-solving, collaboration, and communication with others. Rather, it is a design solution that takes advantage of certain habits users have. Users are not required to interact in social networks, nor is there a need for common objectives or shared values in order to use platforms that employ implicit participation. Such platforms provide the means for certain user activities and benefit from the user-generated content. The user activities performed on these web platforms contribute to the system-wide information management and can be exploited for different purposes, such as improving information retrieval, or gathering user information for market research.

Implicit participation seems to emerge out of nowhere, but it is actually the result of software design that focuses on user actions. Peer-to-peer (P2P) file-sharing systems, such as eDonkey, Gnutella, and Bit Torrent reveal implicit participation in the technical design as well, since they require the user to share a part of his or her hard drive and processing power for the system-wide distribution performance. Commercial services in Internet Protocol Television (IPTV) like Joost or Zattoo, and

IP telecommunication services (Voice over IP, VoIP) like Skype or Gizmo also take advantage of P2P infrastructures for distribution and connectivity. Using these systems automatically leads to implicit participation in sharing hardware and connectivity for distribution purposes. Some systems, such as the above-mentioned IPTV and VoIP services, use implicit participation as a default while other P2P applications, such as the SETI browser or the Folding@home project, require an initial 'opt in' decision to be made by the user. Users installing applications such as Skype, Joost or Gizmo also 'consciously' accept implicit participation by accepting the general terms of use. Similarly explicit is the user's decision to participate when agreeing to share his or her files with other participants and allowing uploading to a file-sharing system. On a technical level, participation is implicit by virtue of its being part of the design, while on the user level, the conscious decision to share files and contribute to the system-wide resource of available files is explicitly constructed in the form of an agreement to share and collect files for further sharing. Implicit participation is generally hybrid due to the implementation of user activities into software design and the inherent interaction of users and information systems.

Explicit Participation	Implicit Participation
E.g. fan culture, activism, cooperating in software development, contributing to Wikipedia and other resources, writing blogs, posting and creating content.	Uploading files to user-created content platforms such as Flickr. Adding tags (to Flickr, Delicious, etc.), using rating platforms such as Digg.com, placing Digg buttons on a website, rating and watching videos on YouTube.
Sharing content in P2P systems, 'donating' processing power to SETI, Folding@Home and others.	Default P2P systems for distribution. Providing 'views', 'click rates' through visiting websites and retrieving content.

Figure 4. Examples of explicit and implicit participation.

Figure 4 differentiates the various actions of explicit and implicit participation using intrinsic and extrinsic motivation as criteria for explicit participation, while implicit participation is channelled by technical design and default settings in the used systems. Participatory culture consists of both modes of participation, that is, implicit and explicit participation. Explicit participation mostly refers to the appropriation of technology by users and the development of technical skills. Implicit participation draws on user habits, such as sharing information and sending each other copies of films and music files. Just by watching a video on YouTube, users participate in generating data, as do users uploading files to Flickr or YouTube. Furthermore, they participate by adding titles, descriptions, and tags to describe their content. This data is then used to improve the system's search engine (Kessler, Schäfer 2009). Automating and facilitating those user activities lead to implicit participation. Thus far, this has been most effectively achieved in Web 2.0 applications, where participation is not only perceived as the possibility for users to do 'whatever' they want, but also where activities are employed for improving information management, where data is simultaneously created for marketing research and advertisement purposes, and where a variety of data is synchronized for different platforms for user-created content. Participatory culture is closely interrelated to its technological features. The latter are inseparably related to explicit and implicit user activities and deserve attention in the analysis of contemporary media practices.

Chapter 3
Enabling/Repressing Participation

Any sufficiently advanced technology is indistinguishable from magic (Arthur C. Clarke).

Discussions about participatory culture often neglect the fact that they are as much about technology as they are about social interactions. Although technology is assigned an important role, many discussions insufficiently analyse the extent to which technology influences emerging media practices. Technology is perceived as somehow magically enabling users to participate in collective production, especially in the discourse on participatory culture. Perceiving technology as having appeared out of thin air leads to a moral framing of participatory culture, which results in analyses dwelling excessively on 'good' or 'bad' consequences. Highly informed by the positive connotation connected to community, participation, or user-led creation, technology is often reduced to the role of a neutral activator, while practice and use become the objects of a myopic moral perception.[1] In order to develop a different understanding of participatory culture, the following chapter will examine key technologies such as the computer, software, and the Internet in light of their characteristic features. Affordances of these technologies which either enable or repress participatory uses of technology are examined with respect to design decisions. Design features may have ideological connotations as well, that is, they may be construed as a mere pragmatic solution to a given problem. As has been argued above, technology is open for interpretation, as are all media texts. Reviewing technology, which is ideologically charged in a participatory culture, reveals that design decisions, which were caused by pragmatic solutions, may be interpreted as ideologically motivated designs at a later stage. This often results in technology being perceived as something with an almost mythical status, which inseparably blends with the popular discourse on participation. In order to untangle this tight web of semantic connections between discourses and technological design in the dispositif of participation, the technologies involved will be examined in light of their specific qualities.

As Norman emphasizes, technology is affected by the qualities of the material used and the design that shapes it (1989:8). These qualities are defined as affordances. In his discussion on design, Norman uses the term affordance in an ambiguous way, one that constitutes a twofold understanding (Norman 1989:9). Affordance describes the material that is used to build or design something, just as wood can be used to design a table, for example, but it also describes the basic qualities of a designed object. As for the table, affordances refer to the possibility to put something on the table's surface. The use of technology is also affected by appropriation, which refers to what users do with a designer's object. A park bench is designed to be sat on, but it is often appropriated for sleeping, because its size also 'affords' sufficient space to lie down on. To prevent this particular use of park benches, designers may add extra armrests in the middle of the bench. This example also makes it clear that politics can be inscribed into the design of artefacts (see also Winner 1986; Latour 1991; Bijker, Pinch 1992). However, as Bernward Joerges convincingly demonstrates, the politics of artefacts are also subject to interpretation, and can be created by inventing a legend.[2] A legend informs the discourse on technology and reveals yet another connection between discourse and design. The many aspects contributing to the construction of technology and the development of discourse are often difficult to untangle.

The basic reconfiguration of our media culture is rooted in the computer, in software, and in the global interconnectedness of the Internet. It fuses technological characteristics with user practices. The constitution of media practices is very much based on the following technological characteristics:

1. the computer as a universal machine, a meta-medium
2. software as an in-material, lossless copiable, modular and tentative resource
3. the Internet as a global infrastructure and tool to connect to social worlds

The computer must to be treated as the basic affordance, the platform upon which the design and use of software operates. The infrastructural features, which connect a multitude of computers to as many users, creates the potential for collective production, and functions as a socio-technical ecosystem for software applications and users.

A profound understanding of the specific qualities of our 'new media' will shape a better understanding for the socio-political dynamics emerging from the collision of old business models and new media practices, as well as an understanding for the appropriate integration of these new practices into the upcoming information society. This is a complex matter due to the dual logic of the above-mentioned qualities. On the one hand, the basic material, which seems to be a rather fuzzy notion in a digital culture, creates affordances in addition to those created in the design of software applications.

3.1   The computer

The Analytical Engine has no pretensions whatever to originate anything. It can do whatever we know how to order it to perform (Ada Lovelace, 1842).

If such a machine were designed in a way that any owner could mold and channel its power to his own needs, then a new kind of medium would have been created: a meta-medium, whose content would be a wide range of already-existing and not-yet-invented media (Alan Kay 1977:404).

Three main features of the personal computer are crucial for contemporary media practices with respect to enabling user participation: a) its ability to serve as a software environment for executing any application that is formulated in an appropriate symbolic code the computer can execute; b) its ability to copy electronic files at almost no cost; and c) its design as an everyday medium. The development of these features has to be placed in a historical perspective. It emerged from the development of binary number systems and the development of calculating machines, and was transformed through different design approaches, which are very much affected by various needs for problem solving, as well as creating markets.

When Ada Augusta Byron King, Countess of Lovelace, described the Analytical Engine in 1842, she was formulating a concept of a universal machine, a machine able to execute any task that was requested of it in a 'machine comprehensible' way.[3] The striking thing about the computers we use today is their ability to function as universal tools, as machines that are not designed for one special purpose, but designed to execute any task provided in symbolic code. These codes are delivered as software. Personal computers made this feature of universality useful to a large group of users, and the Internet and the World Wide Web would later multiply these affordances by distributing them globally and subsequently connecting the social worlds of its many users to individual terminals. The computer functions therefore not only as a machine to execute tasks, but engages in a productive performance with its user (Winograd, Flores 1986:170).[4] The aspect of universality inherent in modern computers has been developed over time, and can be traced back not only to the personal computer, but also to the basic characteristics of the Internet. It creates a design flexibility (Winograd, Flores 1986:170) that enables dynamic productivity to occur in a participatory culture.

As an assistant to Charles Babbage, who conceived an early version of a mechanical computer, with his difference engine and his analytical engine, Lovelace recognized the potential for creation that went beyond the mere calculation of differential equations:

The Analytical Engine weaves algebraical patterns just as the Jacquard-loom weaves flowers and leaves. Here, it seems to us, resides much more of originality than the Difference Engine can be fairly entitled to claim.[5]

This line of thought, while neglected for some time, was taken up by Alan Turing, who devised a concept of universal machines that became a guiding principle for the computers we use today (Turing 1936). Turing's notion of the future applications such a machine would develop is remarkable:

The importance of the universal machine is clear. We do not need to have an infinity of different machines in doing different jobs. A single one will suffice. The engineering problem of producing various machines for various jobs is replaced by the office work of 'programming' the universal machine to do these jobs (Turing, 1948).

This vision already anticipates the transformation of engineering work to programming work, from countless machines to a single universal machine simulating each of the many special machines, and from the work floor of mechanical configurations and tinkering to the office space. It anticipates programming as the main task of work processes evolving from the information machines to come. Turing's universal machine was first and foremost a thought experiment, suggesting an infinite paper tape for storage, which eventually grew into applicable machinery through John von Neuman's electronic computer design (Bolter 1984:47). The most significant feature of the Von Neumann architecture was that it could store data and instructions in one memory and define the central components of modern computing as an input and output device, a memory and processing and control unit. A computer would then retrieve instructions from the store, read and execute them, and continue to do so until the task is completed or the program halted (Ceruzzi 2003:23).[6] The basic quality of an electronic machine – its ability to execute any task that is formulated as an algorithm – was a significant stepping stone for the further development of executable applications and the eventual development into a machine used for office work, leisure time activities, and communication. The separation of software from hardware turns the computer into a basic platform for the execution of any software compatible with the machine's operating system. It consequently turns the computer into a 'software environment' (Nelson 1974/1987:47), and constitutes the emergence of software industries to provide all kinds of applications for a mass market of standardized machines (Campbell-Kelly 2003). The availability of these standardized machines at affordable prices affords access to production means and provides users with the basic platform to execute any kind of software. However, one should not neglect that the decreasing prices for computer hardware are also related to precarious working conditions in the manufacturing industries, especially in developing countries.

BASTARD CULTURE!

Another crucial aspect inherent to electronic computers is the ability to copy files. From the outset, an electronic computer was a copying machine (Parikka 2008:71). The copy is a genuine and inevitable feature of computer technology and is still the basic principle for data transmission.[7] Jussi Parikka emphasizes that the copy became a cultural technique and an aesthetic principle. This exceeds the general appreciation for collage techniques that is familiar from 20th-century avant-garde art, or of remixing in music cultures (Miller 2004), and aims at core aspects of digital culture, such as peer-to-peer file sharing, streaming media, unlimited access to information through downloading and the creation and distribution of software.[8] This new media practice is contrary to many business models in culture industries that rely on the control of distribution, such as the music and film industry (Parikka 2008:73). The ability to copy appears as a core feature of a computer's performance and its affordance to communicate and send data through networks.

While these two affordances (functioning as a 'universal software environment' and a 'copy machine') of computer technology are significant, the development of the computer from an expensive and sophisticated scientific apparatus to an affordable device for common users was crucial for the emergence of participatory culture. The emergence of a market for computers and the development of an accessible device serving all kind of purposes, from office to leisure work, are closely interrelated. This process was very much affected by designing the computer as an easy-to-use medium (Friedemann 1999). The development of graphical user interfaces and software applications in order to make software programming easier and to enable users to write their own code contributed significantly to the development of the personal computers (PCs) we use today. A similar development can be seen in the diffusion of radio sets. As Andreas Fickers (2007) argues, the development of interfaces, such as control panels and tuning buttons, provided an effective distribution of radio to a broad audience. But along with the easy-to-use interfaces and a growing audience came regulation and control, confining the apparatus of the radio to a bureaucratically controlled broadcasting device, thus excluding enthusiastic users, whose technology appropriation has stimulated inventive technological development.

Computers were not designed for convenience by chance; the design development of the microcomputer was highly influenced by the promise of participation. Although in many texts participation has not been explicitly identified as the desired objective, many others focused on the explicit development of technologies and machines to improve the organization of information and the understanding of knowledge. Vannevar Bush's visionary text 'As We May Think' (Bush 1945) does not emphasize an enabling aspect for common users but rather sees his information machines as effective tools for professionals.[9] However, Bush's memex, the anticipated apparatus for information management, inspired other pioneers, such as Douglas Engelbart (1962) and Ted Nelson (1974). These men developed tools and concepts that broadened the use of computer technology for lay users.[10] Engelbart introduced many devices that would make interaction with computers easier and more efficient, such as a pointer, the keyboard and the mouse, the representation of users' actions on a screen. What Bush had anticipated as a research and annotation tool for scientists was for Engelbart an interactive device for scientists, architects, managers, physicians and all other occupations that deal with information (Engelbart 1962:4). In his preliminary report, *Augmenting Human Intellect*, Engelbart describes the computer as a medium for retrieving and sharing information, for writing, drawing and constructing models virtually:

> In such a future working relationship between human problem-solver and computer 'clerk,' the capability of the computer for executing mathematical processes would be used whenever it was needed. However, the computer has many other capabilities for manipulating and displaying information that can be of significant benefit to the human in non-mathematical processes of planning, organizing, studying, etc. Every person who does his thinking with symbolized concepts (whether in the form of the English language, pictographs, formal logic, or mathematics) should be able to benefit significantly (1962:12).

Referring extensively to Bush's concept of the memex, and placing his research in association with it (1962:54), Engelbart proposed a future for the computer that seems so natural today. However, at the time it stood in striking contrast to the expectations engineers and computer scientists had for computers.[11] A general motivation for Engelbart is evident in his notion of 'bootstrapping', building technologies and evaluating them immediately in order to improve them in the next design step. His design vision viewed bootstrapping as a process of technology transfer that would broaden the potential group of computer users (Bardini, Friedewald 2002).

While Engelbart anticipated computer technology as a means for professional use, Ted Nelson explicitly called for the computer to be turned into an enabling technology for all consumers. He argues that everybody has to understand computers, because computers would increasingly determine the shape of life in society. He furthermore anticipated what would come to be called 'hypermedia' as a means for collective production and educational processes (Nelson 1974).

Theories of learning, the quest to improve education and enabling children were significant influences on the work of pioneering computer scientists Seymour Papert, Alan Kay and Adele Goldberg, as well as others who pushed the development of the personal computer further (e.g. Papert 1980; Kay 1990). A radical new step in that direction was the attempt to harness computer technology for children. Recognizing that the potential of computers went beyond facilitating calculations in weapons engineering, they focused on designing an interactive machine for 'children of all ages' (Kay 1972). Inspired by the concepts of learning taught by Jean Piaget, MIT mathematician and computer scientist Seymour Papert developed the programming language LOGO for children as users. Papert was convinced that an interactive approach to computers would have an enormous impact on learning and improve children's knowledge and thinking (Papert 1980). Alan Kay, who had been in contact with Papert and learned of LOGO, Piaget's theories, and the theory of constructivism, developed concepts of human-machine interaction that were directly designed for children. Kay, joining the research facility Xerox PARC in 1970, was not only influenced by contemporary learning theories, but was also familiar with McLuhan's theories (Kay 1990). Consequently, he recognized that the computer had to be perceived as a medium; it was neither a tool nor a machine to be operated by a specially trained person. Instead, it could be used by anyone who had grown up in a computer-related media culture. In his personal review on the development of graphical user interfaces, Kay notes that he was wondering 'What kind of thinker would you become if you grew up with an active simulator connected, not just to one point of view, but to all points of view the ages represented so they could be dynamically tried out and compared?' (Kay 1990:193). As Kay and Goldberg put it, the computer should turn into a 'meta-medium' that would make it possible to simulate all other media (1977/2003:394). This is highly reminiscent of Turing's universal machine. The resulting concept was the Dynabook, a computer that resembles today's laptop. For the Dynabook, Kay and Goldberg turned to everyday actions, such as writing and painting, and tried to work them into the computer system. Similar to Engelbart's approach to translating an architect's work into a computer-aided work sphere, Kay and Goldberg conceived the Dynabook applications by translating everyday actions into computer-aided activities. Recognizing the danger of an application-overloaded device that loses its functionality in an attempt to serve every possible need, the Dynabook was conceptualized as a basic platform on which users ought to write the software they would need.[12] The important thing about this line of thought is that users in Kay's and Goldberg's concept are active participants, who develop the applications they need themselves. Consequently, the computer is perceived as a platform on which basically any program can be executed. Once the basic platform (hardware) is provided, programming applications (software) provide a means for executing any medium whatsoever on the computer. Kay and Goldberg anticipated the complexity of software and its incalculable application in terms of a 'not yet invented media', a blank to be filled in by the ingenuity of users of programming languages, who might build media according to their needs. Future users are therefore invited to participate not only in using the technology but actively altering it through developing software applications. The dream for a Dynabook as an active tool for children of all ages still holds large expectations for the disadvantaged generations in developing countries. Education and the promise of participation are highly evident in the One Laptop Per Child project (OLPC) headed by Nicholas Negroponte.[13] Apple's iPad comes closest to the early sketches of the Dynabook; the iPad does indeed represent a meta-medium for common users, although it is rather expensive and quite limited in comparison with other platforms.

Ted Nelson evangelized the use of computers as an enabling technology and as a means of education; he called for active citizen participation, promoting connected libraries similar to Licklider's concept, but exceeding it with his idea of collaborative work processes for all users. Instead of limiting the information technologies to military people, scientists and intellectuals, Nelson pleaded for free access and collective collaboration processes.[14] Nelson formulated his vision in the ambitious publication *Computer Lib/Dream Machines*, a fanzine-like book containing xeroxed articles, newspaper clippings and many of his own comments on the technological design of computers (Nelson 1974).[15] The book could be read either from front to back or back to front. The front side, *Computer Lib*, anticipated the computer as a comprehensible machine open for anyone to use; the flip side, *Dream Machines*, introduced hypermedia and hypertext as a means for education and collaborative learning.[16] Nelson's message was clear: people had to learn and understand computers now, because computers were entering all levels of society and becoming an important means for administration and governance:

> Computers are not everything, they are just an aspect of everything, and not to know this is computer illiteracy, a silly and dangerous ignorance (Nelson 2003:303).

The promise of empowerment is clearly stated in the illustrations on both the front cover of the book, which features a fist with the caption 'Computer Lib. You can and must understand computers NOW', and the back cover, where a user with a Superman cape flies through a window into a virtual world subtitled 'Dream Machines. New Freedom through Computer Screens'. A countercultural, anti-hegemonic tone pervades Nelson's writing, which urges the reader to recognize the need for acquiring a knowledge of computers, as well as being a call to reject the idea of the computer as a mere scientific machine that cannot be used or understood by laypeople. The secret knowledge circulating in the developer's culture of computer manufacturers who thoroughly affected – in an adverse way according to Nelson – computers' prospective uses had to be made accessible to a broader audience. Nelson calls for design to alter the machine so that it becomes a medium and, as Noah Wardrip-Fruin and Nick Montford point out in their commentary on *Computer Lib/Dream Machines*, Nelson foresaw intellectually what the microcomputers Altair and Apple II realized in design (Wardrip-Fruin, Montford 2003:301).

It is a convincing argument that the development of the personal computer was a complex process that took place simultaneously in different areas of scientific research that are not mutually exclusive, as well as in business-oriented research and amateur circles (Friedemann 1999; Sturgeon 2000; Freiberger, Swaine 2000; Lécuyer 2005). Visions of socio-political progress were informing the discourse and co-developing the mindset accompanying technological development. The way we understand computers has changed in the process, as they have gone from being data-processing machines to interactive devices. It radically altered the initially anticipated target group for computer technology and eventually created an enormous market, which is the point where the claim for participation meets the genuine interest of the entrepreneur, as Ted Turner has pointed out (Turner 2006).[17] The personal computer has given users a technology that is unlike most other artefacts. In addition to its capacity to execute software, it also unleashes creativity and effectively accumulates labour in the collaborative activities of users, who either engage explicitly in cultural production or benefit from the work of fellow users when creating works individually. In the networked society, the computer is not only a 'digital workbench' but functions also as an access point to networked communication and the distribution of files, and even as a multi-media centre. The more graphical user interfaces made the use of software applications and networked services easier to work with, the more users were able to actively participate in the emerging digital culture. The computer apparatus is the linchpin for participatory culture, and will remain so even when its shape changes and increasingly becomes replaced by mobile devices.

Using a computer goes beyond human-machine interaction and, in addition to the logical machinery, it provides access to the realm of binary codes: software defines the infinite number of special machines and media that can be simulated on the universal machine.

3.2   Software

The stuff we call 'software' is not like anything that human society is used to thinking about
(Bruce Sterling).

Mens agitat molem (Vergil, Aeneid, 6,727).

Software is the stuff that runs on computers, and it is an artefact completely unlike anything else used earlier in history. The term software primarily describes all non-physical parts of a computer.[18] The term hardware refers to the physical components (microprocessor, hard drive, motherboard, and peripheral tools, such as the monitor, keyboard, mouse, etc.) that form the material layer for executing, storing and representing software and data.[19] Software itself remains a rather strange phenomenon, falling somewhere in between logic and machinery. Science fiction author Bruce Sterling described it aptly.

Software is something like a machine, and something like mathematics, and something like language, and something like thought, and art, and information... but software is not in fact any of those other things.
The protean quality of software is one of the greatest sources of its fascination.

It also makes software very powerful, very subtle, very unpredictable, and very risky (Sterling 1993:31).

Indeed its very qualities affect the way software is produced, distributed, and used. It is a new, strange form of language that is as effective as machinery. Software is more than just a symbolic language for programming computers, it intrinsically involves the 'cultural practices of its employment and appropriation' (Cramer 2008:173). The quality of software as a symbolic form (often referred to as code), and as a copiable digital artefact, contributes significantly to the emergence of its cultural practice. The computer is the space where the logic of the program is converted into action. In view of software design and its appropriation within participatory culture, three affordances of software have to be emphasized: software is 1) 'in-material', 2) modular and 3) tentative (Rieder, Schäfer 2007:156).[20]

Software is 'in-material'

Software has been often perceived as immaterial, due to its close resemblance to 'human language' and its haptic inconceivability. It cannot be touched physically and it is structured in a symbolic form like language, but its performance impacts the material world. However, software is always 'in-material'; it is not only embedded in data carriers, it also must be perceived in terms of materiality, because it creates means of production. Labelling software an immaterial artefact has been criticized by Matthew Fuller, among others, for 'trivializing and debilitating' its far-reaching and profound material impact on economics, labour practices and social relations (Fuller 2008:4; 2005). However, for the use of software and aspects of participation, the affordance of a language-like structure, which harbours a material inconceivability and is an affordance for any digital artefact to be distributed through copying, is a crucial aspect of software that could be called immaterial, but will be described here as 'in-material' in order not to emphasize its relation to a material world.[21]

Consequently, software is understood as something 'which may defy immediate physical contact, yet which is incorporated in materiality rather than floating as a metaphysical substance in virtual space' (Van den Boomen et al. 2009:9).

A software program is a text written in a programming language observing a strictly defined structure and syntactic rules (Cramer 2008:168). However, software differs from spoken language in that it requires a material data carrier. On the one hand, a software program is a formulation in a programming language, while on the other hand it is the execution of the formulated actions, and it therefore stands, as Latour said, 'between word and action'. Apart from the material data carrier, software requires a basic prerequisite for application; software itself is by virtue of its structure similar to language, but by virtue of its function and effect similar to machinery.[22] The metaphors we use to describe software unveil this characteristic as well, because they are drawn from the domain of both language and engineering. One speaks of 'programming languages', and the task of a programmer is 'to write code', in which 'syntax errors' occur, assembler code is used and a compiler to 'translate' a program into a language the machine can read. People speak of software engineering, and professionals in the field are called software engineers, designers or architects.[23] How close programming languages are to conventional languages becomes clear in the programming language Perl, developed by Larry Wall, who was trained as a linguist. The extensive use of English words in Perl inspired developers to write Perl programs that read like poems, and though the poems may have appeared nonsensical in their context, they nevertheless represented a working program (Cox; Ward 2008:208).[24]

Perligata (or Lingua::Romana::Perligata) derives from Perl's translation of all English words in the programming language into Latin. When executing the program, it translates itself into the original programming language and runs accordingly.[25] These examples demonstrate how similar programming languages are related to the conventional understanding of languages in general: they are designed as languages, and function accordingly. It furthermore shows how technological design is also closely related to its developer's culture. It can be fun or sometimes nonsensical, much like conventional language use itself.[26]

Software is written in programming code, a system of characters that works according to syntactic rules, and it can be distributed like written texts, but unlike conventional texts, it can be executed by a computer reading the program code. In this process the written program code is translated into electromagnetic impulses, which are often called 'zeros and ones'. Software therefore literally exists between words (the programming language) and action (its execution):

> Now that computers exist, we are able to conceive of a text (a programming language) that is at once words and actions. How to do things with words and then turn words into things is now clear to any programmer (Latour 1992:255).

Similar to J.L. Austin's (1955/1990) concept of action through words, one could describe software as a performative artefact. Referring to Austin's notion Florian, Cramer eloquently labels the process of executing symbols in programming as 'words made flesh' (Cramer 2005). In designing software, instructions are given on how to act. Latour therefore emphasizes the programmer's capacity for action and the discursive aspects of technology for representing social programs.[27] Software programs consist of instructions for the executing computer platform, but they also channel user actions. A computer program is not just a script, it is the combination of a script for actions and their performative execution that can be effective as machinery.[28] Programming means enabling action, making things and actions possible. Similar to Ada Lovelace's notion of the analytical machine that 'weaves algebraical patterns', Ted Nelson speaks of programming as a 'weaving of plans of events (and where they are to take place) – the choreography of happenings' (Nelson 1987:40). In this respect, software can be described as a mode of potentiality (Winograd, Flores 1970:170-172).[29] Winograd and Flores, as well as Ciborra, argue that designing software or information management systems in a generally flexible way that is open to interaction, changes and transformations through its users will improve and work better than static, top-down designed ones (Ciborra 2002:44). A similar argument has been made in relation to users participating in design processes (Von Hippel 2005; Abbet 1999; Oudshoorn, Pinch 2003). There are many references in the literature on this subject to the Promethean aspect of software (Bolter 1986), an argument that is reiterated in the debate on participatory culture technology's basic capacity to enable and emancipate. Unlike other artefacts, software can be built on a trial and error basis, as a work in progress that improves earlier steps after evaluation, at the cost only of time and not of materials. The thought experiment becomes the experiment in software programming itself. Tinkering with software is therefore generally an inexpensive but time-consuming activity in the information age, open to anybody who is willing to invest the necessary time.

The in-materiality of software emphasizes that symbolic language, action – meaning actual performance – and socio-political issues of the material world are inextricably linked. A technological constellation that enables users to actually do things with words, something they can accomplish either individually or in collaborative work processes, and furthermore to reproduce their productions at insignificant cost constitutes a substantial shift in amateur culture. The artefact produced in software programming might be labelled as symbolic code, but it can actually execute and accomplish tasks. Software appears simply as language, but it presents technology as a cultural practice, thereby making it nearly impossible to separate technology from culture.

Since software is in-material, embedded in a data carrier, but like all other digital artefacts easy to copy and distribute, software is widely available and highly exchangeable.[30] It forms a vast cultural resource from which modules can be extracted for further development or to build new software applications, which leads to another crucial affordance of software: its modularity.

Software is modular

When the 'programmers' of the 'Typographic Age' – scientists, philosophers, poets and artists – were writing texts, they never conjured anything out of thin air, but benefited from existing common knowledge and a reservoir of publications. In addition to the individual attributes of an author's work, the intertextuality and the abundance of cross-references and citations in discourses show how interwoven the various elements of cultural production are (Barthes 1967; Kristeva 1969; Foucault 1970). Similarly, software programmers use and contribute to a reservoir of existing written code, and they learn from other programs and even use parts of them to integrate into new programs. As stated already, copying is an inherent element of electronic computers and digitized artefacts. A result of this is that program modules can be quickly and easily implemented into other programs. Programming code is not a coherent and solitary artefact, but can be divided into many different elements that can be produced separately and reused in the most divergent programs. As with conventional texts, software builds up a reservoir, a cultural resource that is used and expanded each time programmers write and release code. This is possible because software is modular, that is, it consists of different modules that all refer to different aspects of a given software application. Similarly, the many modules of a software program can be used for totally different programs. In this respect, software design also resembles the practice of DJ culture in which modules (called samples) from various songs are used to create new songs. The rearranging of existing artefacts is a familiar concept in 20th-century arts, from Dada to surrealism; it turned into an artistic practice in Marcel Duchamp's ready mades and was especially emphasized in William Burroughs's cut-up technique, in which a finished, linear text is cut into different sections and rearranged onto new pages (Burroughs 1961).[31] Developed by an artistic vanguard, these media practices anticipated future modes of media reception, and can help us understand cultural production in the domain of accumulation, where fans rearrange media texts (Jenkins 2002; Schäfer 2004; Hughes, Lang 2006; Van Dijck 2007).[32]

In software development it has been a common practice to reuse modules or even offer them in libraries that provide a framework for software development. Like building a house with LEGO bricks, developers can configure a program by assembling different building blocks of code. Educative software for programming uses this distinctive feature as well by presenting already written programs, which students can change or combine and subsequently see the result of their trial and error efforts by running the programs. Many features of software programs have already been written and just have to be integrated into the programming and adapted for the actual purpose. Programming languages and software development frameworks come with libraries that provide entire modules for certain program routines, as well as modules that enable interoperability with other programming languages.[33] The library of the open-source programming language Python offers many modules to relate Python code to other programming languages. Like other script languages such as Perl or Ruby, Python often is described as a 'glue language' because it is highly capable of connecting modules from different languages and enabling interoperability between the different sections.[34]

Modularity not only stimulates reuse, it also enables the subdivision of complex programming work in a number of sections. This way of organizing large software projects is achieved by assigning smaller pieces of programming tasks to different programmers working independently according to their skills, available time and personal involvement, who put all the different pieces together in the end. Here, the modularity of software enables the global organization of complex software projects, creates new work processes, and makes it feasible for large groups of far-flung programmers to cooperate.[35] Modularity is clearly a crucial factor for the appropriation of software and software-based products, since in its totality the provided programming code offers ample opportunity for reuse and a host of potential combinations. In view of the cultural tradition of collage, reuse and sampling, writing software fits snugly into the tradition of building texts that has been developed over the past century and endows software with a specific cultural value. It literally stimulates participation because it motivates the use of modules in existing software, to alter them or develop new applications. It has a significant impact on collaborative work processes, because complex software projects can be divided in many different modules of different complexity and size. Therefore, a large group of developers can participate effectively even by providing only a small part of programming code. Collaboration can take place online, where platforms offer a means of managing, hosting and developing collaborative software projects.[36] In view of emerging participatory culture, the use and reuse of modules has provoked a heated debate on ownership and control (e.g. Grassmuck 2002; Gosh 2005). An urgent question is to what extent this media practice will be acknowledged and accepted in socio-political circles as a leitmotif of cultural production in digital media.

Software is tentative

While a conventional piece of engineering, say a television set, a car or a bridge is considered finished at the end of its development and production process, software remains unfinished. It does not reach a state of completion but a state of stability, and is only released once it is considered stable and most bugs, errors in the programming work, have been removed. The development does not stop there, but continues with the addition of new features, design changes which are made when the user's appropriation interferes with the software's initial objectives. As is the case for physical artefacts, for example, the park bench mentioned earlier, the use of software appropriation is revealed after software applications are published and introduced into the market. But in contrast to physical artefacts, software-based products seem to offer a vast range of potential applications that can differ radically from the original intentions. When software-based products are released into the market, they are actually merely entering another stage of development.[37] Unlike many physical goods, software can be updated, and electronic consumer goods with network connections receive new software updates, often without their users noticing it.[38] Increasingly, companies exploit this not only to improve the software on their products, but also to control their use. Security holes enabling appropriation are then repaired in order to avert certain ways of using the product.

Before release, software is already a process, characterized by complex design phases and a lot of trial and error (Reeves 1992). Software is tentative in terms of its methodology, its development and its use.[39] Despite many attempts to formalize software, software development has not evolved into a formal and structured design discipline, as is the case with hardware engineering. It still remains a heterogeneous process, executed in many different ways, without mandatory or formal guidelines or standardized procedures, a process that is often the result of the very requirements for which software is produced, that is, its rather vague specifications. As software programmer Jack Reeves states:

> Software specifications tend to be fluid, and change rapidly and often, usually while the design process is still going on. Software development teams also tend to be fluid, likewise often changing in the middle of the design process. In many ways, software bears more resemblance to complex social or organic systems than to hardware. All of this makes software design a difficult and error prone process (Reeves 1992).

Software therefore is in a state of permanent development. In general, software is highly complex, and this complexity derives from the fact that almost no aspect of software development is independent from software design (Reeves 1992). All aspects are interrelated, not only to the programming code itself, but even more importantly to a complex and dynamic dispositif of users, machines and graphical interfaces, aspects, in other words, that have to be translated into program routines and taken into account for the overall functioning of the program.[40] Although the practice, developed in open-source software development, of having many eyes exercise control over the code (Raymond 1998) promises increasing transparency and code maintenance, the programs, and especially their interrelations with other programs, databases, information systems and machines through countless interfaces, frequently continue to grow, as does their complexity. Pluralities of users interacting with software amplify the complexity and reveal 'invisible hands', effects of use and appropriation on other software systems. Nevertheless, it must be acknowledged that there are areas of strict software development that result in stable products. Indeed, Bernhard Rieder distinguishes between a 'stabilized' and an 'innovative' area of software design (2006). Automation industries developed engineering processes for software that have a more final character. The software for industrial robots, aeroplane control systems, cars or traffic systems is characterized by more routine and stable design. Computer games, Internet and web applications, open-source software, and software for consumer products in general are more frequently subjected to still unstable parameters, experiment and innovative developments (Rieder 2006:236-237). There is still a significant amount of unexplored territory in this area of software and information systems, which leaves open the opportunity for unexpected discoveries. These often result in inventive appropriations by users that receive much attention and paint a picture of software programming dominated by young, creative men who do things that seem almost miraculous.[41]

In the area of software-based consumer goods, open-source software and many web technologies, the range of the functionality and applicability of software and software-based products only becomes evident during the process of user appropriation. Modules of the software can be used for completely different means other than those intended by the programmers, and the software can reveal features none of the programmers and designers could have conceived. Continuously developing computer and Internet technologies are another aspect that software is required to adapt to. Frequently, errors, known as 'bugs', are not anticipated and only become evident after a software application has been in use for some time. Software is never free of bugs, and their detection is often achieved only by using the software, which therefore requires beta testers and then users to find and report the errors.[42] One practice of user participation that has been employed by game development company Id Software was to publish a beta version of the first-person-shooter game Doom to users, who then enthusiastically played the game and reported bugs, and occasionally even provided necessary patches. The Mozilla Foundation formalized bug reporting by creating an interface for users to integrate bug reporting into the Bugzilla database. Users can also make suggestions for features to be included in future versions of Mozilla software products. Bugs are often used for processes of appropriation as they are a handy way for manipulating software and exploiting it for purposes unintended by the original developers. Bugs in computer games are frequently used to cause a buffer overflow in a computer game console, such as Microsoft Xbox or Playstation Portable. When the system crashes due to the exploited bug, a different code can be executed. This practice is used for modifying a game console to play unlicensed copies of games or install software applications different than those designated by the vendor.[43]

Software is too complex for us to be able to appraise its overall effectiveness and understand the full range of its applicability. In view of its nature, Latour has noted that 'even a software programmer is surprised by her creation after writing two thousand lines of software' (Latour 1999a:283). The act of creation harbours unforeseen complexities, as do the acts of use and appropriation. Latour reminds us that every creator is surprised by his or her creation, and one may add that the use or interpretation of every creation can hardly be controlled by the creator. Much like Barthes's reader, who is a co-constructor of an author's text, users participate in the creation of software by appropriating it, and reveal features not intended or made visible by the original programmers. The program code of the computer game Grand Theft Auto. San Andreas (Rockstar Games 2004) consisted of a mini-game, a game within a game, that allowed users to engage in erotic activities. By making this hidden feature accessible through a patch known as the 'Hot Coffee Mod', Dutchman Patrick Wildenbourg caused a heated debate on the age rating of the 2004 version of Grand Theft Auto.[44] This clearly highlights a qualitative shift from

Fiske's active audiences, who were only active in interpreting media texts and switching between TV channels, to the users in participatory culture who actually change programs. Again similar to language, the user of digital media is not limited to interpretation or intellectual deconstruction, but engages with these new media texts by altering, rewriting and further developing them (Raessens 2005:380-381).

The modality of software has an enabling feature in that it defines software production as a cultural resource. It enables us to treat software in a similar way to other media texts, which can be remixed and combined in a variety of ways. It therefore contributes significantly to the development of software as an important practice of participatory culture. The process of learning how to use and how to develop software is and has often been a social one, which is something stressed by Winograd and Flores, who say that 'the computer is unlike common tools in its connectivity to a larger network of equipment. Its power does not lie in having a single purpose, like a carpenter's plane, but in its connection to the larger network of communication' (Winograd; Flores 1986:170).

This is true of software development and its use. It transforms the cultural practice of dealing with media texts into one with a plurality of more or less skilled users, who subsequently appropriate it in many different ways. Before the Internet, computer subcultures, including computer clubs, 'copy parties' and other locally organized events, were the network that provided the social wetware for hardware and software. With the Internet and its extremely successful application via the WWW, computers and their users were effectively connected to a global network.

3.3   The Internet

The emergence of a global community of learning is a natural outcome of a world in which the production and transportation of commodities finally merges with the movement of information itself (McLuhan 2003:12).

Even if the extent of the Internet's global community remains disputable, the production of digital commodities nevertheless converges with the transferring of information online, as anticipated by McLuhan.[45] As a basic affordance, the Internet first and foremost distributes the qualities of computers and software on a global scale, making them accessible to everyone with an Internet connection. It literally connects individual computer users with a plurality of other users, regardless of their respective geographical locations. Through the Internet, a single computer is situated in a larger network that exceeds the locally confined social networks of the pre-Internet era. In addition to its usefulness as an office machine, it has developed as a convenient communication device.[46] It serves as an infrastructure for distributing data, and through accumulating resources of collectively amassed texts, it simultaneously creates an archive for cultural heritage (Borgmann 2000) and a social memory (e.g. Ernst 2007).

Describing the construction of the Internet would again highlight the dynamic and ideologically tinted interaction between humans, discourses and technology. On a discursive level, the ideology inherent in the technology could be summarized as a) universal access and b) unlimited communication, characteristics that are most radically realized in the basic design of the World Wide Web.[47] However, many more pragmatic arguments were a driving force behind the development of networking, such as the sharing of hardware or data in research projects. Many design decisions resulting in the specific features of the Internet can be traced back to these needs and convictions. It wasn't only Licklider's dream of future libraries that had a major impact on the technical design and the social interaction of computer networks, but also the succeeding generation of engineers' belief in a free flow of information, not to mention their relatively open, non-hierarchical way of working.[48] But the need for sharing expensive computer resources, distributing information technology and winning a large number of users was also influential for the development of a significant diffusion of the Internet.[49]

Unlike other information technologies and networks, the Internet and the WWW are open to a social dynamic. Their seminal success in quick global diffusion and their social acceptance are rooted in a design construction, which both accidentally and by planning constitutes a technology that not only connects hardware and software, but also results in a performative human wetware: Creativity, innovative ideas, tinkering and appropriation constituted the collaborative and individual efforts of a plurality of users. The information infrastructure is social since its development is closely linked to the social context of its participants. As Claudio Ciborra emphasizes, an infrastructure is more than just a set of hardware and software tools, it is also a

> ...formative context [...] able to shape both the organization of work and the set of social scripts which govern the invention of alternative forms of work, the future ways of problem solving and conflict resolution, the revision of the existing institutional arrangements and the plans for their further transformation (Ciborra 2002:70).

Though already in use, both the Internet and the WWW are technologies in the making, and they are transforming themselves as much as they are transforming societies. That happens not only on the level of technological design but also on the level of social organization, as well as with regard to the interpretation of technology and its potential uses. The design decisions made during the development of the Internet and the WWW turned out not only to serve the traditional agenda of participation, but also to offer entrepreneurial business opportunities. A statement by Internet pioneer Paul Vixie emphasizes this double logic of promised freedom and entrepreneurial success inherent in the design of the Internet and the WWW:

> If one of my kids, or anybody anywhere, sits down in front of a web browser and keys in a URL, it ought to just work. They ought to see the same web page that anybody else would see, no matter what country they're in or what their ISP [Internet Service Provider] wants or what their local church or government wants. This universality of naming is one of the foundations on which the Internet was built, and it is how the Internet fosters economic growth and social freedoms. It's what makes the Internet different from old Compuserve, old AOL, old MSN, old Minitel, and everything else that has come – and gone – before.[50]

Crucial to this aspect of social openness was accessibility and a general culture of openness that characterized the design process of both the Internet and the WWW. The traditional concept of universal access to information resources was part of that, as was the non-hierarchical collaborative efforts among its developers. Requests for comments (RFCs) exemplify the openness and collaboration of Internet developers. These documents not only show a work process independent of geographical location, they also reveal the meritocratic attitude of a developing technology. Everyone was invited to contribute to RFCs as long as his or her contributions were interesting and supported the development process. Since RFCs were not limited to technical issues only, they also contain philosophy, humour and socio-political questions.[51] As Janet Abbet emphasizes, ARPANET was already open – although not officially – to users from outside the field of developers or computer science (1999:84). As Abbet puts it, the network provided an 'environment for both frustration and opportunity for its users' (1999:90). ARPANET was difficult to use because of a number of obstacles, but its users were granted the freedom to tinker with its technology, and they were able to connect with each other for mutual support and communication. The users became a crucial aspect in developing the network and even redefining its general purposes once the initial idea of designing a network for sharing pricey computer resources had become obsolete (1999:111). The rather informal and lax management style lowered the bar for users to actively participate and take over the initiative to contribute to the network, which Ciborra considers a crucial factor for the success of information infrastructures (2002:32).

Designing systems applications and organizing their general regulation need to be achieved in a way that affords participation. Similar to software and computers, the Internet and the World Wide Web evince specific aspects that co-define their social use, that stimulate certain uses and repress or avert others. Many of these design decisions can easily be interpreted as ideologically motivated to transform the world into a better place. They constitute the legends that nourish popular discourse and promote the use of the technology to a broad audience. However, many design decisions are pragmatically chosen to stimulate a fast and effective diffusion of the technology and reach a significant number of users. The competitive environment at CERN, where many scientists were working on similar hypertext systems, stimulated Berners-Lee and Cailliau to deliberately design their hypertext system as a very easy-to-use tool that could be extended by anyone at low cost and without bureaucratic obstacles (Berners-Lee, Fischetti 1999). In their design, they built on a resource of a number of already-developed technologies. The mark-up language for creating platform-independent hypertext files, HTML, was developed from already existing SGML and sought to become the 'lingua franca' of the Web (Berners-Lee, Fischetti 1999:45). They deliberately designed the language to be easier than the standard used at CERN to encourage using the Web as a standard hypertext system. Unexpectedly, HTML was used increasingly by end-users who did not bother learning the HTML tags and started creating HTML documents. Publishing in HTML was as easy as writing a text on a text editor, as the following quote from an anonymous web post in 1995 perfectly illustrates:

```
<html>
<head>
<title>HTML is about text</title>
</head>
<body>
Publishing on the web requires text skills, not tech skills!
</body>
</html>
```

Later developments of HTML by editors using interfaces similar to text editors made it even easier, as did the development of web browsers, which increased the opportunities for publishing and experiencing content on the web by integrating possibilities for multimedia and graphics.

In order to stimulate the diffusion of their hypertext system, Berners-Lee and Cailliau published a website on which the WWW was explained, and the necessary software was made available as well.[52] Most of the software was released under a General Public License that allowed others to use, expand on and build applications into the code. Along with this release came a call for participation: via a 'How can I help' page, users were invited to contribute by uploading their own data, writing software, reporting bugs or spreading the word.[53]

By publishing the specifications of HTML (which by then was even further developed) to RFC 1866 in 1995, and by turning it into a public standard, along with the Web's main protocol HTTP, computer scientist Dan Connolly and Berners-Lee opened the doors for further development of the technology to professional and amateur third parties, who drew inspiration from that standard to design applications and new features for the growing WWW.[54] Communicating the WWW to the people at the Internet Engineering Task Force (IETF) led to the standardization of

URI/URL, HTTP, and HTML and simultaneously promoted the web among a critical community that stood at the forefront of technological development.[55]

Berners-Lee and Cailliau benefited from a group of 'early adopters' in the high energy physics community, especially at the Stanford Linear Accelerator Center, which set up the first web server outside of CERN. Scientists had been using the Internet for years and were rather familiar with exchanging information electronically through email or newsgroups (Berners-Lee, Fischetti 1999:50). Introducing the Web to the newsgroup alt.hypertext has been described by Berners-Lee as a 'watershed event' that increased participation and collaboration exponentially (1999:51). The culture that had already developed on the Internet helped the further development of the WWW (Castells 2002:36ff). The spirit of interaction and collaboration led to the swift development of software and rules of social interaction: 'The people of the Internet built the Web in true grassroots fashion' (Berners-Lee, Fischetti 1999:52).

The WWW was by far not the only hypertext system around at that time.[56] But the easy-to-use design, the availability of the software and the unbureaucratic regulation that allowed users to participate on all levels, from publishing and browsing to actively extending the network by adding new web servers, helped the WWW to develop quickly. Another important factor is that the WWW combined two concepts of information media, by 'grafting' a hypertext system on the infrastructure of the already-existing Internet. Publishing on the Web would simultaneously always expand the underlying infrastructure.

Naturally, the World Wide Web was not the first telecommunication-based information system. CompuServe, America Online and the French Minitel system are examples for corporate and bureaucratic attempts at information infrastructures (e.g. Castells 2000:373; Ciborra 2002:39, 42; Berners-Lee, Fischetti 1999:113). Ted Nelson's Project Xanadu is also a noteworthy concept of a hypertext system conceived as a global infrastructure. They all failed, however, to open their systems to a broad inclusion of users. Nelson's Project Xanadu was designed as a 'paranoid' machine storing every document and every hyperlink in an 'eternal' archive and individually identifying every user. Furthermore, it sketched a royalty system of micro payments to compensate any content contributor for visitors browsing its files. Commercial providers were hesitant to allow users to appropriate and expand their information system. Quite contrary to this, Berners-Lee intended to stimulate the social interaction of users to explore and develop more ways of benefiting from the new common information space. As opposed to Minitel or CompuServe, the WWW offered a decentralized approach that allowed other users and institutions to connect the most heterogeneous technical systems to the growing infrastructure. For Berners-Lee, participation was crucial because he and his small group of collaborators were not a powerful corporation but instead were dependent on others to make their vision work. In order to get many users on board, the designers of the World Wide Web attempted to ease use and increase compatibility between different networks by creating a platform-independent application, instead of interfering with established practices and standards.

The public nature of such protocols, the independence from commercial vendors, as well as the possibility for anyone interested to join in and participate in the development process or at least to present their own inventions and discuss the integration of systems and compatibility, created a very fruitful atmosphere. Jon Postel, editor of the RFCs and Internet pioneer, gives three reasons for the successful diffusion of the Internet: 'I think three factors contribute to the success of the Internet: 1) public documentation of protocols, 2) free (cheap) software for the popular machines, and 3) vendor independence' (see Malkin 1992, RFC 1336; quoted in Galloway 2005:121). These principles envision the Internet as a common information infrastructure that can easily be expanded by anyone connected to the network, and grants easy access to the most necessary software for important applications, a principle Tim Berners-Lee and Robert Cailliau adopted for the World Wide Web as well. Berners-Lee purposely decided not to patent the standards and offered the main technologies for free (1999:74, 76).[57] The policy stated that related programming codes could be used for academic purposes for free, and companies not intending to resell the code but who use it 'to participate in global information exchange' would be exempt from paying a fee.[58] The openness of the main technologies and protocols of the World Wide Web represent a social programme, an ideological motivation that is an inherent part of its design.

Unlike a vendor, who would only turn out to be a bottleneck to further development, use, and transformation, the Internet and later the WWW were fundamentally open to participation, allowing users to connect easily, to develop applications and services on the basis of public standards, and to extend the infrastructure without the obstacle of bureaucratic procedures. In this design, the Internet and the WWW were radically different from other applications that offered similar services (Ciborra 2002:43). The Internet and its various applications provide users with the means necessary for social interaction at a global scale, and they provide an infrastructure for the distribution of digital files. Users, either professionals or amateurs, can actively engage in building and further developing many of the applications used for those activities. The Internet enables users to do whatever they want to do with a computer on a global scale, to connect to a multitude of other users and to benefit from the growing cultural resources stored online.

Chapter 4
Bastard Culture

The street has its own uses for technology (William Gibson).

After having examined the affordances of computers, software, and the Internet, this chapter will show how appropriation and design evolve in the extended culture industry. As described in the preveious chapter, the design of software or electronic consumer goods is ambivalent in either stimulating or repressing certain practices. Using two sets of cases, this chapter encourages a perception of participatory culture as a heterogeneous constellation of different participants, either professionals or amateurs, whose activities are deeply intertwined. It furthermore argues for an understanding of participatory culture as a hybrid constellation of information technology and large user numbers interacting in a socio-technical ecosystem. A clear distinction in the resulting labour cannot be made between user and machine-created aspects, instead it has to be accepted as having been co-constructed by both. The first set of cases examines to what extent software-based products can be used in ways not anticipated by their original designers. It furthermore shows that business models can contradict the basic affordances of an artefact and provoke user appropriation to uncloak the device's extended but vendor-limited potential. These user activities qualify for explicit participation in the design process of electronic consumer goods. The second set of cases shows to what extent user activities can be integrated into software design, thereby stimulating the use of software applications, lowering the bar for participation, and creating platforms for user-created content. In this case, user activities manifest themselves implicitly as forms of participation.

Furthermore, this chapter argues that participation extends production and distribution into the domain of audiences and users. As Henry Jenkins extensively argues, many users accumulate and modify corporate media texts. Despite the fact that user and producer blur in intertwined production processes, their specific role either as user or as producer must be defined with respect to the production process, institutional context, legal framing through licenses and copyrights, and their particular relations to companies and user communities. These complex and dynamic connections in explicit participation can be clearly recognized in the analysis of three selected cases of hardware modification.

The case of the modification of the Microsoft Xbox and the leaking of the Xbox Development Kit (XDK) demonstrates how users appropriate corporate design and to what extent the basic affordances of the Xbox have even provoked this appropriation. Ultimately, the Xbox case advocates the recognition of a second step of design development in which the corporate designers formalize many modifications and user activities to work towards a further revision of the design, thus benefiting technologically, and in the last instance also financially, from the input users provide.

The case of the Xbox-Linux-Project explores the work of a heterogeneous user community. Skilled hackers and non-skilled users participate fruitfully in a shared project, and knowledge transfer is enabled through the production of tutorials and a grassroots help service. The Xbox-Linux case is different from the XDK case with respect to motivation. The project thrived on the ongoing dispute between the Linux community and Microsoft. Furthermore, it is an exemplary case of corporate design limiting the affordances of a software-based product. The Xbox-Linux-Project uncloaked the suppressed potential of the video game console Xbox to turn itself into a personal computer.

A confrontation between corporate producer and a user community is examined in the AIBO case. It demonstrates how user communities raise media attention in order to publicly claim their right of cultural freedom. The AIBO case furthermore shows to what extent companies are challenged not only by user appropriation but also by the complexity of their own products for which they fail to provide the necessary support.

After having examined user appropriation as active participation, I argue that user productivity is a heterogeneous process which is often closely linked to culture industries and which often affects the design process of professional consumer goods production. User productivity therefore constitutes an extension of the culture industries rather than an alternative and separate production. In contrast to the explicit participation that has been revealed in the case examples in section 4.1, section 4.2 investigates implicit participation. The case examples show how user activities can be channelled and directed through graphical user interfaces and 'back-end politics' in an 'architecture of participation'. It introduces the notion of participation as a hybrid process brought about by the interaction of large user groups and information systems. As opposed to the previously examined explicit participation, implicit participation often involves unacknowledged labour or implicit, often unconsciously performed labour. These socio-technical processes are characterized by a trend towards automated user participation in order to generate data for improved information management, targeted advertising, and the maintainability of stored data. In implicit participation, the actions of user and producer do not necessarily blur, but rather those of user and information technology, because the labour is performed by both the information system and its plurality of users. Subsequently, I argue strictly against perceiving participation only as a communal activity driven by anti-industry resentment, but rather as user activities that have been developed over the past decade online, and which have now been formalized and translated into software design. Consequently, the cases explored in this section show that the cultural industries successfully constitute business model opportunities by providing platforms for all kinds of user activities in the domains of accumulation, archiving and construction.

4.1 Participation as explicit media practice

Participating explicitly in cultural production through customizing and changing mass-produced serial products has always been an important aspect of amateur culture, as has been the reuse and implementation of products in different ways than initially intended by the industry (Pacey 1983). It is important to emphasize that modifying industrial products is not bound to digital culture, although this practice has become considerably more explicit over the past decade. For example, the impact of amateurs on the development of radio technology has been described extensively (e.g. Douglas 1987; Lécuyer 2005); similar to the radio in the 1920s, the computer was initially targeted at hobbyists and advertised in related special-interest magazines as *Popular Electronics* and *Radio-Electronics* (Ceruzzi 2003:225).[1] The development of the personal computer itself was very much the result of the labour of enthusiastic amateurs. The significance of amateurs in developing hardware and software continued after the commercial introduction of the first microcomputers in the early 1980s. It often took place in computer subcultures and communities of hobbyists, who started to write their own software and exchange it through fanzine-like computer magazines. Another example of software appropriation is gamers creating their own levels, so-called 'mods', or further developing a game. The prime example for successful modifications is probably the first-person-shooter game, *Counter-Strike*, which was modified from the commercial game *Half Life*.[2] In gaming, producers of commercial games recognized how valuable user contribution was, and as a result they are adopting ways of integrating the communities' work into their production processes with increasing frequency (Nieborg 2005). The hands-on activities in the Xbox-Linux-Project, the production of modified chips as well as the Xbox 'homebrew' software scene in general are almost exclusively the domain of male hackers.[3] This is still the case for many areas of digital culture, as for instance in the demoscene and the netlabel scene, or in groups dedicated to the development of open-source software.[4] However, initiatives such as the Genderchangers or the German group Haecksen attempt to provide space and capacities for women teaching women to use, alter and modify software, as well as hardware.[5] Another area showing a higher but not yet balanced percentage of female participation in hardware hacking and software modification is media art.[6] Although only a few areas have been identified where user appropriation occurs explicitly as female agency, such as in the so-called slash fiction (e.g. Jenkins 1997; Kustritz 2003), the promise for a participatory culture – so often formulated as a universal principle – is challenged by the absence or the lack of representation of women actively appropriating hardware and developing software (see also Keif, Faulkner 2003).[7] However, the scope of this research cannot appropriately analyse its case examples with respect to gender relations.[8]

In general, any consumer good is open for appropriation (Akrich 1998). However, modifying software seems to be pervasive, since tinkering with software can take place in online connected communities supporting each other and distributing software at almost no cost. Appropriating software does not require certain craft skills and special tools, but a computer and time to learn to work with software. Furthermore, it is possible to formalize the hack of a software or software-based product in an application or hardware device in order to distribute it widely and make it easy to use for lay users. In appropriating electronic consumer goods, the craft of hardware modification and programming are often combined, extending substantially the range of functionalities of the products in question.

High-school students even use mods for their scientific calculators, and adults find information online telling them how to remove the region code on their DVD players. For hand-held game consoles like Playstation Portable (PSP) and Nintendo DS, a plethora of websites dedicated to hacking and homebrew software have inundated the Internet.[9] Although game copying is a major motivation for using and installing homebrew software, the developing community also offers many more attractive features which are not covered by the actual producers. The Nintendo DS can turn into an organizer, and serves as a music and video player as well.[10] Furthermore, a list of modifications would also include the Roomba Community, which uses the reasonably priced artificial intelligence technology of the homonymous robot vacuum cleaner to tinker with,[11] the iPod Linux project that migrated a Linux distribution to the popular music player,[12] and the 'case modders' who change their computer cases and compete for the coolest, most imaginative and eccentric case, most often accompanied with high-performance graphic cards and tuned processors – 'overclocking' – and water cooling systems, or techniques to decrease the machine's noise level, called 'silent modding'. Modifications therefore also take place at the level of the hardware itself, by replacing or changing the original parts. A second level of modification affects the software, a practice which is very common in gaming but also among electronic consumer goods, which consist of hardware and software. For the original Xbox, even commercial modifications have entered the market; the Taiwan-based company Friend Tech changed the original device by adding a much faster processor, a bigger hard drive and a case that resembled the style of case mods.

Many web shops for computer games and game console accessories offer modified consoles as well. Production and distribution of modchips actually constitute a shadow market that is severely contested by established companies in the field (see chapter 5). It shows that user appropriation can also be commercially motivated. The ambiguous crossover and interrelatedness of professionally working hackers developing modchips, user communities, non-monetary-driven projects, and corporate companies reveal participation is complex. Those connections are revealed when relations and connections of the various participants and the different elements involved in the process of appropriation are mapped, as will be described in the following cases. However, my research has been limited in several ways: it was not possible to identify all actors nor to sufficiently follow and document them. I was confined, to a certain extent, to the 'willingness' of participants to communicate. People from the hacker scene, maintainers of user forums or other expert users were often very open and helpful in providing information as well as in describing their activities in detail,[13] but it was almost impossible to receive statements from companies, not to mention actual interviews with corporate designers or decision-makers.

The trail of the XDK

When developing the Xbox, Microsoft provided a software development kit called the Xbox Development Kit (XDK) to enable third-party developers to create applicable software for the video game console. The use of the XDK was strictly regulated through a licensing policy. Only companies that had obtained a license were allowed to produce and market software for the Xbox. The XDK, however, leaked onto the hacker and homebrew developer scene, which also started to produce software for the Xbox, software not approved by Microsoft. The case of the XDK will reveal connections between Microsoft and the hacker scene and show how hackers and common users collaborated in the production and distribution of applications. It also shows how the leaking of the XDK into the community of hackers created an alternative network of users who produce and distribute homemade software applications and establish entirely alternative gaming networks. A relationship to professional companies participating in the modification of the Microsoft game console is visible as well. However, the most recent Xbox 360 is an example of how a commercial vendor can learn from user appropriation, and consequently develop a design to avert certain forms of appropriation and deliberately implement others.

In 2001, the Microsoft corporation entered the market of game consoles by introducing the Xbox, targeted to compete directly with Sony's successful and top-selling Playstation 2. Shortly after launching the console, Microsoft released Xbox Live, a gaming network offering various services and online multi-player games. Technically, the Xbox was actually a regular personal computer limited to the functions of a game console. It came with an Intel Celeron 733 MHz processor, 64 MB of RAM, an 8 or 10 GB hard disk, a DVD drive, and a network interface. A stripped-down version of the Windows 2000 kernel served as its operating system. As pointed out in chapter 3, a computer is an all-purpose device, a universal machine. Therefore, confining these basic affordances to a 'special machine', a video game console for replaying corporate content, fundamentally contradicts the technical possibilities. It could not have come as a surprise that users would immediately try to unleash the full potential of the Xbox. The Xbox processor would only run vendor-licensed software, whereas software developed with unlicensed XDKs required a modification of the Xbox.

Microsoft's definition of the Xbox as a game console resulted in a discrepancy with its technical specifications. After being released into the market, the contradictory design attracted the attention of hackers and enthusiasts who recognized its capability to perform a broader range of functions. MIT student Andrew 'bunnie' Huang was probably the first to hack the Xbox. He initially posted some documentation of his hacks to his website and published a memo on the cryptography system of the Xbox (Huang 2002; see also Takahashi 2006:56-59). The inconsistency between the product's definition and its actual technical capabilities on the one hand and the collective intelligence of users on the other turned out to be a motor for innovation. The Xbox became one of the most popular platforms for cracked software and so-called homebrew software.[14] The appropriation of the actual Xbox design is revealed in the process of hacking and the many applications developed for modified game consoles. Other game consoles, the Sony Playstation 2 and the Nintendo Gamecube, did not stimulate a noteworthy production of homebrew software. According to game console hackers, the Xbox was relatively easy to hack, and one of its advantages was the hard drive and the PC-like technology, but social aspects should not be overlooked either. The Xbox attracted a group of users that were forming a community and accepting the challenge of hacking the device for various reasons.

A variety of motives drive the labour for hacking a game console. As Linux enthusiasts, the members of the Xbox-Linux-Project were seeking ways to migrate Linux even on the Microsoft Xbox and turn it into a full-fledged PC. Other hackers thought of extending the possibilities of the console and developed extra software for features Microsoft had not supplied it with. The most popular application was probably the Xbox Media Center (XBMC).[15] This is a media player that runs most video and audio formats and turns the Xbox from a game console into an entertainment centre for films, video clips, music, and, of course, games. It supports the archiving of media files on the Xbox's hard drive. Other developers provide games or emulate those from outdated platforms for the Microsoft game console. However, playing unlicensed copies of games remained and continues to be a main motivation for hacking game consoles.

Producing and using homebrew software requires several extra features that open up an entire set of producers, users, hardware, and network effects beyond the original production channels of the Xbox. The leaking of XDK into the homebrew developers' scene reveals an entire alternative actor-network of video game console use. To produce software for a hardware platform, a proprietary toolkit of hardware and software is needed. The XDK could be considered a 'transparent' version of the black box Xbox, and was officially only available to licensed third-party developers. In respect to the black box metaphor it is amusing and noteworthy that the developer's kit was provided in a transparent case, in contrast to the black case of the retail version of the Xbox.[16]

Figure 5. Xbox, developer kit (transparent), consumer kit (black). Image courtesy of Ian Court <www.ianc.net>.

The XDK provides the necessary production means for developing any software for the Xbox. It consists of a software development environment and pre-installed libraries for programming routines. After being available to the user communities, the XDK made it possible to program unlicensed software for the Xbox. Software developed by Microsoft's official third-party developers and those unlicensed applications labelled as homebrew, in other words, are built with the very same means of production but differ in their signed or unsigned code. Since all software for the Xbox was produced without licensed XDKs, their code is unsigned and remains vulnerable to copyright infringement claims. Commercial distribution is therefore out of the question. Furthermore, it is not that simple to run unlicensed software on an average Xbox. Signed code could only be executed on the Xbox processor, which made it necessary to modify the console either by installing a 'modchip', or modifying it through a software manipulation in order to run unsigned code. Modification chips are small electronic devices that will be attached to a printed circuit board of, for example, an Xbox.[17]

The modchip or 'modification chip' appears as a crucial actor that circumvents the proprietary control of executing signed code only. It furthermore transforms the vendor-controlled console into a user-appropriated and user-controlled device, running software which is not intended or approved by the original designers. There are two ways of modifying a game console, the 'hard mod' and the 'soft mod'. In case of the hard mod, the original processor is replaced by a modchip consisting of an alternative operating system that will execute all code. Modchips were developed and produced mostly by European hackers who employed encryption techniques to protect their work from Asian-based enterprises cloning their design and selling it for a cheaper price. Companies such as Lik Sang, Friend Tech, and countless web shops in Europe and the US distributed the modchips for all kinds of gaming consoles.[18] These companies were often targets of lawsuits filed by Microsoft, Sony and Nintendo, who argued that modchips are primarily used for playing copied games. An entire grey market emerged due to the demand for modchips, which are sold by web shops in large quantities. In order to produce a working alternative chip, the modchip producer needs profound knowledge of the specifications of the targeted product, knowledge that is acquired by reverse engineering of the device. Developing a modchip is not a simple amateur activity. It requires knowledge and funding for research and development in order to produce a prototype that meets the requirements and is not easy to clone. For serial production, financial resources are necessary to purchase the technical components. According to a former member of the modchip producer SmartXX, pre-production can cost up to $50,000. Although their production and distribution can be in violation of intellectual property laws, modification chips are produced on an industrial scale and answer the user's desire to do different things with gaming devices than the vendors intended. The producers of both consoles and games feel their business model is being threatened by modchips because their revenues are based on selling games and additional services to the often subsidized hardware of the game consoles.[19]

Using a soft mod does not require opening the game console or touching the original hardware, but circumvents its control mechanisms and allows the execution of all code as well. When 'softmodding' the Xbox became a common and easy thing to achieve, Microsoft reacted by declining warranty claims and excluding modified consoles from the Xbox Live network. In response, user communities developed their own alternative networks like Xlink Kai to exploit Local Area Network (LAN) technology and relay the gaming from the console via a desktop computer over the Internet to an alternative network. It even allows compatibility between Xbox, Playstation, Nintendo, and hand-held consoles such as the Playstation Portable.

It is not quite clear how the XDK came into the hands of hackers. In interviews, homebrew software developers and members of user communities often speak of the 'XDK leaking into the community'. There are many hints of unofficial relations between corporations and hackers, a recent one being linked to an incident in 2005, when stolen development kits for the next generation console Xbox 360 were found in the house of the Austrian hacker Hamtitampti, a member of the modchip producer SmartXX. In a statement he denied the accusation of having stolen the development kits but admits that SmartXX got hold of them and had notified Microsoft directly thereafter. According to Hamtitampti, whose house was raided by the police, Microsoft tried everything to avoid a public lawsuit, attempting to withdraw the initial complaint of theft, and even paying his lawyer.[20] It also appeared that private investigators such as the German Prevent AG collect evidence against people committing copyright infringement. These private investigators often have good connections to the police authorities and unfortunately are often consulted as experts on matters of copyright infringement despite their obvious bias towards industry interests.[21] However, many of those connections remain undisclosed, and more often rumours and speculations haunt the scene. One of the unverified speculations is the rumour of modchip producers illegally buying intellectual property from a Microsoft employee. If the leaking of the XDK to the user communities was indeed something that Microsoft was aware of, this would complicate the actor-network even more, with the corporate actor using the users while pretending to oppose their activities.

In any event, the leaking of the proprietary knowledge in the form of the XDK can clearly be traced to the many homebrew applications that were developed with it. By far the biggest platform for the distribution of these applications is the ftp server Xbins.[22] Figure 6 shows a screen shot of the folders stored on the ftp server Xbins as of October 2005; it reveals the vast amount of applications provided there.

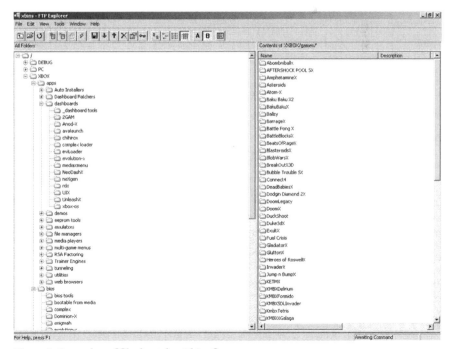

Figure 6. Screenshot of files hosted at Xbins ftp server.

For each access to download files from Xbins, users have to get a password and a log-in name from a channel in the Internet Relay Chat (IRC).[23] The maintainers of Xbins emphasize that they are not supporting 'warez' – illegally copied and distributed games – just homebrew software, meaning unsigned code that is produced with the XDK. When retrieving a password and a log-in, users receive a note that the server contains only homebrew software, and that each user will be allowed to download 30 files only, because 'We do NOT tolerate GREED and you shall be banned if you break this rule' (see screenshot, fig. 7).

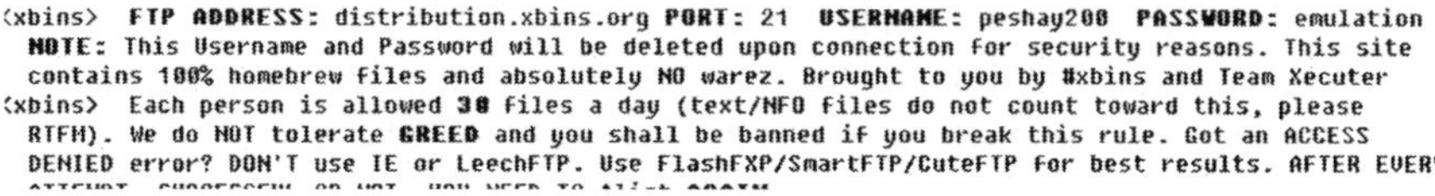

```
<xbins>  FTP ADDRESS: distribution.xbins.org PORT: 21  USERNAME: peshay200 PASSWORD: emulation
    NOTE: This Username and Password will be deleted upon connection for security reasons. This site
    contains 100% homebrew files and absolutely NO warez. Brought to you by #xbins and Team Xecuter
<xbins>  Each person is allowed 30 files a day (text/NFO files do not count toward this, please
    RTFM). We do NOT tolerate GREED and you shall be banned if you break this rule. Got an ACCESS
    DENIED error? DON'T use IE or LeechFTP. Use FlashFXP/SmartFTP/CuteFTP for best results. AFTER EVERY
```

Figure 7. Snippet from Xbins dialogue for log-in and password retrieval.

For users with less ftp-server experience, many files are distributed through the popular open-source platform Sourceforge.net or through file-sharing systems, such as BitTorrent. The file-sharing programs are also used for distributing copyright-protected software and games. Distribution of software therefore primarily occurs via three channels: a) ftp servers such as Xbins, b) websites such as Sourceforge.net, and c) P2P file sharing systems or file hosting services.

The widespread unlicensed use of the official Microsoft XDK reveals unacknowledged ties between Microsoft and/or their licensed third-party developers with the homebrew scene. As Hamtitampti from SmartXX points out: 'Not only the XDK leaked: It is a mystery inside the hacker scene until today how it was possible, that a 4GB source code tree (including the complete Xbox kernel) and test applications had leaked onto the Internet. Some modchip operating systems, like Xecuter, were completely built out of this source'.[24] It might be possible that an employee of a third-party developer accidentally or deliberately leaked the code.

Since the XDK found its way to software developers outside the established software and games industry, it is evident that hacker and homebrew developers form just another group of third-party developers. Members of homebrew development communities suggest such leaks should take place more frequently so that software could be developed in a quicker and better way. With XDK, Microsoft offered a device for developing applications for the Xbox to professional software providers, but when it leaked into the hacker community, the chain of development extended to another network. Indeed, it has reached the hacker and user communities, who use the same tools as professional producers. They extended the production of the Xbox by introducing new functions, developing new interfaces, and redefining the original device. These are not only activities performed by hackers, nor are they, as often alleged, a counter-action against the proprietary and commercial producer, but they are closely linked to the playfulness of hacking, as well as to commercial interests. The motivations for appropriating an electronic consumer device are as diverse as the developed applications. Here, an entire branch of software production is emerging independently from the official third-party developers for the game consoles. A grey market for providing hardware and services to run unsigned code as well as copied games on official products is emerging along with the homebrew communities. Their relation to user communities is evident on the websites of the game console scene.

The most popular online platforms for game console users include Xbox-scene. org, Gamespot, and Kotaku.com. These websites are crucial for communication and presenting news to the user community. They serve as a virtual drop-in centre where new users, or 'newbies', can find information and support. Forum discussions treat all kinds of elements related to game consoles. Hacking is a topic, as are the possible features of unreleased hardware and software. Discussions revolve around gaming, exploits, cheats, and ways to work through different games. These websites also contribute to the media hype generated before the release of new game consoles, and in the case of the Xbox 360 and Playstation 3, discussions about the performance of processor and graphic cards, and of course debates about the hackability and possibilities of software development through the community are rampant. Online magazines and special-interest magazines covering news about information technology, computers and gaming are creating attention too. Important hacks are covered there, and developments regarding legal issues about modchip production are being carefully monitored.

A website like Xbins.org serves as a web catalogue for the contents of the eponymous ftp server, while Xbox-scene.org is important for promoting homebrew software applications and hacker groups. Modchip producers and companies distributing the modchips and computer, game supply, and modified game consoles often place advertisement banners on user community websites and link to them from their own websites. Advertisement banners of the official game console producers can also be found on community websites. Friend Tech promoted the book *Hacking the Black Box* by hacker Andrew 'bunnie' Huang. The modchip producer SmartXX links with a banner to the website of the Xbox-Linux-Project. Sometimes hyperlinks represent social connections as well. In the case of SmartXX and the Xbox-Linux-Project, some members participate in both projects.

Community websites are a crucial aspect in the actor-network of game console hacking. They serve as portals and platforms for the various groups connected to game consoles: hacker and development groups, modchip producers and their distributors, producers of graphic cards and other hardware suited for gaming, weblogs about gaming, mainstream and special interest media, and naturally the actual game console producers, whose official websites are often linked to the popular community websites. Figure 8 shows the hyperlink clusters of the community website Xbox-scene.com. This network reveals connections between the official Xbox.com website, the user community Xbox-scene.com, as well as to the modding scene, represented, for instance in the websites TeamXodus.com, SmartXX.com, or the distribution platform DMS3.com. Links are also visible to the Xbins.org website, which provides most of the homebrew applications. Other links lead to the official Xbox website, and several hacker groups, as well as various modchip distributors. Figure 9 maps a selection of hyperlinks between various websites related to the Xbox and its modification. The figure describes step one of the design and appropriation cycles that the Xbox has undergone. It is clear that the leaking of the XDK created an entire additional set of producers, users, applications, media appearances, and a set of relations that connects hackers with modchip producers, who are related to distributors, who again advertise on community websites.

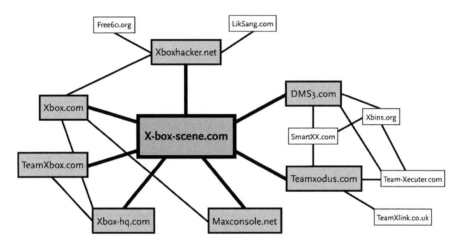

Figure 8. User community Xbox-scene.com, selected links.

It has to be acknowledged that both the officially released and the leaked XDK turns third-party developers, as well as hackers, into users of production means developed by Microsoft. This software giant controls the output by licensing policies which designates one code as rightful, while it relegates the others to the fringes of legality. Licensing fees are necessary in order to compensate for the subsidized hardware that does not earn profits. Circumventing the limitations in design and licensing policies is considered a direct threat to the original vendor's business model.

User appropriation redefined and changed Xbox into a media centre and computer bypassing the built-in limitations and copyright protection systems. When Microsoft started to control the execution of unsigned code by accessing the device through the Xbox Live network, the company actually attempted to avoid appropriation and again changed the definition of the Xbox. The device then became a platform users would purchase just to access specific services. The product was not under the control of its owner, who purchased it, but was open for the producer to access and modify any time. As a result, the Xbox Live alternative networks, like

Xlink Kai, were developed to free users from vendor dependency and allow all kinds of gaming platforms to join in.

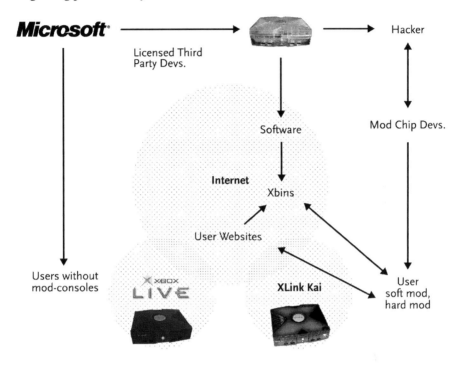

Figure 9. Mapping of the main actors in XDK case.

The original Xbox underwent a transformation due to user appropriation; completely new features were developed, and a use now became possible that contradicted the vendor's business models. This transformation took place in an actor-network of communities, developers, media platforms aiming to represent communities and publishing-related news, and a range of technologies, such as the XDK, modchips, software bugs, source code repositories and ftp severs, as mapped in figure 9. When developing a new gaming console, Microsoft took into account the many experiences gained from user appropriation for the new design. Microsoft focused on increasing security features and attempting to avoid hacking. 'There are going to be levels of security in this box that the hacker community has never seen before', announced Chris Satchell from the Xbox Advanced Technology Group.[25] Homebrew software was not Microsoft's main concern, explained Andre Virgnaud, member of the Microsoft Xbox team, in his weblog, but 'piracy' was. Microsoft's response to the appropriation of the Xbox through modchips had to be a design that would integrate as many attractive features as possible that users might miss, but above all exclude possibilities of playing copied games.[26] The Xbox 360 was released in late November 2005, and crucial changes to the design were made. The

Xbox Live network was extended and made available for all users in a basic network service. More services and games were made available through upgrades. Also the operating systems required regular updates and made it difficult to be replaced through an alternative on a modchip. Along with connecting users seamlessly to the producer's network, many features from homebrew software were integrated into Xbox 360. The media centre resembles very much the homebrew Xbox Media Center. The previously 'leaked' XDK was literally incorporated into the new design as an integrated development kit, known as the 'XNA'. Now both professional and amateur developers could build applications for the Xbox 360. The problem of signed and unsigned code was abolished by offering a free version and acknowledging every user as a potential licensed developer. Joining the 'Creator's Club' for a annual fee of $99 would legalize the distribution of homemade programs. Noncommercial applications may be distributed and executed on Xbox 360.[27] Reasons to modify the game console for homebrew software no longer seemed warranted. However, many Xbox enthusiasts are unhappy with the new design and claim that the quality of homebrew applications, customized user interfaces, and other features is rather poor in comparison with those available for the old Xbox. And indeed, the Xbox 360 immediately stifled the homebrew scene's output, and hackers lost interest in making developments for the Xbox 360, either due to the annual fee, or the requirement of developing in Microsoft's .NET Framework on which the XNA is based.[28] Furthermore, it seems the Xbox 360 is not as popular among hackers as the old Xbox. Modchip production for the Xbox 360 also changed radically due to the fact that the hack cannot be protected with cryptography. The modchips can therefore easily be copied and reproduced at low cost by 'cloners' who copy modchips and produce them en masse in Asia. Many modchip producers, such as SmartXX, pulled out due to a lack of revenues. A Xbox 360 hack allows one to play copied games, but does not allow the execution of a different operating system. It is therefore impossible to install and run homebrew applications like it had been on the Xbox.[29]

The trail of the XDK reveals several important aspects of participatory culture: users and producers converge to an extent that requires defining the individual role of a participant at any given state of the production process according to his or her social context, institutional affiliation, access to either licensed or unlicensed means of production, technical skills, and the mindset motivating his or her labour. Furthermore, the XDK case shows how user appropriation and corporate design decisions are intertwined and stimulate one another. It demonstrates clearly that participation is not a homogeneous activity of users, but that companies are actively engaged in the process, too. In the context of participatory culture, the case of the XDK highlights an extension of the culture industries into the sphere of users and consumers who actively – driven by various motives – participate in further developing original designs by means of appropriation. Furthermore, it demonstrates how this labour can be integrated, or at least be beneficial, for new design developments by corporate producers. Following the 'leaked' XDK and the unsigned code produced with it reveals strategies of corporate control in response to the use of modified Xboxes. Microsoft employed several strategies to ban or discourage unapproved use. It is also recognizable how user appropriation explores the entire range of computer technology and software to circumvent those strategies of control and produce alternative solutions. However, these activities cannot be perceived as an independent culture detached from the world of corporate production, as both are closely linked to each other on so many levels.

A penguin on Bill's black box: the Xbox-Linux-Project

The Xbox-Linux-Project differs in an important respect from the XDK case. Its objective to install GNU/Linux on the Xbox disconnects it from the need to develop with the Microsoft Xbox Development Kit (XDK) and provides an alternative operating system and alternative software for the Xbox.[30] Instead of the original stripped-down version of Windows 2000, a GNU/Linux operating system was developed and successfully installed on the console. This accomplishment furthermore demonstrates an ideological impetus by 'liberating' the consumer from the vendor's control and turning the limited functionality of the game console into an adequate and reasonable personal computer, based on hardware that is subsidized by Microsoft. Other motives for hacking the Xbox were to learn more about hardware architecture, reverse engineering and cryptography (Huang 2003), as well as writing a Linux-based operating system for a game console that resembled common IBM PC architecture. The idea of the computer as a multi-purpose device, accessible and available at low cost to anyone, was a driving motivation behind the project and visible in its communication. The Xbox-Linux example shows not only a clear collision of media practice and a business model, but also a confrontation of different socio-political mindsets. The project received a lot of media attention, and members attended important conventions, like the 2004 German Linuxtag or the prestigious conference of the Computer Chaos Club in 2004 and 2005. Because project members were presenting themselves in public, a coherent appearance was necessary and thanks to the effort of project leader Michael Steil, specific presentations, images, and film files were produced for Xbox-Linux. The focus on the Microsoft versus Linux narrative increased its popularity, and was conveyed by setting the Linux penguin mascot, Tux, on the Xbox and presenting it that way both at live events and in downloadable videos on their website. The image of the penguin sitting on the Xbox made it easy to grasp the significance of the difficult process of migrating the former Microsoft game console to a Linux computer. It furthermore aimed to illustrate the right of customers to tinker with their purchased goods and articulated a call to limit the obstacles companies try to impose on their clients in order to prevent them from modifying their product. The project especially inspired activists and Linux enthusiasts who either were fascinated by Linux running on

Microsoft's game console or were already dreaming of hundreds of thousands of Xbox-Linux systems being shipped to developing countries as cheap computers to diminish the digital divide. The Xbox-Linux-Project is embedded in an anti-proprietary software culture, and, referring to Walter Benjamin's notion of author as producer, a specific socio-political attitude is affecting the appropriation of a greater potential for participation (Benjamin 1934/2003).

Founded in 2002 by German computer science student Michael Steil, the rather small group of five to ten project members managed a great deal of reverse engineering on the Xbox to develop a GNU/Linux distribution for the console.[31] The project was funded by an initially anonymous sponsor some time later, and after the project began to grow, they organized a hacking contest in order to find a way of executing non-system code without requiring a modchip; the winner would receive a prize of $100,000.[32]

Clearly their activities contained an ideological overtone. The welcome screen on their Xbox-Linux says (see fig. 10), 'Welcome to your box', emphasizing the possessive pronoun, and referring to the alleged collective intelligence and the community ideals of open-source software and active participation:

You don't have to be a passive consumer of corporate content. With Linux you can plug into a world of sharing and contributing, you can be part of a worldwide community where ideas and software are free.[33]

The appropriated Xbox shows that this was not an empty claim, but rather something realized in the modification of the design. The members of the Xbox-Linux-Project were primarily Linux enthusiasts, not gamers. Demonstrating a distinctly playful attitude, they sought the best ways to hack the Xbox in order to execute Linux. As Xbox-Linux-Project member Ed states, 'It is about porting Linux on proprietary devices, but once I see Linux booting on them, I see the objective realized and lose interest in further development work.'[34] Another ideological motivation emphasized on the project website and frequently disputed in the press was the fact that the Xbox was being sold at half the price of a regular PC but offered equivalent features (Takahashi 2006:58).

A first booting of GNU/Linux was achieved in August 2002 but still required a modchip. Nevertheless, the press release announced:

This is a landmark in the struggle for control of the Xbox, which features PC-like hardware, an Intel CPU, a standard hard disk drive and DVD drive. Microsoft had been counting on the purchasers of the Xbox remaining passive consumers of paid-for content [...] However with the first release of Xbox Linux, consumers will soon have a choice to connect to the normal Internet, using normal browsers, and run any Linux programs for free. They will also be able to play any audio (e.g. MP3) and video content they choose without restrictions.[35]

In March 2003 hacker Habibi_xbox won the hacking contest by booting Linux successfully without using hardware modifications.[36]

Figure 10. The welcome slide of Xbox-Linux.

The hacker took advantage of a software bug known as a 'buffer overflow' that emerged in the save/load game function of the game *James Bond 007: Agent Under Fire* (Electronic Arts 2001).[37] Instead of loading the game, the Xbox would allow any code to run after the buffer overflow crashed the system. The procedure is possible with other games as well, such as *Mechassault* (Microsoft Game Studios 2002), or Tom Clancy's *Splinter Cell* (Ubisoft 2002), where bugs have been found that can be exploited in the same way. The members of the Xbox-Linux-Project created a software called Mechinstaller that facilitated the soft mod of an Xbox. It is noteworthy that commercial software was not only exploited for uses not approved by the original designer again, but also that this appropriation was then quickly formalized in a new software application, such as the Mechinstaller, and easily distributed. The fact that the solution was eventually provided by a Microsoft-produced game added an additional flavour of hacking beauty. However, Microsoft used its Xbox Live network to update the consoles' software and close the security holes that were exploited by hackers. By accessing the users' game consoles, the company attempted to exert a certain amount of control after releasing the product into the market. As mentioned earlier, software updates became a strategy for companies to maintain control of their products and to adapt their software to prevent user appropriation.

Software updates can also be used to exert a certain amount of control and prevent users from violating the terms of use from certain services and warranty claims. However, this dynamic has lead to a competition between users and companies. The corporate design attempts to regulate the use, while users appropriate the new design version again, or circumvent it by re-installing an earlier firmware version.

Aside from the Xbox-Linux-Project, other opportunities for softmod were further developed and led to the production of easy-to-use cartridges and softmod manuals that helped less-skilled users to modify their game console. The Xbox-Linux-Project increased assistance to less-skilled users by writing a detailed step-by-step manual for modding the Xbox and installing a Linux distribution.[38] A group of enthusiastic users offered their help to less-skilled users. Eventually, the Xbox-Linux-Project provided a 'boot CD image' that users could download to set up the Linux operating system. Here, the hacking process itself transformed into a stable solution, enabling unskilled users to modify their Xbox on their own. By 2006, the developers had succeeded in running Linux on the Xbox in a stable way, and in reducing maintenance to a minimum. That year, the project was awarded the Community Award in the category of hardware on the prestigious Sourceforge.net website, where the Xbox-Linux-Project was hosting their software.

The Xbox-Linux-Project can be described as an active, straightforward software development venture with an efficient division of labour. Along with the core developers, a group of 5 to 10 people and another group of approximately 35 users helped to maintain the project by extending the website, writing and translating manuals, providing artwork, and answering user questions. Inexperienced users could look up skilled users in a database and visit them in real life to have the game console modified. Here, the project benefited significantly from the efforts of those who actively took part in developing the community. According to core members of the Xbox-Linux-Project, enthusiast users, who were less skilled in hacking and programming, were crucial in assuming the task of explaining the application and processes to really inexperienced users. Hacker Ed from the Xbox-Linux-Project appreciates the collaboration of less-skilled users as much as the collaboration of experienced hackers. He says that the core developer group would not have the time to maintain the mailing list and answer all kinds of questions.[39] As a result of volunteer efforts, the Xbox-Linux-Project page, in addition to being in English, is also available in German, French, Spanish, Polish, Dutch, and Finnish. This is yet another demonstration of the dynamics of user communities in developing technical skills and sharing knowledge.

Again, the Xbox-Linux-Project shows that computer technology can be used differently than intended by their original designers just by changing the devices' operating software. The Xbox served as a software environment for the 'special machine' designed as Microsoft 'Xbox software', which then was replaced by the Xbox-Linux software. As the Xbox-Linux-Project unfolds, it shows the capability of users to accumulate resources in order to set up and accomplish a hacking and software-developing project. Many tasks were fulfilled in a semi-professional way, and some participants were professional programmers or computer science students. Nevertheless, a significant contribution came from a group of computer game or GNU/Linux enthusiasts collaborating for various reasons and according to their personal capabilities and skills. It shows that community-driven collaboration works even with a limited common objective. The only objective was migrating Linux on the Xbox, which became for some members an anti-Microsoft mission, and was perceived so by the press, while for others the main objective was the technical challenge of hacking the Xbox. It is an example of explicit participation, a conscious undertaking, well received by the press, that raised funding and media attention, and allocated the necessary resources to achieve the set objectives. This successful appropriation demonstrates the extent to which software-based products are open to modification and how their basic affordances affect later use. An Xbox has little in common with its original design once GNU/Linux is booted on the device.

Hacking the AIBO and teaching Sony to back off

The AiboHack case is a prime example of the valuable contribution users can make to sophisticated electronic consumer goods by offering support to other users and developing additional features for the product. It furthermore illustrates how user communities may defend their cultural freedom to modify products they have purchased. When Sony tried to shut down the distribution of non-corporate software for the robot dog AIBO on Aibohack.com, user communities generated attention for their case and made mainstream media news.

   In 1999, Sony introduced a highly sophisticated product into the market of electronic consumer goods. The AIBO[40] is an electronic robotic dog with abilities to learn and to express different 'moods'. Equipped with a camera, touch and audio sensors, a memory stick, 16 MB RAM, and a 32 bit processor, the pet could walk, orientate itself to its surroundings and respond to user actions.[41] The dog was like the Japanese hand-held digital pet, Tamagotchi, in that the owner had to pay attention to it and could influence its learning processes. The AIBO provided an advanced set of interaction possibilities due to its touch sensors, audio interface for voice commands, and various ways of expressing different moods. Like all software-based products, the AIBO was open to modification and could offer a wider range of functions than its original designers imagined. Similar to the cases discussed above, user community websites served as important media platforms for exchanging information and contacting other AIBO owners. Furthermore, the websites facilitated communication between skilled users who were able to develop programs for the AIBO and less skilled users. The US-based hacker known as 'Aibopet', who calls himself 'just a robot hobbyist', was among the first to examine the AIBO.[42] On his website Aibohack.com, he started to publish small programs he had developed to extend AIBO's abilities. Using his software only required a Sony memory stick applicable to the AIBO product model in question. Aibopet's programs were extensively promoted on the AIBO community websites. Besides offering new programs and receiving ideas for new ones, Aibopet answered questions and offered support for less-skilled AIBO owners. Although he offered applications and services free of charge and was actually adding value to the AIBO, and also despite the fact that he was very much appreciated in user communities, he was threatened by a cease-and-desist letter from Sony in 2001: 'Sony is excited about your enthusiasm for AIBO, but is very concerned by the manner of distribution of your original contents.'[43] In a meeting with Sony representatives, Aibopet tried to explain that his distribution of applications would not harm sales or the development of AIBO. In fact, the opposite was true, since Aibopet was offering support the company was not able to maintain and he was expanding the value of AIBO to users, since Aibopet's programs made the robotic dog much more attractive. With programs like Disco AIBO, the little robotic dog was able to dance to tunes on the radio, AIBO Scope captured the pet's perspective and Bender AIBO made the dog talk like the homonymous robot in the popular TV series Futurama. Aibopet explained in the aforementioned meeting why Sony's $500 software Master Studio was not suitable for developing applications like Disco AIBO and demonstrated the free software extensions he was offering on his website. Actually, the extensive use of these programs required users to buy more memory sticks from Sony. Obviously this was a case of a skilled user actively participating in the enhancement of a product's value, and he even provided competent support, thus constituting user participation and diminishing the gap between corporation and consumers. Up to that point, the problem seemed solved:

> In the intervening months, while discussing various AIBO things with Sony/ ERA/ERC representatives, no 'legal' issues are raised. I (foolishly) believe they understand the value I provide to their product line, for free. I believe they will let me, at least implicitly, continue my work. Even at Robocup (early August) nothing was mentioned to me on the topic by ERA/Sony representatives. In fact I received an embarrassing amount of praise, including some from the Japanese engineers.

But on 26 October 2001 a second letter required Aibopet to suspend offering 14 of his AIBO programs on his websites because of violating intellectual property laws.[44] This points to an interesting dynamic inside larger companies. Engineers involved in research and development can appreciate user appropriation differently than people from the legal department. However, the management probably is more open to the concerns of the legal advisers who then can dominate the companies actions with their proposals and strategies. In response, Aibopet shut down his websites Aibohack.com and Aibopet.com entirely, but not without publishing

Sony's letter first. He also asked all websites mirroring his download section to discontinue that too. When Aibopet published that letter, it was picked up by the user community websites and a process of agenda setting was initiated that would soon hit the mainstream media. Sony's cease-and-desist letter shows how user communities can generate attention and how special-interest websites, mailing lists, and commercial media are interrelated. Figure 11 shows how the news spread from community websites to media such as the *LA Times* and the *New York Times* (Schäfer 2004:69). On Friday 26 October, the closing of Aibopet's websites was announced on the several AIBO user community websites, such as Aibosite.com, Aiboworld.co.uk, and Aibo-life.com. Users immediately began writing online petitions, demanding Sony to suspend legal threats, and they even called for a boycott of Sony products.[45] The next day the news was featured on the important platform Slashdot.org, a website on information technology news and related issues. When Slashdot features articles, related websites can easily collapse under the volume of visits, a phenomenon called 'the Slashdot effect'.[46] The week following Slashdot's report, special-interest media from all over the world covered the altercation. 'Sony Dogs Aibo Enthusiast's Site' read the *LA Times* headline, and the widely read German technology forum *Heise* announced 'Aibo Hacker Gives Up'. The articles were joined by many newsletters, mailing lists, and other websites linking to them.[47] The story was discussed on the influential mailing list Nettime, one of the oldest forums for critical commentary on the Internet and related political issues, and it was being circulated on web forums and on mailing lists dealing with questions of copyright and the Digital Millennium Copyright Act (DMCA). It also appeared on the English and Japanese *Wired* magazine's news, the English and Japanese edition of ZDNet, the *New York Times*, *Newscientist.com*, and elsewhere.[48] Within a week, the news had spread worldwide, especially in technology and digital culture-related media, fostering a sense of community among the different AIBO user websites.

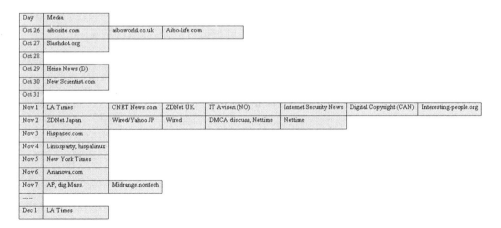

Day	Media						
Oct 26	aibosite.com	aiboworld.co.uk	Aibo-life.com				
Oct 27	Slashdot.org						
Oct 28							
Oct 29	Heise News (D)						
Oct 30	New Scientist.com						
Oct 31							
Nov 1	LA Times	CNET News.com	ZDNet UK	IT Avisen (NO)	Internet Security News	Digital Copyright (CAN)	Interesting-people.org
Nov 2	ZDNet Japan	Wired/Yahoo JP	Wired	DMCA discuss, Nettime	Nettime		
Nov 3	Hispasec.com						
Nov 4	Linuxparty, hispalinux						
Nov 5	New York Times						
Nov 6	Ananova.com						
Nov 7	AF, dig Mass.	Midrange.nontech					

Dec 1	LA Times						

Figure 11. Media coverage of the AiboHack-Sony confrontation (Schäfer 2004:69).

The news appeared at a time when audiences were becoming sensitized to issues pertaining to the DMCA. Users were alert to the fact that companies would use the DMCA, a confining adaptation of copyright law, to limit their freedom in using products according to their needs and also use it to stifle critics and exclude unwanted competition from the market.[49] The news of Sony's cease-and-desist letter reached already alarmed audiences in various 'issue networks' (Rogers 2005) related to debates about the DMCA, including music file sharing and downloading, free software and the threat of software patents, consumer rights, and digital citizenship. Even in communities not involved with the AIBO and its related groups, the case became another example of repressive copyright law. One could claim that the widespread concern about DMCA-related actions taken by corporate companies against programmers and customers led to a more rapid dissemination of news about AiboHack. In the eyes of the media, the David-versus-Goliath image of enthusiast users fighting for their cultural freedom against a major enterprise made the story an easy pick, which the Wired headline 'AIBO Owners Biting Mad at Sony' attests to.[50]

Loyalty has been described as a participatory relationship (Sennett 2006:64) which is increasingly present in organizations with high social capital. Although it may be going too far to characterize loyalty as the driving force behind the uncoordinated but effective actions of user communities and individuals, a shared understanding of values and a common sense of defining cultural freedom formed the ideological base of these actions. As William Uricchio has pointed out, a form of civil engagement emerges when companies confront their users with legal action (Uricchio 2004). This seems very much recognizable in the actions of the AIBO fans and their 'ad hoc allies' in related issue networks. Although not necessarily united by the same interests and causes, Sony's actions provoked a concerted, albeit not centrally organized, response.

Forcing Aibopet to shut down his websites made several things clear: a large community – the AIBO users affiliated to the different AIBO user websites – felt their cultural freedom was under attack and perceived the company's actions as deeply unfair. The communities immediately took the initiative and generated attention for the case, contacted Sony with petitions for settling the issues with Aibopet, and threatened to boycott the company's products. Postings in many online forums made it clear that Sony had not only been unable to offer the necessary support a sophisticated product like AIBO required, but they even lacked the proper documentation and help manuals as well. The posting with the subject 'Shame Sony...' by user Dale to the blackboard system at Aibosite expresses clearly what AIBO users thought in general about Sony and Aibopet:

Subject: Shame Sony...
Posted By: Dale
Date: Sunday, 28 October 2001, at 2:42 p.m.

Hi everybody.

I just want to say, how angry I am for Sony for causing the closer of Aibohack. If it wasn't for site such as Aibohack or this one [bbs.aibosite.com], I would have never of purchase an Aibo with his extra's.

'THE AIBO MANUAL IS UTTER CRAP.'

IT TELLS YOU NOTHING. MY AIBO TRIES TO COMMUNICATE BUT THE MANUAL TELLS YOU ABSOLUTELY NOTHING ABOUT THE TONES OR BODY LANGUAGE. IF WE DO NOT KNOW THE LANGUAGE THEN HOW CAN WE UNDERSTAND.

Because of Aibohack and this site, I could understand my new pet and enjoy him.

SONY YOU HAVE DONE IT AGAIN. STUFF YOU I NOT BUY ANOTHER AIBO, OR ANY OF YOUR ENTERTAINMENT ROBOTS AGAIN 'UNTIL YOU GET YOUR ACT IN ORDER'. SONY STOP BEING AN ARSE HOLE TO YOU CLIENTS, 'WE PAY YOUR BILLS AND WAGES'

Dale

[punctuation, emphasis in capital letters, and spelling in original posting][51]

This posting highlights problems that are deeply related to both the complexity of the software and Sony's corporate structure. Poor documentation is a recurring problem in software development and software-based products; it often affects the field of open-source programming, where small developing communities usually do not have the resources or do not see the need to provide manuals and documentation. In the case of the AIBO manual, it became clear that it did not sufficiently explain the product and its nature. The electronic pet was far more complex in its body language and communication than the manual suggested. According to Aibopet, who had been spending up to three hours per week answering user questions through e-mail, each launch of a new AIBO model increased the number of questions users sent him.

Despite Sony being a huge enterprise with many different departments, the AIBO saga is a perfect illustration of the right hand not knowing what the left hand is doing. While the research and development department produces highly complex products, departments responsible for customer relations and marketing are unable to meet customers' needs. On the level of product promotion, Sony underestimated the tentativeness of the AIBO, a product that was open to modification and further development by users due to its technological features. This aspect manifests itself also on the technical level. The software Sony provided for users to edit programs for the AIBO was confining and poorly designed. The AIBO editor developed by Aibopet in early 2000 worked much better than the pricy AIBO Performer Sony provided. His AiboPet Editor was eventually implemented in a new version developed by Sony and released in 2001 as Master Studio Editor.[52]

A community of enthusiastic users will always come up with more ideas for a software-based product than any marketing brainstorming session will achieve. In a digital age, in other words, vendors should recognize that their software-based products are destined to be further developed once they enter the sphere of users. Acting accordingly, they try to reduce the gap between users and the corporation, which would benefit the company's interest in improving products, services, and customer satisfaction. This is even more true in the case of a product like the AIBO, which fascinated computer novices and artificial intelligence researchers alike. Since both groups could meet on user community websites, a profound knowledge exchange took place between them. A more alert company would have recognized an opportunity for winning over those platforms as an interface between corporation and customers. When Sony failed to appreciate the user communities and Aibopets' software development, they missed out on the chance to engage actively with the communities and learn from consumer needs or stimulate collaboration. According to Aibopet, Sony employees were only passively following developments in the user community.[53] Eric von Hippel has convincingly argued that users' participation in research and development, for example through user appropriation, can contribute substantially more to innovation and product improvement than market research surveys (Von Hippel 1988). The paradigm of corporate control might stifle many innovative ideas and slow down improvement processes for products. A participatory culture is challenging management theories to question their approaches of control and feedback in order to develop more advanced strategies to integrate user activities into their development processes.

The detailed knowledge Aibopet acquired by hacking the AIBO models became a valuable resource to the rest of the community, as did the extra features offered on Aibohack.com.[54] But this knowledge also spread to communities where users were increasingly capable of supporting each other and providing answers to frequently asked questions. The communities appeared to be an important link in creating and maintaining a knowledge base on the product in question and stimulating improvement and further development. The tight-knit cohesion among different user websites and affiliation with multipliers like Slashdot.org and influential media like Wired magazine guaranteed the necessary attention and might well have exerted considerable pressure on Sony.

So far, the AIBO example demonstrates:

1. the significance of user communities and social networks
2. the impact of media and representation channels that cover users' issues
3. the importance of skilled users as agents of improvement, innovation, and support

Under the surface of advertisement, marketing campaigns, and product definitions, products start leading their own lives no matter what kind of spin the company presents them with. Software-based products, software applications and their appropriation by users constitute a new area of conflict that requires all participants to develop ways of interacting with each other in order to adapt to the new situation. Companies that refuse to acknowledge that their own product is barely under control, far too complex and sophisticated, and therefore partially unfamiliar to its creators, can lose the product, their clients, and eventually the initiative to engage in the market. The conflicts caused by colliding mindsets and challenged business models lead to reconfigurations of company-consumer relations. Ultimately, Sony withdrew its claim against Aibopet and, on 23 November 2001, just four weeks after the cease-and-desist letter was sent, Aibohack.com was up and running again. Sony decided to become more open to the community and announced an open software development kit, the Open R Software Development Kit. Aibopet was invited to beta-test the software. According to Sony Austria executive Helmut Kolba, the experience with the AIBO community generated change. The company realized that a top-down approach to software-based products was not working. But even today, years after the Aibohack incident, many companies have not managed to establish a productive relationship with their most enthusiastic customers. As Aibopet pointed out, Sony was merely granting the freedom to tinker with AIBOs, and while Sony employees were lurking on the AIBO community sites, no real interaction took place, let alone collaboration. But Sony integrated many of Aibopet's designs and improvements into new AIBO models and their related software. In January 2006, Sony announced that they would discontinue the production of AIBO. A still very active community remains developing applications as well as maintaining their social networks, where they share their dedication to their electronic pets.

Heterogeneous participation

The type of user participation presented in the cases above has to be characterized as heterogeneous. Such a view refutes an image of user groups as mere hobbyists working solely in their leisure time, intrinsically motivated by their opposition to commercial production. Especially in the case of the modification of electronic consumer goods, the initial producer, hobbyists, and commercial third-party developers are closely linked, and individuals participating in this production often belong to more than just one of these groups simultaneously. Participation is in the first place heterogeneous with respect to the active contribution and the status of the user. The user might be a computer novice but also an expert and employee of a corporation or a hobbyist. The term user can also describe a company using several tools developed by other producers. Users are heterogeneous in their status within the various stages of the production process, as their respective use of tools is heterogeneous with regard to licensing or unlicensed use. In the second place, the motivation to participate is equally heterogeneous and far less related to the frequent claim that participants are primarily fans. But in all cases their participation is explicit rather than implicit. The reasons for participation are often related to the development and execution of technological skills, the aspect of doing something that was not initially intended by the original producer, and of course the aspect of developing a distinguished personal profile for competing in an online community.

Examining exemplary cases of appropriation and the interrelationship between users and corporate designers illustrates that collaboration between users and producers unfolds at many different stages of the design and appropriation process. Depending on their involvement and technical skills, users perform different tasks. The majority of users just employ the applications and services offered by those users who are more involved in the process of production and modification. A comparatively small group of expert users provides content and services and develops new software. But less-skilled users also contribute to the development of new software by formulating their wishes and posting new ideas. This actor-network is characterized by heterogeneous activities and collaboration between different participants.

The teams of hackers seem to be quite small. The main group developing Xbox-Linux consisted of five people handling the bulk of the programming. Various phases of the project took place in temporary collaborations between people who were not necessarily members of the team. The same is evident on the larger scale of community websites and in various hacking groups. Even if a user group could be identified as a group of people interested in a certain electronic consumer product, the group itself would be very heterogeneous. Members differ in motivation, involvement and skills. For example, the majority of game console users are solely interested in playing games without having a need to connect to a user forum. Another large group uses community websites for information, news, and to learn about 'cheats' and 'exploits'. Maintaining a forum or a website and participating actively in the process of communication online does not necessarily require technical skills, but social skills and time are crucial. Users that have no programming skills may also assist by beta-testing software; their feedback helps developers make improvements. The game developer iD Software was the first company to invite users to beta-test new games. Users were glad to participate in the process of game development and even wrote patches for the bugs in the software.

A smaller group of users is able to program with software development kits and write complete applications or hack software. They build software such as the Xbox Media Center (XBMC). They often refer to less-skilled users or beginners as 'noobs', and exclude them from their communications because this stifles their work process. However, on important community platforms, such as Xbox-Scene.org, hackers and less-skilled users can and do communicate. The platforms are important for channelling attention and promoting hacks and homebrew applications.

In an attempt to categorize members of the heterogeneous user groups, one could differentiate them in terms of their motivation (gaming, hacking, social networking, etc.), involvement (time, participation, social network, etc.) and skills (from playing games to hacking). In the case of game console users this could lead to the following provisional taxonomy:

Lay user: uses the console for gaming, usually an unmodified console

Expert user/gamer: uses the console extensively for gaming, often a modified console, uses lots of copied games, participates in online communities for gamers, possibly provides plug-ins, manuals, FAQs and administrative tasks for the community

Expert user/modder: uses the console often for activities other than gaming, participates in extending the functions of the console, is able to write code, provides applications, installs modchips or software solutions that are equivalent to modchips, often helps common users obtain modified consoles

Expert user/hacker: mostly interested in the technical aspects of consoles, hacking the platform, and providing applications for various uses, able to work with developer kits and debug kits

An example of an expert user/gamer would be Xwarrior, who is active on Xbox-Scene.com and who calls himself a 'frequent gamer, playing at least a couple of hours a day, posting a lot on a forum, and chat with some friends'. He describes the Xbox-Scene.com platform as a place 'where noobs ask all kinds of stupid things, but it's also the place for developers to get some attention'. Xwarrior writes patches for programs that don't work well and does some beta-testing. His motivation is 'the fun of it'.[55] The development of software does not take place on a platform like Xbox-Scene.com but in small teams, who usually maintain a website. The Xbox-Linux-Project core development group or the Aftershock Team would be an example of a small group of expert users/hackers who program homebrew software for the Xbox.[56]

In the conventional thinking of the culture industry, a group of professional producers develops artefacts for leisure-time audiences. This clear-cut distinction between work time and leisure time, between monetary-based professional and non-monetary activities, and voluntary labour can no longer be sustained. Neither is it possible to draw a picture of an emerging alternative form of production, because it is often difficult to separate professional from intrinsically motivated production. The distinction is particularly difficult to make among those who actively participate in open-source communities, fan culture or other communities developing knowledge and producing artefacts. Professional web designers participate in the collective production of frameworks and other means of production on a global scale, means which are crucial to their local business for developing customized web applications.

User participation has a profound impact on the process of design. The resulting design formalizes many aspects of appropriation and integrates them into new design developments. It can even exceed what Andrew Feenberg observed about lay participation in design processes:

> Lay initiatives usually influence technical rationality without destroying it. In fact, public intervention may actually improve technology by addressing problems ignored by vested interests entrenched in the design process. If the technical professions can be described as autonomous, it is not because they are truly independent of politics but rather because they usually succeed in translating political demands into technically rational terms (Feenberg 1999:89).

As Eric von Hippel argued in Democratizing Innovation, many software-based products are actually significantly improved and developed through appropriation by users. As opposed to many accounts of participatory culture, Hippel does not refer to fans, but to professional users, for example, librarians and medical technicians improving the products they use (Von Hippel 2005). While Feenberg's notion of lay participation focuses on the level of socio-political engagement, Von Hippel's examples describe engagement on the level of technical design. In software-based products, both aspects often appear simultaneously. As the example of the concerted actions of AIBO users illustrates, technical appropriation and socio-political activities unfold in tandem because the use of the products in question affects a cultural practice that needs to be established and defended against other interests. This argument has been made with respect to information systems in general (Ciborra 2002) and the Internet (Abbett 1999), where users are recognized as crucial factors not only for the development of new kinds of use but by virtue of their constituting a cultural practice along with shared values and an understanding for technology's cultural meaning. In that respect, appropriation of design not only changes products but affects society (Bijker, Law 1992). Speaking of participatory culture therefore means acknowledging users as active agents of technological change.[57] But rather than perceiving their labour only as a radical grassroots movement, an anti-hegemonic subcultural achievement, or an alternative mode of production, an adequate understanding of such phenomena needs to acknowledge the deeply intertwined relations between the sphere of 'amateurs' and 'professionals'.

4.2   Participation as implicit media practice

The hacking and modifying of electronic consumer goods described in the previous sections suggests that participation is generally understood as an explicit activity that is either intrinsically or extrinsically motivated. It is a conscious and voluntary act of participating in cultural production that I have labelled 'explicit participation'. The example cases discussed above, in other words, connect community-based production processes with a high degree of communication and an organizational structure for project management. But alongside such explicit forms of participation, there are also others that are neither intrinsically nor extrinsically motivated, but rather are motivated by the design of an information system itself with a low degree of communication among participants, which take place in a social structure that cannot be described as a community. Many popular Web 2.0 applications and services serve as a platform for the kind of user activities described in section 2.2 as accumulation, archiving and construction. These web applications provide the environment for media practices that have been developed earlier, but are now formalized in an easy-to-use interface.

Participation can in fact also be formalized as a default design feature that unfolds as an implicit activity. This form of implicit participation is intrinsically related to the Internet and the World Wide Web. As explained in chapter 3, a collaborative structure is already inherent in material aspects of the World Wide Web. Furthermore, the underlying design of the Web 2.0 has been described as an 'architecture of participation' (O'Reilly 2005), a term that clearly points to an understanding of participation generated by design options rather than community spirit. This is not new to the Web 2.0, but has become very much evident in many of its most common uses, such as file sharing.

Peer-to-peer (P2P) file-sharing systems thrive on implicit participation in that they provide designs that require each participant to contribute processing power and storage space. The development of file-sharing technologies evolved from sharing music and video files and stimulated developers to build technologies that would be able to handle the up- and downloading of ever-growing file formats. This design improvement enabled the speed of downloading files to increase. Although file-sharing services like Napster have been too hastily perceived as P2P communities, the strength of P2P actually lies in reducing the need for mutual social relations and community-based organization. The legacy of Napster is that it provided an easy-to-use application enabling users to search and actually find music files without being bothered to interact socially with the person providing those requested files. Napster showed how user activities can be perfectly implemented into software design, so that they become easy to perform and even automatized. Simultaneously, the P2P application provides an interface that connects users and their stored files with other users' search requests without requiring them to communicate. These systems offer a platform for a large number of users who benefit from better search results and performance when more users participate. As opposed to community-based organization, where software applications support user communication and collaboration, software design constitutes the crucial and central aspect of socio-technical ecosystems. While individual participation is the key factor in communities or teams, in socio-technical ecosystems the plurality of users is the more significant factor.

When using a P2P file-sharing system, users are not just taking part in the explicit act of file sharing by downloading or uploading, they are implicitly contributing with their hardware and processing power to the system-wide infrastructure. Their implicit participation extends the overall socio-technical ecosystem. As the sharing of hardware is a default setting in P2P file-sharing systems for participation, web-based information management services implement participatory media practices into their technical design by channelling user activities through the graphical user interface. This started with the easy-to-use interfaces of weblog software, which facilitated methods of setting up, editing and maintaining websites, and continued in Web 2.0 applications.

The different domains of user participation referred to as accumulation, construction, and archiving often merge in Web 2.0 applications.[58] Web 2.0 applications provide even unskilled users with an opportunity to connect databases, synchronize various data streams into one or more applications, and publish and edit content online (O'Reilly 2005). Described by O'Reilly as 'harnessing collective intelligence', application programming interfaces (APIs) enable users to connect various applications and sources and use them for different purposes. Instead of keeping data closed and hidden in a database no one may access, service providers share their information through the API. Sharing information and offering many possibilities for third parties, whether they be officially licensed partners, common users or just creative kids, has been recognized as an easy way of expanding business opportunities. In fact, the mostly misguided celebration of what is perceived as the openness of API's is actually just another way of controlling data.[59]

Another aspect of implicit participation is the sheer pragmatism of handling large numbers of users. Instead of administrating requests for advertising, Google assigns, with its Adsense service, the labour to the users who can freely install it on their websites. Users advertising via this service can do so by means of a handy interface. The information management system then delivers ads to the appropriate websites connected to the Adsense database (O'Reilly 2005). Just as Cisco Systems significantly changed the means of dealing with customers through a web-based catalogue and electronic order system, Google built interfaces enabling all users to advertise their products through Google Adsense or place adverts on their websites. While Cisco Systems and many other companies share databases with licensed suppliers and identified clients, Google simply opened theirs up to everybody by providing an appropriate API. This approach is just another formalization of user requests and service provider responses, but fewer personnel are needed for communication and administration, and it is open to anybody without prior subscription or contact with the service provider. Although many Internet technologies display features of implemented user participation, as is evident from hypertext, P2P distribution, and distributed computing, the Web 2.0 is perceived as a significant shift towards the integration of user activities into new business models. The beneficial effects of a network of users can be incorporated into software design, something referred to by O'Reilly as the 'architecture of participation'. O'Reilly also anticipates that taking easy-to-use interfaces can lead to commercially successful applications that take advantage of user activities (2005).

Principles of this architecture are APIs for the synchronization of databases, the use of free text meta-data that can be added by users, possibilities to create, publish, and share all kinds of content, and a general interoperability that allows users to integrate the content into different websites or applications. The significant value provided by users is often described as user-generated content. Providers such as Flickr, Delicious, MySpace, and Facebook indicate a shift in media industry from providing content to providing platforms and information management systems where content will be generated, stored, organized, shared, and expanded by users. The increased visibility and efficiency of user activities, as well as the huge numbers of individuals using these Web 2.0 applications, is leading to an understanding of a new generation of web tools that are explicitly aimed at user participation and offer a default design for their use (Uricchio 2007). Ciborra has pointed out the importance of user participation in information management systems, emphasizing the need for easy-to-use, adaptable, and hackable technologies that allow users to tinker with them and modify them (Ciborra 2002). This is exactly what popular web applications try to emulate, although in a way that allows the platform providers to exert control over user activities. Providing access to data through APIs led to the emergence of the 'mashup', which can be described as a collage of various websites and databases. A prime example is Google Maps which provides geographical data, images, and maps in different resolutions of almost every conceivable geographical location. Users can access these data through the API and route them to their own websites and applications. Available tools include easy-to-use mashup editors that provide a web interface where users can relate the different sources and apply their individual filter settings with a simple drag-and-drop method.[60] A commercial project such as Plazes integrates information on users' geographical location (retrieved either through the IP address or the GPS data of a cell phone) on Google Maps.[61] The website Flightwait.com combines data from American airports and a map of the United States on flight schedules to show delays in real time.[62] Flickrvision shows the upload of pictures to the Flickr database in real time and relates them to the geographical location of the uploading user.[63] Trendsmap tracks trends in Twitter in real-time by placing frequently used words on a map.[64]

Aside from the creation of mashup sites that rather qualify for explicit production, the most profitable user-generated content is in fact data. These data might be personal information users add to their profile pages in 'social-networking sites', their communication routed over e-mail and messaging services or merely the information of how many users are watching which video. Every click will be tracked, and log files assemble user data according to profiles and stored content. Users can rate content, indicate inappropriate postings, and participate in the indexing of the vast amount of data. Information organization becomes a key function of the information architecture in the Web 2.0. When posting content to websites, users contribute to the information management system by adding title, descriptions or comments. In view of these technologies, participation has to be differentiated in terms of the voluntary production provided in user communities as well as by commercial third-party developers, and the incidental and hybrid participation of large numbers of users in combination with information technologies. While the explicit participatory culture of fans, activists and 'prosumers' has been described as the labour of enthusiastic communities that often might inherit critical connotations or aspects of a new folk culture (Jenkins 2006b:132), or which might appear as a subculture phenomenon, participation in Web 2.0 occurs as an implicit aspect of clever software design. It is achieved by designing information management systems and their graphical user interfaces in ways that subtly channel user actions.

Information management

Websites such as Delicious and Flickr have become extremely popular and are often used as prime examples of the Web 2.0. Their aim is to achieve information management through a large number of users, and can be seen as typical socio-technical ecosystems. Noticeable in these systems are the different layers of social interaction and the use of meta-information, that is information about information, for organizing stored content. 'Tags' are used to improve semantically correct information retrieval. Tags are free text meta-data that can be attached to any content stored online. The best analogy is to that of a Post-it describing the object to which it is attached.[65] A tag could be any keyword, such as the title of a song that is stored in an audio file, or the title or the description of a picture, website or a video file. The words used as tags can be chosen by the user independently of any formal classification or regulated terminology. Tagging differs in this respect from any classification or taxonomy. It is just a form of meta-information that is organized by the semantic structuring process of the information management system (Hammond et al. 2005a, 2005b). Users' freedom to choose whatever text they like has led to tagging being labelled as 'social bookmarking', emphasizing a collective production of 'folksonomies'. The term 'folksonomy' stands for user-generated taxonomy, although the contribution of free text meta-data is in fact neither a taxonomy nor a classification or an ontology (Golder; Huberman 2005). 'Social bookmarking' and 'folksonomy' are perceived in popular discourse as yet another example of the social progress and 'democratizing' effect of the Web 2.0.[66] The social aspect of tagging is reflected in the number of users contributing to the information management system, simultaneously constructing an efficient semantic organization of content. The expectation is that users adding keywords to files and websites stored online will improve the accuracy of retrieved information. The problem generally associated with information retrieval has been clearly articulated by Winograd and Flores:

> If the problem is narrowly construed as 'Find a book, given specific information' then the system may be good. If we put it into a larger context of 'Find writings relevant to what you want to do' it may well not be, since relevance cannot be formalized that easily (Winograd, Flores, 1986:167).

The problem, in other words, results from the inability of machines to understand the semantic content of files. It has been suggested by the World Wide Web Consortium (W3C) to create and attach machine-readable meta-information to files stored online. Unfortunately a large part of online content lacks these very meta-data, or the person who configured the meta-information is using terms unknown or inappropriate to those searching. Free text tagging provides two promising perspectives for information organization on the Internet: Firstly, it describes the semantics of files stored online as a Post-it added to a website, a photo or a video file and the like; secondly, it is realized as a flexible technology, not dependent on a hierarchical classification of fixed terms, and not limited to specially skilled or authorized users who are able to add and change meta-information. Every possible term can be used as a tag. Furthermore, meta-information is not exclusive or static; other users can add information, hence the files can be described in several ways, and can be labelled with different keywords. Search engines cannot read and identify all files. Video and audio files, pictures and many websites, cannot be read by search engines and can only be identified if machine-readable data describe the content. So what tags do very well is to compensate for the semantic limitations of information technology, because the free text meta-data can be read by machines and are useful for users as well, because users can attach any keyword to the file in question. Users are free to act without the restrictions of regulations and the limitations of classification systems and taxonomies. The use of free text keywords directly stimulates large numbers of users to add any keyword to improve their own information retrieval or the visibility of the content they store online. But it also generates a plurality of input that can be used for automated information management.

Often such tags are represented in the form of a 'tag cloud', usually as an alphabetical listing of the keywords (tags) used in a given information management system, such as Flickr or Delicious, but also on weblogs for a quick navigation to postings related to the keywords represented. The size of the letters indicates how frequently the tag was assigned to stored content (see fig. 12). The tag cloud became an emblematic icon of Web 2.0 and can be found as a representation of related keywords on any Flickr and Delicious user account. Many other websites use the tag cloud to offer a quick overview of frequently used keywords and a way of navigating to entries featuring those keywords. However, the practice of 'quick-and-dirty' tagging made the representation of keywords in a tag cloud less attractive. Redundancy of keywords provided rather boring results.[67] On these websites, each of the keywords is a hyperlink linking up with the collection of data using this specific keyword. Tags become a way of navigating through stored data and connecting to stored files. They furthermore construct semantic 'neighbourhoods' of the stored files and users.

Top Tags
What this blog is about

animation **art** bbtv **comics** **copyfight** disney environment food **funny** games green innovation **kids** make a difference **maker** music old school safety science **video** audio boing boing tv **book civlib** **happy mutants** if you don't like something change it **maverick** spirit **photo** **steampunk** today

Figure 12. Tag cloud of keywords used on the BoingBoing weblog, retrieved from Technorati.com.

Participation and the collective generation of content are facilitated by implementing an interface design that stimulates users to provide tags to the files they upload. The interface also may enable social interaction between users but does not rely on it. Social interaction becomes only one of many options. The overall system is not dependent on the extrinsic and explicit participation of individual users, but on a plurality of users contributing to the system by simply using it. The labour generated on the platforms reflects the hybrid interaction of a plurality of users and the software bound together in a socio-technical ecosystem.

How participation takes place on an implicit level will be briefly illustrated by considering Flickr and Delicious, which are prime examples of information management in Web 2.0 applications and qualify as representative examples of the phenomenon of non-intrinsic and non-explicit participation. They furthermore demonstrate how users and technologies act interdependently in a socio-technical ecosystem. The implicit participation engaged in by users of these sites requires us to review what has been described as explicit participation, namely the terms of community, the social network, and motivation.

BASTARD CULTURE!

Flickr is a popular photo website ranked 32 on the Alexa Global 500 statistics for the most frequently visited websites (July 2010) and provides space for storing, sharing, and commenting on photographs online.[68] Each user account consists of a photo album that can be organized into different sets, a contact list, a list of groups the user is subscribed to, and a list of the user's favourite photos taken by other users. Users can add any other user to their contact list, as they can add any other user's pictures to their list of 'favourites'. The social network is therefore not necessarily reciprocal. Social contacts can be divided into 'family', 'friends' and 'contacts', and different privacy settings for stored pictures can be designated to each of these profiles. Users can also join and found 'groups' on Flickr. These groups revolve around all kinds of topics and can consist of as few as one or two members or as many as several thousand members. When uploading photos to Flickr, users can easily add meta-data and attach a title, description, and several tags (keywords) to each picture. By providing this information, users contribute to the system-wide database where the tags and all other added information such as titles, descriptions, and comments is accordingly organized by semantic structuring processes. For example, if a user uploads a picture of the Eiffel Tower in Paris, she might add 'Eiffel Tower' as a title, and 'Paris' as a additional tag, or she might add 'sunset', 'clouds', 'night' or 'summer vacation 2007', depending on the situation the picture represents. She could even attach the geographical data of the location to the picture through an interfacing connection with Google Maps, that allows Flickr users to drag the photos onto the location of a map where the picture was originally taken: the system will then add the geographical data to the picture.

The information management system will organize a photo according to the tags. The more pictures and information are added, the better the system organizes them semantically. As a result, personal tags, such as 'summer vacation 2007' or something like 'Jeff's birthday party' will not affect search requests that are not directly aimed at these topics. Many photos labelled as 'Paris', 'Eiffel Tower' or 'night' will form a cluster most likely consisting only of night shots of places of interest in Paris. Unnoticed by most users, data are already contributed through the exchangeable image file (EXIF) data. These data are meta-data attached to each image taken with a digital photo camera and contain, among other kinds of information, a record of the camera model, date, time, and camera settings. These data can be used for extensive statistical analysis of camera use, the popularity of the models used, and the number of photos shot with the different cameras.[69] Users generate even more data by viewing other users' pictures. Subscribers with a paid account can retrieve these data on a daily basis.[70] On a system-wide level, all this information is used to improve search results. Through an interfacing connection to the Yahoo Search engine, the meta-data of pictures are used to respond to picture search requests. Here the labour of users is leveraged to the benefit of the companies providing the service of the photo-sharing platform, and collective labour is constituted by means of implicit participation. Many features are automated, such as the transferring of EXIF data, while others are implemented into the interface design as part of the tagging options. Being a side effect of user activities performed on such an information management system, the resulting labour is of course used without any acknowledgement for their having improved commercial services.

Although Flickr does provide examples of communities and tight social networks, the important distinction to be made here is that participation takes place accidentally by simply uploading pictures and adding a title or tag to it, which is not necessarily caused by an intrinsic motivation to improve search requests. It cannot be denied that there is an important motivation the Flickr design takes advantage of, namely the potential number of views their pictures might receive. Users think of ways to tag their pictures as effectively as possible in order to attract a large number of views. This can also be seen as a motivation for joining a group dedicated to a certain topic. The more groups a photo is posted to, the more views one receives. Several groups introduced rules saying that they only accept pictures not exceeding a certain limit of group posts. However, the motive of receiving attention might also be mentioned as crucial for users who modify electronic consumer goods, but it would not sufficiently account for the amount of labour accomplished in those user communities, nor would it sufficiently account for the number of photos stored at Flickr and the meta-information added to them. The difference between a community developing a modification for a computer game or a fan culture platform and a massive multi-user information management system is that in the latter case a large number of users make comparably small contributions, such as adding meta-information, and the way in which these interact with the software design. As opposed to the communities in software development, gaming, modding or fan culture, the participation in massive, multi-user information management systems is not rooted in a common interest for a given subject, neither does it require the intrinsic motivation of individual users to expand a given cultural resource or the will to contribute to something.

The information management system Delicious displays features similar to Flickr's, but it is even less dependent on social interaction. Delicious is a popular website for storing one's favourite web bookmarks, that is, web addresses of websites (URLs). Users browsing the World Wide Web can post all websites they want to bookmark to their Delicious account. While adding a link, users attach meta-information in the form of tags as well, mostly choosing keywords they associate with the website in question. If other users have already bookmarked that site in question, the information management system suggests keywords other users have used as appropriate tags. The Flickr.com website, for instance, has been posted to Delicious by over 79,000 users who tagged it mainly as 'flickr', 'tools', 'photo', 'photos', and 'sharing'.[71] When adding a new URL, the system already suggests tags based on tags that were attached to the same website by other users. Again, users are participating in the creation of an information infrastructure just by storing content online that is furnished with meta-data. Users and the stored

URLs form clusters and paths for navigation. Looking up an URL on Delicious leads to a collection of URLs of the individual users who have already added that URL to their individual bookmark collections. The relation between the individual user, the plurality of all users, and the information system can be easily recognized in the Delicious tag cloud, as displayed in figure 13. The tag cloud represents the most frequently used keywords, and highlights the keywords the individual user is sharing with other users. By clicking on a tag, a hyperlink refers you to a chrono-logical list of stored websites that are labelled accordingly, and another list shows the most active users contributing to the keyword in question. Although it is pos-sible to use 'social' features in Delicious, such as establishing a personal network with other users and recommending posted websites to them, or looking up their bookmark selections, the social interaction is even more fragile than in the case of Flickr and less cohesive as well. Users cannot prevent others from adding them to their network, but they can refuse a mutual connection.

Figure 13. Screenshot displaying popular tags on Delicious.

Again, the meta-information provided by the plurality of Delicious users creates ways of navigating, and by clicking on the keywords a user added to the posted websites, they will find not only their own postings but those of all users using the keyword in question, and it is subsequently possible to browse the bookmark lists of other users and find related links. Participation is again taking place at an im-plicit level that does not require any identification with a community, product or activity, rather it serves pragmatic features, such as achieving better search results. The effectiveness of the overall information system is determined by the number users adding meta-information to it, the software design channelling the user actions and organizing the input information, and yet also by the graphical user interface that encourages easy and intuitive use. But Delicious offers us more than just a system for storing bookmarks online, since it relates the bookmarks to the collections of similar tags and users storing bookmarks accordingly. This enables users to find other websites through the semantic clustering that allocates them around keywords and users. Without mutual communication, users can benefit from their various collections of links.

The features of implicit participation make particular sense in the area of archiving. Just as Napster was actually a system for organizing information and creating an index file of locations available for downloading, many Web 2.0 applications are 'engines' for effective information management, unfolding in user activities and automated information processing.

These examples show a different quality of participation. Here, participation takes place incidentally, but is nevertheless a contribution to a form of cultural production, namely the construction of information resources and ways of navigating through them. While explicit participation showed how heterogeneous the activities, motivations, practices, and objectives are, implicit participation reveals that the media practice is extremely hybrid, consisting of interactions between users and technologies. It furthermore shows that aspects of participation can be automated and integrated as design features into information management systems, allowing participants to perform activities without the need for social interaction, and even allowing the providers of a system to benefit from user activities without acknowledging their contribution. The design of these technologies can be set up to stimulate certain activities and stifle others, and, as will be discussed in chapter 5, this objective can be seen as an attempt to implement user activities into certain business models or to enable users to achieve certain skills and qualities.

Data collections

The large libraries and information storages Paul Otlet, Vannevar Bush, Ted Nelson and Joseph Carl Robnett Licklider were proposing have turned into a somehow anarchic form of floating archive online. Generally, the Internet and WWW provide a means for publishing content different from conventional archiving. However, collecting, distributing, and maintaining data constitute rather 'floating archives' than a stable and organized collection of entries in a traditional archive. The media practice referred to as archiving in chapter 2 reveals a notable convergence of explicit participation and implicit participation. Users participate explicitly through creating, maintaining or contributing to data collections, but users can also participate implicitly by improving the information management system simply through retrieving files from the archive. This media practice indicates a rather heterogeneous, if not anarchistic and often coincidental way of organizing and storing information online. What traditionally was perceived as an archive, namely a local storage of artefacts determined by a filing system, an input control, and policies for maintenance and access, is challenged by the new technologies. Now user participation has become a crucial aspect in creating data collections, filing, maintaining, and processing information. While traditional archives were maintained by professionals and were subject to regulations stating what is worth preserving and in which categories it should be filed, floating archives are more like a dumping space for all kinds of files.

Unlike 'analogue' archiving, the storing of information in digital media is not determined by storage space. The ever-increasing capacities of data storage devices and the decreasing costs of storage space lead to a media practice that has been characterized by Lev Manovich as the 'post-compression condition' (2005).[72] Manovich claims that unlimited storage capacities also profoundly affect the production of art. While art in previous centuries was forced to compress reality and represent, for instance, entire narratives in one single painting, the post-compression condition even allows the real-time archiving of events and preservation of unlimited quantities of information in databases (Manovich 2005). What Manovich calls the post-compression condition is characterized by an attitude of storing first, selecting later.[73] This process can even take place in real time.

A noteworthy project anticipating a media practice that comes close to real-time taping a user's life is Gordon Bell's *MyLifeBits* (Gemmel et al. 2002; Bell; Gemmel 2007). It aims to record an individual person's entire day by capturing all kinds of information, from weather data to geographical location and pictures or video files and sounds from the events of the person's day.[74] Made from common consumer electronic devices, the Australian media artist Nancy Mauro-Flude has built a bag that serves as a tool for recording images, sound and tracking geographical position data. Such a device can be used for collecting records for a personal diary-like archive, but it can also be used as a tactical medium for grassroots journalism, and is therefore providing means for participation. Mauro-Fludes device also automatically scans its environment for open WLAN access to transfer the recorded data to a remote server for archiving.[75] Projects like the Mauro-Flude's *Bag Lady 2.0* or Bell's *MyLifeBits* anticipate a media practice of perpetual recording and archiving in what Manovich calls a post-compression condition.

While traditional archives applied filtering before storing artefacts, filtering is now used to select from the vast amount of stored information those pieces which seem to be worthy of being used for further purposes. Due to the decreasing costs of storing information or even large files online, and due to the increasing possibilities of gathering and distributing all kinds of data, archiving became an almost pervasive media practice, wherein much of the labour is done by users, while commercial services seek opportunities to collect and exploit the collected information. Companies such as Rapidshare, Megaupload, and Flyupload offer cheap online storage capacities for large quantities of data. Others offer services for specific kinds of data, such as Flickr or Photobucket, which offer users a system for archiving photos, and YouTube for uploading videos. Nevertheless, the emergence of these services indicates that storage and traffic do not come for free, and particularly when a certain scope is exceeded, they require large enterprises for funding, maintaining, and marketing those services. It demonstrates the extent to which participatory culture often spreads on corporate platforms. Beside commercial services, there are countless data collections in the domain of users.

The plurality of different formats, data carriers – either offline or online – and the Internet, with its hypertextually connected web servers, constitute a void filled with data. The term 'archive' might not be appropriate to describe the often unorganized, widely distributed, redundantly stored, coincidentally filed, and often not systematically indexed information. The archival chaos began with the challenge of preserving earlier generations' artefacts. Just as nitrate film required copying on more durable film, or acidic paper often leads to reprinting books on acid-free paper, the basic format of data carriers in the digital age has changed as well. The digital heritage is divided into many different formats, machines, operating systems and file systems. Storing data in one format does not guarantee durable archiving. Many programs that can be run on outdated computers or video game consoles would not be accessible anymore if users or companies didn't reformat them to work on current gaming devices. Many classic computer games are available with what are known as emulators, software that emulates the original machine on a current device. The format data are stored in, and the devices they are stored on, are changing faster than the archival process itself. But in general data on digital devices do not disappear over time, as is the case with acidic paper or nitrate film. Electronically stored data vanish when someone consciously or accidentally deletes them. Along with the plurality of allocated data on the most different of machines, data carriers or online databases, data collections are heterogeneous in their indexing system, their meta-information, and their relation to retrieval and search technologies. While the established archive has been an institutional setting with a curating policy, a coherent filing system, and durable maintenance, the data collections on the Internet can be accumulated and often accessed by anyone.

In an attempt to categorize the many different kinds of existing archival systems or information management practices, the following forms can be distinguished: organized archiving, personal archiving, and massive archiving. Each category describes different layers of participation. The interrelated dynamic of users and information technology is explicitly visible in user activities aimed at organizing information. This activity is heterogeneous also with respect to professional organizations maintaining archives or communities and individual users who employ information technology to provide data collections and access. In the case of web-based applications, personal archiving is an explicit activity performed on a platform that exploits it simultaneously as implicit participation. Massive archiving, on the other hand, describes automated processes of archiving and a high degree of implicit participation.

Organized data collections

Organized data collections maintained according to curatorial guidelines, filing systems, and systems of information management and retrieval are those that most resemble established analogue archives. These data collections do not need official or institutional approval and can be constructed by any user as long as storage and traffic capacities are provided. Often, users can add further data to a collection. Noteworthy examples are Internet Archive, Scene.org, and the Project Gutenberg. The Internet Archive's Wayback Machine provides documentation of websites back to the year 1996 and carries out regular web crawls to archive a global snapshot of websites. Furthermore, the Internet Archive hosts a collection of films that are in the public domain, as well as an audio and text collection.[76] As Uricchio emphasizes, this archive is crucial for providing access to the first decade of the World Wide Web through systematically preserving the dynamic, constantly changing, and unstable media technology (2009). Scene.org is an archive for audio files and demoscene files, facilitating daily traffic of up to 200 gigabytes.[77] It is an example of a community-based archive, preserving and maintaining the creations of a fragmented part of digital culture.

Project Gutenberg is one of the oldest digital archives attempting to provide access to public-domain books. Supported by thousands of volunteers, books are scanned and made available in plain text and HTML, totalling over 20,000 freely accessible books.[78] As opposed to the information management implemented in sites such as Flickr, Project Gutenberg primarily thrives on explicit participation and a selected group of people responsible for maintaining and organizing the archive, as does Scene.org. However, the Wayback Machine is an approach to archiving that implements participation and automates it (Rogers 2004:14). The websites indexed in the Wayback Machine are indexed through a plug-in users may add to their browser. After this initial explicit act, the collection of data is delegated, and websites will be reported automatically to the Wayback Machine.[79]

Personal data collections

Along with the large organised data collections that are most often stored on servers, archiving online includes personal data collections that can either be stored on servers (web-based) and/or on clients (on the user's PC).

The most simple examples are e-mail archiving applications or software for organizing music, video and text files, or hyperlinks.[80] Basically the archiving application helps users create an index that enables fast retrieval of all kinds of data that might be stored somewhere on the user's hard drive or online. Index and content can be separated and are related to each other through hyperlinks. Commercial Web 2.0 services, such as Flickr and Photobucket, provide users with storage capacities and useful tools for information retrieval. With Delicious, users can add information and tags to the websites they store in a personalized structure and relate them to the entirety of stored web sites in the information system. This activity may only serve the user's personal need for information management, but the user can also share stored information with other people. However, regardless of the users' motivations, they do, by the same token, participate implicitly in improving the system-wide database. The more users add information to the system, the better the overall information system becomes in terms of information management and retrieval. Despite the fact that users archive their own personal files, their activities exceed the scope of personal information management and affects the system-wide platform.

Distributed data collections

The most striking aspect about storing files online is massive participation (Uricchio 2004a; 2009). Through distributed computing, processing power and bandwidth can be shared, facilitating the distribution of even large files. An initial download of a program automates these processes, making it necessary to connect the user to a file-sharing network. The use of such an application indicates how explicit and implicit participation blur into each other.[81] While users on Flickr, YouTube or other Web 2.0 platforms often don't see to what extent they implicitly participate in creating value, users of file-sharing systems are often aware that they explicitly share a part of their hardware and processing power. A prime example of explicit participation in distributed computing is the SETI@home browser, where users can 'donate' their computer's idle time to process signal analyses of recorded data.[82] In file-sharing networks, users also participate at this technical level by contributing processing power and storage capacity to the overall network, but they also participate at a content level by uploading files for sharing. The boundary between explicit and implicit participation blurs in these examples, as does the boundary between user-driven and machine-facilitated participation. Posting video files on the Internet Archive's database or on YouTube is a conscious and explicit process, while adding tags, viewing clips on YouTube, commenting, rating, and so forth constitutes, at least at some level, also an implicit participation in information management. When participating in a file-sharing network, parts of the hardware are implicitly used for extending the network's distribution quality.

Technologies such as P2P file sharing thrives on the participation of a large number of users. The more people participate in a P2P file-sharing network, the more files become available and the faster the distribution. For services such as YouTube, Flickr, MySpace, and Facebook, which are all in the top ten of Alexa's web traffic statistics, large numbers of users have a similar effect. The more people store and tag their photos on Flickr, the more accurately the search can cluster and retrieve photos according to search requests.

This kind of archiving also differs from a conventional understanding of archiving in that the stored data and the index or referring meta-data do not need to be stored together. Through hypertext, users can navigate from an index directly to the stored data. The separation of storage and index is a feature widely exploited in peer-to-peer file-sharing systems. P2P file-sharing systems are mainly distinguished by their being either centralized and decentralized. The Napster file-sharing system employed a central server hosting the index of all available files. Decentralized systems, such as Gnutella or eMule, resort to a choice of available files generated in real time from available nodes and therefore do not represent the overall availability of files. In both cases, index and actual files are separated and only hyperlinks refer from index to file. The index may represent all the features of an organized archive, but the related data can be stored on many different locations. File-sharing systems facilitate the separation of index and content. The BitTorrent protocol used for P2P file sharing formalizes the separation of index and stored file. A Torrent file refers to a certain file, for example, a video. Once downloaded to a user's computer and opened in a BitTorrent client, the Torrent file connects to an index of other users where the requested file is available, and starts downloading pieces of it until completion. The BitTorrent protocol enables faster distribution of files, exploiting characteristics of massive participation. The more often a file is downloaded by users and stored redundantly, the faster the file can be distributed. Storing files, as well as the creation of indexes, open many possibilities for user participation.

Countless user websites publish links to files stored on share-hosting services, such as Rapidshare and Megaupload. These commercial services are therefore enriched by users searching the contents and publishing hyperlinks to stored files. Similarly, BitTorrent files are published on countless websites, relating media files to a Torrent file, which can facilitate the distribution of the advertised media file. One of the most famous search engines that indexes from P2P filed data is the Pirate Bay. This controversial web platform operates under constant legal threat from various associations in the film industry. It is an oft-repeated accusation made by the music industry that file-sharing systems are used for illegal purposes only, but in fact they offer a legal way to cut costs on traffic expenses. Several copyright owners and other services deliberately use these systems to distribute their content and avoid hosting files on their own servers and spending money on traffic.[83] They take advantage of a plurality of users hosting their files and participating in circulating them through file-sharing networks.

Napster, the first P2P application, has already demonstrated how little social interaction is required for participating in a socio-technical ecosystem. Automating several processes in the search for indexed files, and their distribution through the connected computers, delegates many processes of sharing files to an application, and lowers the bar for participation. Users participate implicitly, sharing parts of their hardware by default; and they participate explicitly by contributing files to the collectively shared resources, or by generating websites that refer to stored files. The media practice of archiving is a crucial extension of the existing cultural resources and is fundamentally transforming the availability and accessibility of media texts. Here, the explicit participation of users is important for collecting and digitizing artefacts, and making them available online.[84]

The media practice of archiving reveals socio-technical ecosystems of interacting information technology and massive user numbers.[85] A great deal of the distribution work is delegated to machines, while it is often the activities of explicit users that provides the content and related information. Similar to the information management systems mentioned above, P2P file-sharing systems are also socio-technical ecosystems thriving on large user numbers and constituting a platform for performing search requests and file distribution accomplished by an interaction of large user numbers with information systems. The easier and the more automated these interactions become, for example, through easy-to-use interfaces and automation, the more popular and more efficient those services can become as well. It has to be emphasized that the dispositif of participation is affected by the hybrid interactions between users and technologies, both of which are subject to popular and scholarly discourses as well as the result of design decisions (such as affordances) that are, yet again, produced discursively and through other user-technology interactions (appropriation and design).

Hybrid participation

Participation has thus far been distinguished as either explicit or implicit. Explicit participation reflects conscious, voluntary, often intrinsically motivated activities; it is often community-driven, based on mutual social relations and communication. Implicit participation, on the other hand, depends on the formalization of user activities as default functions in the technological design. It has been described as heterogeneous with respect to its various participants and their social context and role either in user communities, corporate businesses, or political groups and the blurred boundaries in between these. It is also heterogeneous with respect to users' motivations and mindsets. By implementing user activities as default options into software design, participation can be perceived as a hybrid interaction of information technologies and users. Of course, hybrids of human and non-human actors can be recognized in many dispositifs, but it has to be emphasized that taking the aspect of hybrid interaction into account transforms the understanding of participation.

Human capacity for action becomes intrinsically related to information technology. But instead of perceiving the technology in a McLuhanian way as a cause shaping a participatory culture, it instead emphasizes design choices made by designers and business leaders to formalize user activities in an interface design and the application's back end. Despite the fact that interactions between humans and non-humans are evident from the descriptions in the many examples above, the quality of user activities implemented into an application's GUI design and back end has a different quality. With reference to Katherine Hayles, implicit participation could be described as an emergence of complexity, constituted in the dynamic interaction of information technology and a plurality of users (Hayles 2007). Hayles notes that 'differences in complexity notwithstanding, the human and computer are increasingly bound together in complex physical, psychological, economic, and social formations' (Hayles 2007:101). In socio-technical ecosystems, this complexity seems to multiply. A multitude of users from the most divergent social contexts and networks are engaging with a plurality of software applications that are connected to many other computer networks, databases, other applications, and software agents. The technology is defined by an opaqueness resulting not only from graphical user interfaces, translating software processes into easy-to-use icons and simplified commands, but also through the general inaccessibility of many of the technologies used. Although users generate content, engage in social relations, mash websites and data streams, affect the visibility of posted articles by means of ratings and number of clicks, which is all computer-mediated and facilitated through software design, the machines operate on the 'dark side' of the interfaces, and are too often neglected in discussions and critiques about user activities.

Users might be aware of some of the routines performed by their e-mail program in order for them to receive and send e-mails, and users also have an understanding of the role technology plays in their daily activities when using a computer. But in the case of implicit participation, the question has to be asked whether users are aware to what extent the software is using them?[86] The *Time* magazine article mentioned earlier demonstrates perfectly how the opaqueness of software hidden under glossy interfaces and praised by enthusiastic promoters emphasizes what users do, but neglects what the information machines do. While on the surface, users still can perform explicit and even critical activities, the underlying structure uses these activities to improve information management and often serves commercial interests. The aspect of hybrid participation has to be emphasized, to point out the role of automated information management, data generation, and its synchronization with other mashed information systems.

As has been shown above, these systems, whether Web 2.0 applications or systems of distributed computing, produce labour and deliver results. These results are neither man-made nor machine-produced, but are the outcome of a dynamic interaction between a plurality of users and artefacts. These hybrids appear in the most diverging contexts of contemporary Internet use. They facilitate complex distribution processes, such as P2P file sharing, enable the accumulation of processing power, such as distributed computing projects, and improve information retrieval and semantic data clustering in information management platforms that are constructed as socio-technical ecosystems, where the plurality of users and the 'realm of pure technology' (Hobart; Schiffman 2000) meet. Hobart and Schiffman describe the almost inaccessible areas of technology such as 'search engines, agents, and algorithms' as pure technology; these, in linguistic terms, are determined by syntax rather than by semantics (Hobart; Schiffman 2000:204). Without changing the basic aspects of technology, free text meta-data and the interfaces stimulating and facilitating their use often compensate well for the lack of semantic information organization. Providing keywords or tags and other meta-information, users increase the overall potential for organizing and retrieving information efficiently. Furthermore, they affect the organization, display, and representation of stored content either by simply retrieving it or even more by explicitly rating, commenting on, or reporting it as inappropriate to the maintainers of the information management system. The participation is hybrid to the extent that the information management system and the plurality of its users construct and organize content together. Describing participation primarily as explicit activities by users neglects the agency of the software design that channels these activities. Releasing a software design immediately leads to interactions of an unknown plurality of users that will use, appropriate and reuse the design in several ways, often in ways that are unknown to or unexpected by the designers. However, many user activities can be structured and formalized in the information management system's design and the user interface, and this is occurring more and more frequently, as the media practice of online culture and social interactions is better known today than a decade ago.

As indicated above, participation takes place on both levels, the level of explicit participation and the level of implicit participation. Contributing deliberately to an archive, either by uploading files or even more by generating the files in question first, since this is achieved through the labour of those volunteering in the Gutenberg Project, is an act of explicit participation. Fans publishing collections of their favourite subjects online or creating websites to present them are contributing actively, too.[87] The former video game producer Atari was not represented online at all for years with the exception of websites created by devoted fans who posted all kinds of material online related to the history of the company. Former employees and enthusiasts set up an entire online museum.[88] User can browse early Atari advertisements, scan boxes of Atari products and related manuals, as well as use the Atari games themselves. Although developed for a technically different platform, they are available through emulators simulating the original machines. Those collections often operate in the grey area between fandom and copyright infringement. The previously mentioned Xbins ftp server is another prime example of users filing programs and archiving them for further use and distribution.

Many data collections are created by fans or enthusiasts who want to provide access to a well-maintained and organized archive of their favourite subject. Collecting, indexing, and even commenting, aside from the technical aspects, such as providing the necessary web space, the interface to browse and access the collection, are valuable labour that in many cases makes content accessible that would be forgotten or lost. Users therefore make a very important contribution to the maintenance of cultural heritage. Most often this labour does not pay off financially but serves intrinsic goals. Other collections offer possibilities to efficiently retrieve files and bypass ensuing payment. Recent lawsuits against corporate file-hosting services, such as Rapidshare, made explicit that their service is regarded to primarily serve purposes of copyright infringement.[89] User activities that involve storing, presenting and distributing media content are a perpetual source of corporate legal action and form one of many domains where old business models and the use of new technologies collide.

But the activities go beyond the labour of collecting, uploading, and presenting collected data online and increasingly involve the management of information, and generating meta-information for improved information retrieval. While archives in previous centuries executed a strict input control and maintained a system of categorizing and filing, the Internet just consumes everything users store on the many different web servers. Indexing information online takes place in a retrospective process through search engines' web crawlers. And these machines are not capable of indexing all websites or data stored online, which leads to the emergence of an unknown data void, irretrievable and impossible to rate. With the advent of the Web 2.0, software design is able to create information management systems that implement user activities and offer handy techniques to add supplemental meta-information at will to every website and a plurality of files stored online. This significant change in channelling user activities to improve information systems will be discussed as default participation.

Chapter 5
The Extension of Cultural Industries

The previous chapters described a participatory culture unfolding through user activities that increasingly affect the production and distribution of media texts and software. This participatory culture is part of a media practice intrinsically affected by the qualities of related technology. Simultaneously promoted and represented in a popular discourse on social progress through technological advancement, this cultural practice manifests itself as an extension of established production routines of media texts and consumer goods. As explicit participation, it shows an active involvement of users in co-producing, appropriating and changing media texts and software-based products of the established industries or even independently creating media content and applications outside the industry's production channels. In this process, corporate producers are confronted with users who deliberately change the original design and develop software-based products further. Additionally, the bypassing of traditional distribution channels for media content through Internet applications has been a serious challenge for industries whose business model explicitly revolves around the control of distribution. I have labelled this process an extension of the cultural industries, where production and distribution are extended into the realm of the user. But this extension appears to be twofold: on one hand, the quality of the new technologies described in chapter 3 constituted an extension of production and distribution channels into the realm of the user, but on the other hand, the culture industries started to extend themselves into users' media practices by integrating user activities into new platforms and services. This ambivalent quality of media practices and technology is also recognizable in the accompanying discourse. While it hastily started out to celebrate the participatory potential of users who were now seen as media producers, liberated from the top-down culture industries, the industries' extension as platform providers for user-generated content is now often criticized as an exploitation of free labour. And indeed, the twofold meaning of the extension of the cultural industries constitutes dynamic interactions between corporate producers and user collectives that raise issues of socio-political quality.

The following chapter conceptualizes participatory culture as an extension of the cultural industries. It deliberately refers to the critical connotation of culture industry as formulated by Theodor Adorno and Max Horkheimer, but it does not strive for a Marxist understanding of participation. The agency of corporate companies, their influence on decision-making processes, and their ability to control – and increasingly to exploit – cultural resources have been neglected in many of the romanticizing accounts of user participation. It is also necessary to emphasize the emergence of new and very powerful media corporations that might not directly produce media content, but do provide and control the platforms on which users not only create media content, but increasingly also their social life. Subsequently, the socio-political consequences of user participation will be discussed as confrontation, implementation, and integration.

Confrontation refers to the collision of a new media practice and the established conventions of production, and describes how attempts are made either to change the legal situation in order to preserve the conditions under which old media practices had functioned, in spite of the possibilities offered by new technologies, or to design technology in a way that would prevent appropriation. Implementation describes the extent to which the new media practice can be implemented into software design. It sees the ability of enterprises to successfully exploit new tendencies and take advantage of them. Unlike confrontation, implementation is less obvious and attracts less attention. It is a subtle and often neglected process that takes advantage of certain user activities. Primarily taking place at the level of design, implementation channels user activities to create new business opportunities. Integration refers to how the new media practice can constitute an integrative approach to production and labour. It harnesses many values and practices developed over the past decade. On a global level, users are collectively participating in creating and developing resources and means of production that can in return be employed locally for commercial purposes. Their approach to copyright and patents, as well as collaboration and business models, is clearly distinguished from the established cultural industry model, which rests upon the exploitation of copyrights.

While confrontation aims at preserving old business models, both implementation and integration employ emerging media practices for new modes of production. To use an old Chinese saying, 'when the wind of change is blowing, some are building shelters but others are building windmills'. The DMCA, Trusted Computing, and software patents are shelters for weary giants, while P2P, Web 2.0, and open-source software might be windmills in a digital age.

BASTARD CULTURE!

5.1   Confrontation: fighting participation

Technological design is the key to cultural power (Feenberg 1999, 86).

Established business models are seriously threatened through the appropriation of corporate design and commercial media texts, as well as through uncontrolled global distribution channels. Losing control of the distribution of digitized artefacts is a crucial factor in the clash between old business models and new media practices. The many confrontations between users and corporations, monopolistic conglomerates, legal administrations, and participating civil society are deeply rooted in a process of renegotiating power relations in view of the new technologies. As Feenberg summarizes:

> Because technologies have such vast social implications, technical designs are often involved in disputes between ideological visions. The outcome of these disputes, a hegemonic order of some sort, brings technology into conformity with the dominant social forces (p. 89).

Design decisions and proposed legal regulations represent different ideological viewpoints. The confrontations provoked by certain aspects of new media practice have been reported widely in mainstream media. For example, a heated debate took place regarding the open and collectively produced encyclopaedia Wikipedia.[1] GNU/Linux, and open-source software in general, was attacked for years by Microsoft and through attempts by established industry players to preserve their role in the market, which is based upon large patent portfolios (Van den Boomen, Schäfer 205). Recent years have seen a extensive campaign by the music and film industries to prevent online distribution, and to criminalize downloading in general (Patry 2009). Especially in the media industries, one business sector has been characterized as a 'copyright industry', a term describing those companies whose business model mainly revolves around the exploitation of the copyright on copyrighted products, often labelled 'public goods' (Siwek 2004).[2] Those media products were easier to control and to commercially exploit when distributed as 35mm film, vinyl records or in print form, but in digitized form they can be copied without loss and distributed uncontrollably. The term 'public goods' is of course misleading and creates an association with 'commons', goods that are legally open for public use and make up the cultural resources. Hesmondhalgh therefore speaks correctly of 'semi-public goods' to indicate their limited accessibility (2002:17). Such scarcity is in fact created artificially in order to reduce the distinctive risks of the media business, high production costs, volatile business and the relatively high chance of failures, by tightening control over distribution and market regulation through copyright policies and vertical market organization (e.g. Rifkin 2000; Hesmondhalgh 2002). This business model came under severe pressure through the digitalization of media products and the ability to distribute them at almost no cost. The new and barely controllable distribution channels constitute an extension of the conventional culture industry, as is the case for collecting and accumulating media texts online and providing access to them. Altering and changing existing or producing new and related media texts not only extend the established production channels, but produce additional texts, which are intertextually linked to the original media texts and reflect a process in which media reception is intertwined with the creation of new media texts (Uricchio 2004a; Jenkins 2006b).

Many confrontations have taken place in an area that has traditionally been defined as the 'fair use' of media content, but which becomes highly controversial under the Digital Millennium Copyright Act (Lessig 2001:187-188; EFF 2004). Within the sketched cultural production of users (see fig. 4), this is applicable for activities of accumulating, archiving, or distributing and commenting on media content produced within the realm of established media industries. Modifying hardware or software and violating terms of use, patents and copyrights often leads to confrontations as well. Confrontations are caused by:

a. threatening the existing business model by either changing hardware and/ or software, or distributing content outside of the industry's controls (e.g. modchips; criminalized file sharing of music and audio files, bypassing regional limitations of distribution)
b. threatening the business model by introducing an alternative model that delivers competitive products (e.g. open-source products, free music downloads, creative commons, open access, collaborative knowledge construction, as in Wikipedia)
c. accumulating large quantities of media content and granting uncontrolled access and use to third parties, either paid or unpaid, depriving copyright holders of control (e.g. fan sites, fan archives, file-hosting sites, etc.)
d. changing, satirizing or appropriating media products (e.g. game mods, commentary, critique on media content)

Here, old business models and new media practices collide. As has been argued in previous chapters, many debates are caused by conflicts resulting from medium-specific (technological) qualities and their social use. Confrontations grow out of the new quality of generating knowledge and using computers, the Internet and software, hence the 'material' aspects of digital culture.

In view of the examination of the material aspects of computer technology, software, and the Internet, it becomes clear how closely and mutually dependent media practice and material affordance are. Wikipedia turns the conventional process of compiling an encyclopaedia upside-down and provokes pessimists to mourn the decline of expert culture, as does the principle of open access publishing that aims at the quick, non-bureaucratic, and easy publishing of academic papers without paying large sums to publishing houses that usually thrive on the free labour of scholars and scientists, as well as on the tax-funded subsidies of libraries.[3] Open-source software, such as the GNU/Linux operating system, threaten the concept of proprietary software. Figure 14 presents examples of general confrontations between media practice and material affordances. It defines the elements threatening established ways of producing and distributing artefacts or the creation of knowledge. Furthermore, figure 14 provides examples of new media practices and to what extent they threaten established business models or modes of cultural perception.

Name	Practice	Confrontation	Attacks	Opponent
Wikipedia	Collaborative production, free use, non-monetary-based distribution	Classic construction of knowledge and understanding of expertise	*Encyclopedia Britannica*, *Microsoft Encarta*, etc.	Representatives of conventional knowledge institutions; defenders of 'expert culture'
GNU/Linux	Collaborative, open-source, non-monetary-based distribution	Classic production model, proprietary software, software as commodity	E.g. Microsoft Windows	Microsoft, SCO, and other software patent holders
P2P networks	File sharing	'Channeled' distribution versus 'distributed' distribution	Control of distribution channels	'Copyright industry' in general (music and film industries)
Modified chips for game consoles	Executing non-vendor code, playing copied games	Product definition, product design	Business model of Microsoft, Sony, Nintendo	Microsoft, Sony, Nintendo
Open access	Publishing academic papers online and granting free access	Internet-based practice of free information and classic publishing	Established distribution and sale of academic books through just a few publishers	E.g. American Association of Publishers (AAP), Elsevier, Sage, Springer, etc.

Figure 14. Examples of confrontations provoked by media practice and material affordances.

Digitized video and audio files challenge the industry's building of a business model around control of distribution. Modified hardware and software turn game consoles into open-media entertainment platforms and threaten revenues by making obsolete the purchase of additional features, such as games, remote controls, and online services. Furthermore, modifying hardware and copying media texts generates new markets – often criminalized as 'product piracy' and 'copyright infringement' – and significant revenues.

However, not every confrontation will inevitably lead to a lawsuit; many are merely attempts to regulate the emerging media practice according to the logic of the media industry of pre-Internet times. At stake are large profits and market dominance, controlled by corporations engaging in friendly competition, defending their slice of the pie by any means necessary, from discrimination by lobbyists to direct pressure on decision-makers and legal administrations. The design and definition of technology and its use become highly political in these arguments. Confrontations with powerful companies and industry associations probably lead to political awareness and organization among those who embrace and defend the new media practice. Figure 15 presents a number of incidents that received mainstream media coverage in order to stress the frequency of legal confrontations and identify the actors participating in them. User participation has to be examined in the context of the larger debates on the legal issues of computer technology.

The new participation of former audiences as active users transpires into a 'battle royale'. The altercation takes place on three different levels: the level of popular and public discourse, the level of technical design, and the level of legislature. On the level of popular and public discourse, all participants seek to communicate their concepts and arguments and to discredit competing practices and their promoters. On the technical design level, the respective visions are implemented into technology, and the respective media practice is subsequently channelled. The level of legislature reflects the actual process of manifesting and regulating the respective technological concepts and media practice in laws. The discursive character of technology and its development, of design and designer's cultures, ideological connotations and socio-political visions, and the organization of markets is clearly evident in the disputes and confrontations caused by design and appropriation in the current media practice (Van den Boomen, Schäfer 2005). The outcomes of these confrontations will deeply influence the regulation of technology and determine the cultural freedom of its users.

In defending their cultural freedom and their way of using computer technology and the Internet, users' explicit participation enters the zone of public debate and decision-making processes, stepping beyond the closed and limited communication confines of the interested parties. Users start acting as citizens and claiming civil rights for their actions. They seek to transform their knowledge of technology into a legally protected practice, and hence integrate specific forms of technology use into society. Aside from the example of the AIBO user communities attracting media coverage for their cause, there are plenty of other examples illustrating how media practice is set on the public agenda.[4]

The UN declared open-source software as worthy of protection during the World Summit on the Information Society in 2003. Increasingly, GNU/Linux and open

Case	Subject	Consequences
Etoys vs. Etoy (US 1999-2001)	Domain: US-based online toy shop requires domain from Swiss art group and files lawsuit	a) Art group launches online resistance and sabotage acts b) Decrease of Etoy's stock value after losing lawsuit c) Netactivism
RIAA vs. Napster (US Dec 1999-May 2001)	File sharing: popular band Metallica and rapper Dr Dre, supported by RIAA, sue Napster	a) Napster shut down b) Development of second-generation P2P protocols
Buma/Stemra vs. Kazaa (NL 2003)	File sharing: Dutch copyright organization sues KaZaa	Kazaa cannot be held liable for user actions
Operation Digital Gridlock (US 2004)	FBI action against a closed file-sharing network, six houses are searched and one Internet provider's offices	Conviction of four operators of file-sharing servers known as the Underground Network
Operation Fastlink (2004)	FBI and international authorities search and seize 120 sites in 12 countries, over a hundred alleged members of the warez scene are affected	47 convictions
Operation D-Elite (US 2005)	Homeland Security works with FBI to shut down the bit torrent network EliteTorrents. The MPAA assisted in the investigation.	Conviction of six operators from the EliteTorrents network
Operation Site Down (US 2005)	FBI and international police authorities seize hardware and software in 10 countries to dismantle the biggest warez groups	Five convictions in the US, many scene members went into hiding, several sites went offline and several groups were discontinued
MGM vs. Grokster (US 2005)	File sharing: MGM and MPAA sue file-sharing network Grokster	Grokster discontinues file-sharing application
Raid on European piracy scene (GER, A, NL, PL, CZ 2006)	Authorities search offices, houses and confiscate servers and equipment	Participation of the German copyright enforcement association revealed in illegally distributing activities through use of 'honeypots'
Raid on Pirate Bay, (SWE 2006)	Under MPAA pressure, Swedish authorities raid the Pirate Bay office, confiscating servers	Political scandal, international attention and support for Pirate Bay; improvement of their infrastructure

Case	Subject	Consequences
Stolen Xbox 360 development kits (UK, GER, A 2005)	Theft: authorities raid the house of Austrian hacker and member of modchip team SmartXX, who got hold of stolen Xbox 360 development kits	Microsoft tries to halt investigation later and allegedly pays the hacker's lawyer and expenses
Operation Tangled Web (US 2007)	Homeland Security sides with FBI for nationwide raid of 32 shops providing modchips	No known results as of June 2010
Stichting BREIN vs Mininova (NL 2009)	Dutch trade association requires torrent site Mininova to seize distributing links to copyrighted files	Mininova loses lawsuit and removes not only links to copyright-protected files but all torrents due to lack of reliable filtering

Figure 15. Confrontations involving authorities' actions and lawsuits.

source in general were perceived as transparent, democratic, fair, beneficial to society, and inherently anti-commercial. Despite the fact that none of these attributes correctly reflects open software or the diverse and heterogeneous participants engaged in developing and using it, it creates the image and general symbolic capital of Linux and open-source software. In 2003, Monica Lochner-Fischer – a politician from the German Social Democratic Party and a trained computer scientist – campaigned with the slogan 'More Linux, More Freedom'. In an interview with the online magazine *Telepolis*, she emphasized the relevance of meeting politicians in person to explain to them how software patents would affect labour, business opportunities, and cultural freedom.[5] When a coalition of lobbyists and politicians tried to launch patent laws favourable to the big players in the software and automation industry, a heterogeneous front of activists responded by making the issue public. Going beyond the circles of business and programmers, the software patent issue reached the mainstream media in 2004, and in 2005 the European Parliament surprisingly refused the EU commission's directive on software patents (Van den Boomen, Schäfer 2005:60-61).

When it became known that American authorities might have pressured Swedish authorities into engaging in a battle against Pirate Bay, the result was not only public outrage about the interference in national sovereignty, it also resulted in the establishment of a Swedish political party called the Pirate Party. In the wake of events in Sweden, Pirate parties sprung up in other European countries as well.[6] Although these parties are unlikely to wield political influence, they put the question of file sharing and related media practices on the public agenda. Well-known politicians and established parties have begun to recognize the potential of gaining votes by promoting the cultural freedom of users.

The material aspects of software-based products caused the development and research process to also be extended into the sphere of users, whether amateurs or professionals who improved and modified the original product into a derivative. Jenkins describes this process as convergence culture, in which top-down corporate strategies interact or collide with bottom-up user activities (Jenkins 2006b:243). The possibilities for consumers to react to top-down strategies have increased exponentially, and companies are well advised to take into account users' abilities for generating attention and their tactics in defending their cultural freedom. Furthermore, a number of publications have convincingly shown that innovation and improvement are not limited to conventional research institutions and companies (e.g. Abbet 1999; Oudshoorn, Pinch 2003; Hippel 2005).

Modchips, grey markets, and big business

The case of modified game chips illustrates how the conflict about design, affordance, and appropriation manifests itself at various levels, that is, in popular discourse, in technical design, and in legal actions. In the case of game console modification, for instance, the conventional business model of such consoles is threatened. André Vrignaud, a member of the team who developed the Xbox, explains on his weblog that the industry in fact uses an 'attachment' business model that lets their clients benefit from subsidized hardware with the intention to make a profit by selling attachments, such as games, online services, or additional hardware.[7] In other words, using the game console as a platform for software that turns it into something entirely different implies that the purchase of such attachments is no longer necessary, and that users can benefit from the subsidized hardware by using it for activities for which they would otherwise have to buy much more expensive devices. Vrignaud's weblog, which is arguing from the point of view of the industry, is one of many channels available for discussing the question of modchips. Vrignaud even assures readers that, in principle, it would be fantastic if users customized the game consoles to their own specifications, if it weren't for the modchips that the industry simply cannot condone because they enable the playing of illegally copied games and would have a damaging impact on the business model. Users, on the other hand, often feel patronized by companies regulating the use of the devices for which they paid considerable amounts of money. On gaming platforms, in special interest magazines, and in other technology-focused media, modchips remain an issue that is discussed regularly. The dispute about modchips, however, does not frequently make mainstream news, with the exception of spectacular cases, such as the above-mentioned raid on a SmartXX team member in Austria in October 2005 or the United States-wide raids of modchip shops in August 2007. Unlike the issue of distributing music and video files, which falls under the intellectual property industries concerned, the issue of modchips rarely finds its way into the mass media and instead stays within the sphere of the participants involved. The original inventors resist unsolicited modifications of design or legislature condoning it, and actively engage in investigating violations of their intellectual property and file lawsuits in order to protect their interests.

At the design level, detection systems try to recognize modified game consoles and then exclude them from connecting to extra online services; in addition, firmware updates that are regularly downloaded on consoles prevent the use of homebrew software. Encryption technologies implemented in chips impede potential cloning and redistribution. Users who want to use homebrew software have no other choice than modifying their gaming device. As a consequence, they often lose warranty guarantees and are excluded from additional services, such as the use of Xbox Live services in the case of the Xbox. In 2009, Microsoft excluded 600,000 Xbox360 consoles from accessing Xbox Live and related services due to alleged violation of their terms of use.[8] Another strategy on the design level is to open up possibilities for a strictly controlled form of participation. The Xbox 360 and the iPhone offer development kits and distribution channels for third-party provided applications, regardless of whether these are developed by professionals or enthusiast users. Through providing the means for production and the distribution platforms, the companies can actually control user appropriation more effectively. Apple recently banned the application MailWrangler, a user-developed e-mail client, from its App Store, allegedly to avoid 'user confusion' with the Apple provided e-mail client. At the legal level, modification is hindered by the expiration of warranty claims for modified consoles and by legal actions against modchip producers. Modchips are simply prohibited by US law according to the DMCA. The DMCA, which was proposed initially by lobbyists in the media industries, helps corporations like Microsoft, Sony, and Nintendo to impose their definition of media use onto customers. In countrywide raids, US Customs and Homeland Security shut down many distribution nodes of modified chips. The dominant corporations made efforts in Australia, the US, and Asia to ban the production of modified chips. The legal argument completely disregards the added value provided by modified chips and does not take into account practices that are in fact perfectly legal, such as executing homebrew software and making back-ups; instead it focuses solely on the possibility of playing copied games. The industry and law enforcement authorities emphasize the allegedly huge losses of revenues due to 'pirated games'. The authorities, however, have not only adopted the industry's position, but also the way in which the industry lobby describes the modchip producers. As Julie L. Meyers, former assistant secretary of Homeland Security and Immigration and Customs Enforcement (ICE), stated after the 2007 raids: 'Illicit devices like the ones targeted today are created with one purpose in mind, subverting copyright protection'.[9] According to Homeland Security, modchips stood to cost copyright-holding industries an annual loss of $250 billion, which is what they used to justify the severe measures they took. However, these are figures almost impossible to verify, and they are usually provided by the industry associations themselves. Authorities repeat these unverified claims mantra-like over and over again. Robert Schoch, head of the Los Angeles ICE office, commented on the 2009 arrest of a 27-

year-old college student accused of modifying computer game consoles: 'Playing with games in this way is not a game – it is criminal. Piracy, counterfeiting and other intellectual property rights violations not only cost U.S. businesses jobs and billions of dollars a year in lost revenue, they can also pose significant health and safety risks to consumers'.[10]

What is rarely mentioned in the media or in statements made by the companies concerned are the revenues modchip production and sales are generating. And if numbers are mentioned, they appear to be as unverified as the industry-produced figures of alleged losses due to so-called piracy and counterfeiting. Producing modchips is not a leisure activity of some enthusiastic amateurs, but requires funding for research and development, division of labour, sophisticated skills in building hardware, and programming encryption, a supply chain producing the actual chip, and a distribution system. Since the labour is illegal, it actually becomes an organizational challenge. According to an former modchip developer interviewed, 'Development and production costs add up to $25 per unit, which are sold for $28 each. The minimum of units built for a generation of modchips are approximately 40,000'. With sales between 300,000 and 400,000 modchips for the first Xbox, the interviewed modchip producers estimated to have gained a market share of 35% at the time. In order to start building a modchip, initial costs for development and the purchase of components add up to an estimated $600,000 for 40,000 chips.[11]

Although the production costs of modchips indicate a rather large business scale, the labour is achieved by only a few participants. While a small team develops the modchip, the actual production is outsourced to a manufacturer,[12] and a variety of online web shops distribute the chips to users. At the local level of device installation, the business is not run by criminal, money-laundering companies as the industry's accusations often claim, but instead it is primarily organized as a rather small type of business that involves semi-professional, enthusiastic gamers. Their activities answer a considerable demand of users to remove the limiting design features of the original vendors whose business model does not fit the technological quality of the distributed devices. That business model can only be upheld by criminalizing the modification of game consoles.

Actions such as shutting down modchip distributors, suing gamers for installing these devices into game consoles, and excluding modified consoles from online services just foster images of David and Goliath, with hackers battling against a much stronger opponent that – in the perception of the communities – can influence legislation and thus buy justice. Furthermore, police activities often seem to be of a symbolic nature. The 2007 Operation Tangled Web (see fig. 15) was undertaken with apparently considerable efforts, but the targeted web shops were up and running as of July 2010.

The wide diffusion of modchips indicates the emergence of a grey market that is closely connected to the established market for game consoles and their related products. It is clear that modchips are not necessarily used for 'illegal' activities but actually enable users to find many other legal uses for their devices that the original vendor does not provide. However, the game console producers cannot participate in this market without cannibalizing their outdated business model which is clearly not fit for the digital age. It can only be upheld by the law and law enforcement through criminalizing the production, distribution and use of modification chips, and through limiting the cultural freedom of users to tinker with the devices they actually paid for.

Open-source software, from hobbyists to business

Off-the-shelf software for microcomputer home users was more or less invented by Bill Gates when he wrote the oft-quoted 1976 'Open Letter to Hobbyists'.[13] Blaming users for exploiting the labour of programmers by using their programs without paying, Gates formulated a vision of software as commodity. The benefit for hobbyists would be efficient off-the-shelf software that could be produced commercially once users understood that they had to pay for it. This production logic and ideology have been labelled as the 'Cathedral' by Eric Raymond, who distinguishes it from the logic of the 'Bazaar' that applies to open-source software (Raymond 1998). Hobbyists' software might never have troubled Microsoft, but when GNU/Linux became more successful among IT professionals, it was less the software itself than the logic of its production and distribution that raised concerns in Redmond. The degree to which Microsoft felt threatened by GNU/Linux's fundamentally different approach to software creation and distribution was disclosed in the legendary 'Halloween documents'.[14] These documents reveal that Microsoft had plans to use a strategy called 'fear, uncertainty, and doubt' (FUD). This strategy had an impact on popular discourse and legal matters, and Microsoft duly attempted to exert tremendous influence in these spheres. However, publishing the Halloween documents was part of the popular discourse as well, first attracting Linux enthusiasts only, but soon spreading as news across mainstream media channels. In an attempt to frame Linux and open source in general as risky and unfavourable design, Microsoft tried to launch a funny message. In October 2000 it displayed an advertisement in c't, Germany's most important computer technology magazine, stating 'an open operating system does not only have advantages' (see fig. 16). The claim was illustrated with mutant penguins. The message was perceived differently by Linux enthusiasts; they celebrated being officially recognized as worthy of anti-propaganda campaigning.

The Microsoft-Linux confrontation is, like the campaigns waged by the music and film industries against file sharing, the most visible and broadly distributed conflict. It ranges from software-developing communities to the European Parliament, affecting decision-making processes about software patent regulation, and constitutes a vision of critical technology production that promises to be applicable to many different sectors of cultural production and socio-political issues. Microsoft vs. Linux represents the most fundamental conflict in the different ways one can perceive software and its production.

Figure 16. Microsoft advertisement in c't October 2000.

Communication strategies were developed by all participants, creating competing rhetorical frames through the use of metaphors, associations, and images to shape the perceptions of technology accordingly (Van den Boomen, Schäfer 2005). Through these discursive strategies, each side's argument was supposed to be communicated by the media to win public opinion and the assent of decision-makers. With respect to the practice of sharing programming code and publishing under what are known as copyleft licences, such as the GNU Public License or the Creative Commons licences, Microsoft representatives often tried to manufacture a link between these licences and copyright infringement, communism, and the exploitation of creators and inventors, as the following statement of Bill Gates demonstrates:

> There are fewer communists in the world today than there were. There are some new modern-day sorts of communists who want to get rid of the incentive for musicians and movie makers and software makers under various guises. They don't think that those incentives should exist. [...] But the idea that the United

States has led in creating companies, creating jobs, because we've had the best intellectual-property system, there's no doubt about that in my mind, and when people say they want to be the most competitive economy, they've got to have the incentive system. Intellectual property is the incentive system for the products of the future.[15]

The same argument has been used widely also by the music industry, which has run many campaigns advocating the protection of creativity in order to fight file sharing. Such statements, however, conceal that patents and copyrights also serve as instruments of market regulation and control. In other words, the promoters of software patents and the promoters of strict and long-lasting copyrights for, among other things, music and films, often refer to culturally shaped associations: the Microsoft rhetoric relies on associating its products with the 'free market' that is glorified as a democratic institution where customers can choose the best products. It is somewhat ironic that a Microsoft white paper promoting the free market as a realm of fairness guaranteeing customer choice and product competition should be entitled 'Enabling the Marketplace to Decide' (Smith 2005). But by secretly investing in the SCO Group, a company which owns the intellectual property rights of some Unix code, Microsoft held shares of a firm that then started suing big corporations that used GNU/Linux systems for copyright infringement.[16] Expensive and disruptive lawsuits against IBM, Novell, Daimler Chrysler, and others eventually led to the downfall of SCO, which was unable to prove any infringement upon its intellectual property, but it was able, for quite some time, to efficiently spread the fear of potential lawsuits among companies using GNU/Linux. In response to SCO accusations, websites were put up to comment on the Microsoft strategy,[17] hackers defaced the SCO website,[18] and Linux communities organized and financed responses to defend Linux from being criminalized.[19]

In order to 'enable the marketplace to decide' Microsoft teams up with governments and offers educational services to secondary school students to train their IT skills. The focus here of course is exclusively on Microsoft products. Similar to the music and film industries, Microsoft offers complete teaching materials to train the students in a biased understanding of copyrights and patents. In an attempt to convince them with 'scientifically' verified data, the Microsoft campaign 'Get the Facts' provides results from Microsoft-financed surveys on the costs and risks of Linux use and the benefits of using the software from Redmond.

On a technical level, Microsoft tries hard to avoid opening its application interfaces to third-party developers. Bundling as many applications as possible into the operating system, the market of messenger services, Internet browsers, and media players is dominated by Microsoft solutions that are offered to clients as a default setting. The Microsoft-Linux confrontation lost its spark when the open-source company Novell started to collaborate with Microsoft on licensing questions in 2006.[20] However, it remains a telling example of how different approaches to working with software eventually lead to confrontations and severe competition for market leadership.

The issue of participation is a crucial factor in the conflict between Microsoft and Linux. While the software giant applied the logic of mass-produced goods to a digital artefact, the open-source developers followed a different logic. Software has been increasingly perceived as a cultural resource that is difficult to build for a single company, but more easily developed by communities. It goes without saying that developing open-source software is not necessarily an altruistic quest undertaken by devoted programmers for counter-hegemonic reasons (e.g. Van den Boomen, Schäfer 2005:48; Weber 2005:66).[21] Furthermore, Gosh et al. convincingly showed that many programmers receive monetary compensation for what they do (2002). However, the economics of open-source software do not work like that of off-the-shelf software; instead, it thrives on a community of programmers creating software as a resource free for all to use, extend, and improve. Based upon access to this resource, new business models revolve around customized software solutions and services. The means of production are created collaboratively, and can be transformed into profitable business opportunities (Gosh 1998; 2005; Raymond 1998). The confrontation between Microsoft and the open source communities is very much founded in this fundamentally different logic of production and value creation. It is notable that open-source software production fits very well within the logic of global networks, community, and team-based work processes as well as the media practice of creating commons-like resources that are freely accessible and expandable. Microsoft's business model relies very much on strict market control and regulation, achieved through various anticompetitive strategies, including contracts with retailers that forbid sales of competitor's products, regulative patent licensing, the abovementioned FUD strategies, and naturally through exploiting its market dominance by bundling various applications inseparably with Microsoft Windows.

Music and movies, the unbearable lightness of P2P

The industry will take whatever steps it needs to protect itself and protect its revenue streams... It will not lose that revenue stream, no matter what (Steve Heckler, 2000).[22]

Copyright owner's problems are market problems, and they can only be solved by responding to market demands: strong copyright protection cannot make consumers buy things they do not want to buy (William Patry, 2009:38).

The 'battle royale' between the music industry and consumers shows how Internet and software applications challenged an established industry and are reconfiguring it for good (Alderman 2001; Renner 2004; Patry 2009). While bandwidth and traffic costs postponed the problem of digital distribution for the film industry for a few years, the music industry was confronted with it when university student Shawn Fenning released Napster, a program that searched for music files and downloaded them to the user's computer (Lessig 2001:130-132). Once music was ripped from compact discs and turned into MP3 files, the files could easily be distributed through e-mails sent from one person to another and eventually affect the basic organizational logic of the music industry (Benkler 2006:51-52). As Yochai Benkler points out, the copyright concept in the music industry relied on difficulties of mechanical reproduction, which made it too expensive to reproduce and distribute music. That obstacle was overcome through digitization and a worldwide infrastructure for inexpensive distribution. In addition to uncontrolled distribution, the music industry also felt challenged by a new media practice of creative appropriation. The practice of remixing and reusing music, which had already proved a significant cultural aspect of music cultures such as Hip Hop, spread into the plurality of users who wanted to share their creations with their friends.[23]

In the wake of what's called the Internet revolution, the music industry completely misunderstood the reconfiguration of cultural industries and changing consumer needs and habits. Perceiving every illegal download as a missed sale, one of the world's most powerful industries turned to complaining about the unacceptable misbehaviour of their audience, calling them thieves, creativity killers, criminals, and even terrorists. On the level of popular discourse, the music industry and its lobbyists started campaigns that are correctly framed by William Patry as 'moral panics' (2009).

The music industry bluntly translates unauthorized copying into theft, neglecting the fact that if someone steals a purse, the purse is actually taken away from its owner, whereas a file that is copied does not disappear. The most frequently aired recent anti-piracy advertisements in cinemas and on DVDs shows someone stealing a handbag, breaking into a car, or shoplifting, and the subtitle confronts the viewer with: 'you wouldn't steal'. Between the short scenes depicting theft, a girl sits in front of a computer watching a file downloading. This parallel is clearly equating downloading a video with theft.[24] From another perspective, however, one could say that the scarcity that determined business models in the age of mechanical reproduction is simply no longer appropriate for the age of electronic distribution. The strategy of labelling all copying by common users as piracy has been counterproductive in the sense that it has blurred all distinctions between common users and professional copyright piracy.[25] Equating downloads with theft and brutal street robbery has not been widely accepted by audiences of the music and film industries, who in fact see a conflict between their common-sense perception of copying for private purposes and the severity of legal actions against downloaders.[26] William Patry assumes that the aggressive campaigns are intended to cloud the music and film industry's failure to change:

By framing the debate as bipolar, between good (property rights) and evil (immoral youths who steal property), issues are semantically shifted away from the failure of copyright owners to rationally advance their own economic interests, and toward abstract principles, such as rewarding creators and punishing pirates (2009:29).

Indeed, the image often stressed in industry campaigns is that of the artist who cannot be creative without the incentive of royalties. However, critics maintain that most of the revenues in the music industry do not go to the original artists, but remain with the major distributors.[27] Both sides make use of scientific research to support their arguments, the music industry claiming that there is proof linking decreasing sales to the increasing use of file-sharing systems and CD burning (e.g. Siwek 2007). However, other surveys are unable to verify this relation and instead see decreasing sales as being related to changing media consumption habits, such as a general decrease in music consumption and cinema attendance, which has been replaced by an increase of other activities, such as playing computer games, chatting online, etc. (Oberholzer, Strumpf 2004).[28] Furthermore, the figures presented by the industry, whether on the quantity of alleged job losses or revenue losses, are not only impossible to verify, they also appear to be simply made up.[29]

To defend durable copyright laws, positive associations are employed, such as art, creativity, the free market, monetary reward as an incentive for invention and creation, the original is better than the copy, a commercial product is more reliable, better maintained, safer, and more trustworthy than one developed in loose collaboration, etc. Simultaneously, negative associations are created to describe the emerging media practice, which is often labelled as communism, piracy, theft, irresponsible, destructive, not creative, stifling creation and invention, and destabilizing industry and employment. These associations are communicated through the many channels the media industry owns and serves, and through public relations efforts at conferences, business fairs, boardroom meetings, public talks, and podium discussions, and they are often supported by consenting newspaper articles. Sponsored teaching material is handed out to schools and teachers for free to teach approaches to copyright issues protecting the interests of film, music, and the software industry.[30] In public-private partnerships, industry associations sponsor these teaching materials that contain endorsements in the form of prefaces by politicians, who completely disregard the biased information.[31]

Most important to the music industry's confrontation with file sharing is the significantly new logic of distribution and production. The logic of distribution has changed profoundly as the Napster example illustrates. In that case, participation is not only the sharing of music files among a circle of friends, it's also the automated delegation of information to a socio-technical ecosystem of information technologies and a plurality of users. At the level of the individual user, participation starts with providing a part of the hardware to the system of distributed computing and with uploading files to the total collection. The information system then index-es the files and distributes them according to user requests. With the recent intro-duction of BitTorrent technology, larger files can be distributed much faster. Dig-itizing media content and sending it through computer networks has become the standard mode of distribution. Media therefore arrive in a format users have begun to increasingly prefer for consumption. Participation in file sharing goes further on a semantic level. Users exchange opinions on music and films, they recommend different artists to each other, and refer them by linking directly to their works. The monolithic structures of the old media industries could not offer appropriate platforms for such a vast social interaction and would not allow the fast, unbureau-cratic, and often unpaid distribution of files. And they have missed out on the op-portunity to offer anything that even comes close to resembling this media prac-tice.[32] At the production level, new technologies make the production of music cheaper. Producing music, especially electronic music, does not require expensive studio time any more. Many artists are able to produce their entire work in the comfort of their own apartments. But production costs have been decreasing for the music industry as well since the advent of the compact disc, which has not re-warded consumers but instead has required them to pay higher prices for content that had simply been re-released in the new formats. This is the logic of re-releasing material from the archives that the Hollywood film industry has practised success-fully for a long time. First by selling films that were no longer distributed to televi-sion networks, and then by releasing films on videotape, and later on DVD. It ap-pears to be typically for an industry that is not innovative but dependent on other innovators (Patry 2009:198).

Interestingly enough, responses to the challenge of digital distribution resulted in only a few attempts to provide alternative and legal download possibilities, which generally failed because boards of directors in the big music business were too hesi-tant. Fearing they would lose control over their catalogues by licensing them to a new distribution method, music publishers missed the opportunity to make a timely entrance into an emerging market and helplessly witnessed the rapid diffusion and encouragement of an alternative distribution practice. A significant portion of the existing music industry's catalogues has meanwhile been spread by means of the emerging networks of peer-to-peer file sharing. Furthermore, these networks devel-oped a source for music and films that is hardly available or completely unavailable through official distribution channels.[33] The success of online distribution, as well as that of remixing and electronic music production, is based on the qualities of digitized music. It makes it very similar to the qualities that have been identified for software (see chapter 3). Music appears to be as modular as software: It is as easy to distribute, and the accumulating resource of existing music provides a vast archive of modules (called samples) to use and reuse for new productions (Hughes and Lang 2006). Editing software made the remixing of music files easier, and even users lacking skills are able to scatter their humble productions over the web.

At the legal level, business executives and lawyers tried to enforce copyright laws and gain compensation payments from users. The music industry's wave of random charges against Internet users aimed at creating a general fear of downloading music. But looking back at the attacks by the Recording Industry Association of America (RIAA) and its equivalents in Europe in recent years, one has the impression that while other industries were trying to adapt to new technologies, the music industry tried to establish monetary punishment as a new business model. The legal crusade of the music and pictures industries began by adapting the copyright law in 1998, which resulted in the DMCA, which has been widely discussed and criticized (e.g. Vaidhyanathan 2001; Lessig 2001:187-188; 2004:157-161; Benkler 2006).[34] In an attempt to introduce the restrictive legislation of the DMCA on a global level, film and music industry associations aligned with other industries thriving on intellectual property and put forward the controversial Anti-Counterfeiting Trade Agreement (ACTA) in 2008. It requires legal enforcement of copyrights and intellectual property, including monitoring Internet downloads and even depriving users who download from illegal sources of Internet access. As of 2010 ACTA has seen various rounds of negotiations in international committees and is about to be implemented into European law. By suing mothers for their children's downloading, harassing teenagers, pushing universities to filter their Internet traffic or to turn over their students to authorities, and confronting suspected file sharers with incredible penal fees, activities of copyright enforcement have shaped the public image of the contemporary music and motion picture industry. The request of the copyright industries for strict and repressive law enforcement is about to seriously threaten civil rights, since the measurements require a complete surveillance of users's internet traffic.

At a technical level, the battleground witnessed the flushing of file-sharing systems with corrupted music files. Companies such as *Overpeer* were inundated by orders from music companies and industry associations to flood peer-to-peer networks with corrupted files. In order to do so, they set up fake networks of virtual file-sharers to distribute the corrupted files.[35] Poorly advised popstar Madonna lent vocals to a fake file pretending to be one of her songs, but when played, the user would hear her say 'What the fuck do you think you're doing?' In response, her website was hacked with a message reading: 'This is what the fuck I think I'm doing', displaying links to download all songs from her album *American Life*.[36] According to the emerging media practice, her vocals were used for remixes that were distributed online.[37] Another strategy used by the music and motion picture industry was to set up something called 'honeypots': servers that offer content for illegal downloading. In order to get the IP addresses of users downloading and spreading content, the music and film industry started to distribute their own content in bogus ways.[38] The work was done by dubious companies, often employing former members of the police. Such social connections also enable the industry to work together closely with the authorities and often even accompany the police on raids against individuals suspected of piracy and copyright infringement. Due to a lack of competence in this matter, the authorities often cooperate with the industry's agents and even allow them to evaluate confiscated material. The entire matter has been extensively described and criticized by the German computer magazine c't.[39]

In another attempt to respond to the challenge of uncontrolled digital distribution, the motion picture and music industries exerted pressure on what was known as digital rights management (DRM) or Trusted Computing (TC).[40] The latter term was coined and primarily supported by the Microsoft Corporation to battle software piracy and to provide a means for authentic user identification. DRM, dubbed by critics as 'digital restriction management', involves techniques to limit the ability to copy and play media content. These technologies are directly aimed at limiting the affordances of digital artefacts, as described in chapter 3. In a world where electronic computers by definition rely on copying processes, the film and music industries intended to reintroduce the original in the form of massively produced but individually signed and identifiable copies. Effective DRM is impossible to achieve on an exclusively technical level; it requires enforcement on the legal level as well (Bechtold 2003). Not only have all encryption and copy protection systems been hacked quickly, the industry also failed to deliver products that customers could play without encountering additional problems. Many CD and DVD drives refuse to play copy-protected data carriers, precisely because 'playing' involves 'copying'. DRM prevents the possibility of playing files on different players, such as a portable MP3 player or a computer. The biggest failure in the many embarrassing attempts to cope with the new technologies can be attributed to Sony, who distributed music CDs that secretly installed a rootkit on users' computers. Similar to a Trojan horse, the rootkit works invisibly in the background but offers third parties the possibility of monitoring and even taking control of the infected machine.[41] When IT security specialist Mark Russinovich blew the whistle on Sony in October 2005, they aggravated the scandal by offering a deinstallation program that actually installed additional surveillance features.[42] The disgrace reached its height when it was revealed that the copy protection software was itself infringing copyrights by using open-source code.[43] Although only customers from the US and Mexico were affected, the scandal made mainstream news in Europe as well. In addition to several lawsuits and a recall of the affected products, Sony BMG suffered significant damage to its image and reputation.[44] These examples also indicate that a strict enforcement of copyright law inevitably invades citizen privacy and therefore constitutes a means of repression.

The absence of legal and affordable download possibilities and the concerted actions of the film and recording industry associations and copyright-holding companies probably even encouraged file sharing. The film and music industries might have underestimated the impact of their aggressive actions. Due to an obvious misunderstanding of consumer needs, the qualities of digital technology, and their difficulty to adapt their business model accordingly, these industries have caused themselves considerable harm. All successful online music services are provided by companies which do not originate from the established music industry. Through their own incompetence to communicate their interests and concerns to audiences, these huge industries are now estranged from their former target audiences. As Lawrence Lessig has eloquently argued, these actions may very well be responsible for a sceptical attitude towards the law, because young users start to view the law as wrong and learn to live with what are considered illegal activities.[45] The legal actions of the music industry are in complete contradiction with a common sense of justice. The industry's adversarial actions infused music consumption with an emotional element that is not only felt among file sharers but which is also evident in the netlabel scene, which distributes their own productions free of charge. The German netlabel Ideology called its label sampler 'Never Mind the Industry'.[46] The plans of the major labels to stop the use of file-sharing protocols by filtering on internet service providers can be countered by the argument that file sharing actually increases the visibility of independent artists. That file sharing does not necessarily harm music sale revenues is evident from successful businesses like CD Baby, eMusic, Beatport, FineTunes, and others. The above-mentioned distributors all sell their music files without any DRM or watermark. As opposed to the rather homogeneous hits of the music industry, these vendors focus on specializing in a variety of independent music and newcomers, and they use the advantages of digital distribution to limit costs; consequently, they have no need for large corporations with bloated administration and expensive marketing and, in addition, their artists even benefit from higher provisions. The way the music industry reacts to new media practices is caused by the failure to innovate and to transform its business model according to the media-specific qualities of new technologies.

The social use of technology and media becomes clearly visible in the confrontations they provoke. The disputes resulting from media practice and technology's material aspects can be perceived as a process of negotiation. It is part of an implementation process of technology into society. The confrontations described above are obviously suitable for media attention. There can be no doubt that media practices are raising socio-political issues and triggering emotional responses. Indeed, their ideological overtone represents social issues and debates. Although confrontations are often highly visible and therefore appealing for describing the collision of old media industries and the new media practice, and although they lend themselves well to making the David versus Goliath comparison, a critical view of the culture industries' achievements in using these media practices for extending their revenues is necessary. The dynamic of confrontation describes a conservative reaction to user participation and technology appropriation. It is opposed to change and seeks to foster old traditions through legal protection, and consequently constitutes a permanent threat to innovation and technological advancement. In contrast, others thrive on the new opportunities and the participatory practices of users. New media practices create new business opportunities that result in a very different perception of participation. Here, the culture industry implements user activities into new services. Instead of colliding with users, the appropriation of technology design channels user activities. This view will be discussed in terms of implementation in the following section.

5.2   Implementation: controlling participation

The emerging media practice was celebrated as the rise of consumers, who would become emancipated users and producers, freed from the tyranny of being limited to simple consumption of what the media giants were broadcasting. The question, however, is whether users have actually been able to free themselves from the top-down production processes of the cultural industries. Or, conversely, to what extent have enterprises succeeded in incorporating users' media practices into new business models? Despite all the enthusiasm for users as producers and for user-generated content, the question of whether power relations have really shifted or whether, on the contrary, existing structures of production and distribution have simply been adapted to new forms of practices still needs to be answered. The previous section described how new media practices and conventional business models have collided, causing different forms of confrontation. This section on the implementation of user activities will argue that it is in fact possible to take advantage of several of the previously discussed media practices and simultaneously channel user activities by means of graphical user interfaces and software design. Implementation describes how the conventional culture industry and new emerging businesses in the field managed to take advantage of media practices afforded, and resources provided, by the Internet. Companies have acknowledged the user activities described in previous chapters in terms of accumulation, construction, and archiving, and instead of fighting them, they offer services, production means, and infrastructures to facilitate these user actions. Implementation here literally means implementing user activities in the software design of an application and employing user participation for commercial purposes often without acknowledging their labour.

The game industry was among the first to take advantage of fans' labour and started to stimulate the construction of additional levels in computer games or the modification of entire games (Nieborg 2005). The Xbox 360 is the result of a process of implementation, too. Not only has Microsoft adopted many of the design suggestions that were realized thanks to homebrew software in the graphical interface and design of the Xbox 360, but the company has also devised a strategy to regulate the practice of homebrew software by providing an integrated development kit.

Fans and the labour they perform on media texts can in fact be easily implemented into the production logic of the media industry. Once corporations producing media texts learn that the activities of fans and users actually benefit their original

Platform	Kind of Platform	User Activities (labour)	Elements of Control
Star Wars MashUp (Lucas Film)	Fan site, providing tools for creating *Star Wars*-related content	Producing media content (videos, images)	Creation and presentation limited to the platform's interface, filters nudity; all user creations belong to Lucas Film
Second Life (Linden Labs)	Virtual world (paid and unpaid accounts)	Producing virtually all content from clothes, to houses, enterprises, and community building	User may earn money in the Second Life infrastructure
Facebook	Social networking site	Providing personal data useful for market research and advertising, creating applications, building groups	API allows application integration; right to exclude users without notification or explanation; Facebook owns all uploaded content
Flickr (Yahoo!)	Photo storing/sharing	Uploading images; creating meta-information, building groups, establishing networks	API allows mash-ups; right to exclude users without notification or explanation regulating pornography; censorship
Delicious (Yahoo!)	Bookmark storing / sharing	Posting private/public links, creating meta-information, building groups/networks	API allows mash-ups
YouTube (Google)	Video storing/sharing	Providing videos, producing click rates, meta-information, ratings, comments, building channels and groups	API allows mash-ups; right to exclude inappropriate or copyright-protected material, excluding pornography
Twitter	Micro-blogging	Providing posts, building networks	API allows mash-ups
Rapidshare	Online hosting service	Uploading and sharing files	Control of uploaded content, claims to ban copyright infringements

Figure 17. *Web platforms and generating value through users, control through service providers.*

products, and that they are easy to stimulate and to exploit, it's but a small step to grant users a certain degree of cultural freedom. In return, the creativity of users will be controlled, and all rights to commercial utilization will be reserved for the corporations. The Web 2.0 services provide platforms for self-representation, social networking, and publishing websites (e.g. MySpace, Facebook, Friendster, Blogger, etc.), infrastructures for storing and distributing files (e.g. Rapidshare, Megaupload), selling possessions (e.g. eBay), publishing photos (e.g. Flickr, Photobucket) and videos (e.g. Vimeo, Google Video, YouTube), or a means to modify commercial media texts as level editors for computer games (e.g. Unreal Tournament) and video editors for films (Star Wars MashUp Editor). In all cases, the offered services or production means revolve around the (generally unpaid and unacknowledged) labour of users, who modify media texts, create content, or distribute it. It characterizes a significant shift in culture industries from creating media content for consumption towards providing platforms where content is created either by users or where copyright-protected material is modified according to the platform provider's terms.

Implementing user activities takes place as explicit participation by providing interfaces for creating media texts like the Star Wars MashUp Editor does. Here, users explicitly use the cultural resource of the copyright owner for remixing media texts and creating new ones. It takes place as a form of implicit participation in socio-technical ecosystems such as Flickr, where user activities improve information management for the Yahoo search engine. The following case examples exemplify the dynamic of implementation as it is unfolding on a web platform such as StarWars MashUp, where corporate content is remixed by users. Online hosting services, such as Rapidshare, do not offer corporate content for user created remixes, but offer an infrastructure that invites users to share files. Web 2.0 applications such as Flickr, Facebook, Twitter, and Delicious show a high degree of formalizing user activities as default design setting.

Figure 17 shows a list of platforms that have successfully implemented user activities and whose technical design (software) and legal design (as defined by software licenses as terms of use and end user license agreements, or EULAs) channel user activities.[47]

Trapped on Death Star. Let the fans do the work

For years the very successful fan platform TheForce.net has been one of the main websites for Star Wars fans to share their enthusiasm about the films and to engage in the production of fan films.[48] They have always been wary of lawsuits being filed by the Lucasfilm corporation. Comments in their web forum maintained that as long as they didn't earn any money with their homemade videos they wouldn't get sued. In fact, the fan forum was always to the benefit of Star Wars since the website and the fan productions heightened credibility and encouraged enthusiasm in a way the corporate communication machine was unable to. The *Star Wars* theme appeared in all kinds of media texts. A group of Unreal Tournament gamers participated in the 2003 Make Something Unreal Contest with a 'Star Wars mod' and was ranked among the finalists, the winner of which would be awarded a prize of $1,000,000. Lucasfilm subsidiary LucasArts allowed the group to continue to participate in the competition and keep the prize money if they won. The strategy of Lucasfilm was rather unclear and frequently limited to letting the fans do whatever they wanted to do as long as they could not generate any revenues. In 2007, LucasArts seemed to adopt a strategy of implementation and announced that people could use images from the *Star Wars* films to produce remixes and upload their work to the corporate website Starwars.com. Although parent company Lucasfilm announced this as a huge concession to fans, the cultural freedom granted by the copyright holder is of course strictly regulated and shows how the implementation of participation is related to the technical design and legal level of discourse. By providing an easy-to-use editing software, they already incorporated certain aspects of the ostensible appropriation. The *Eyespot* editing software prevented nudity and pornography in the remixes. Furthermore, the selection of *Star Wars* film samples offered by Lucasfilm is only available in streaming format, as are the final fan-made productions, in order to prevent users from downloading and reworking the samples in other media editors or posting them elsewhere. A centralization of control was achieved by limiting the right to upload to the corporate website only, where the editing policies were enforced by a team pre-screening every fan-made *Star Wars* film before it got published.[49] Uploads to other websites were simply banned. The *Star Wars* example provides a clever, easily applicable model for media industries to establish tighter bonds between their products and their consumers. Having recognized that the creativity of users is actually helping them to increase their revenues and maybe even to polish their image damaged by lawsuits and cease-and-desist letters, Lucasfilm protected their interests in a more subtle way and shifted from controlling the original media text to channelling fan labour and preventing them from participating in potential revenue-generating activities.[50] The editing technology is crucial in this relation. Providing a tool that is far simpler than many film editors, the copyright owner can attract more- and less-skilled users, and simultaneously maintain control by imposing the discursive design of the film editor on the users. The advantage for Lucasfilm is that it can in fact stay in business without having to ever produce another *Star Wars* episode. The fans continue feeding the saga and in order to do so have to use the resources and means provided by Lucasfilm and, moreover, they create meaningful community activities, entertaining films, images, and promote *Star Wars* merchandising.

As Lawrence Lessig rightly asserts, this form of user participation is in fact degrading the user, who thus is turned into 'the sharecropper of the digital age'.[51] At a legal level, exclusive rights to fan-made productions are granted to Lucasfilm, allowing them to exploit the labour in any form whatsoever without any compensation to the creator. The terms of use stipulate that 'Lucas grants you a non-exclusive, non-transferable, revocable, limited right and license to access and use the Star Wars Supplied Materials solely for the purpose of mixing the Star Wars Supplied Materials with Your Posted Material,' and the user in return agrees to grant 'Lucas, its licensees, successors and affiliates a perpetual and irrevocable, exclusive, royalty free, world-wide license in all rights, titles and interests of every kind and nature.'[52]

The example of Lucasfilm demonstrates that the culture industry is in fact capable of shifting from creating media content to providing platforms for using existing content or creating user-generated content. The practice of remixing, changing, and altering existing media content by fans is implemented into a proprietary platform that channels these user activities and ties them to the strict regulations of the content provider. The media texts form a resource from which users can draw the raw materials for their own media creations. However, all their labour and creativity are subject to the copyright holder's regulations, not only with respect to commercial aspects, but also with respect to control and censorship banning unwanted user creations. Users and fans become unpaid co-workers using their creativity and imagination to extend, further develop, and market the original product. The commercial rights are completely in the hands of the corporation, which has no obligation whatsoever to compensate the creators, nor to respect their moral rights. A professed openness is used to grant access to the original text, but only according to defined terms of use and always without the possibility of benefiting themselves by putting their creations to commercial use.

Hosting file sharing, thriving on piracy

Services such as Rapidshare or Megaupload facilitate the distribution of large files, and are described as one-click hosting services.[53] Revenues are generated through advertisement and premium accounts, but all the distributed content is completely uploaded by users. Many of these services implicitly take advantage of the practice of file sharing and copyright infringement. Although their terms of use do not condone it, a large part of the stored files are distributed illegally.[54] The fact that Rapidshare and Megaupload are ranked among the top 20 websites in the Alexa Global 500 list not only indicates the popularity of online file storing and sharing, but also that the large numbers of users generating this traffic require a solid infrastructure that also needs ample funding for covering traffic costs. In August 2007, Rapidshare announced it had a total of 3.5 petabytes of disk space and 140 GB/s of Internet bandwidth which was continually increased to 10 petabytes of disk space in 2010.[55]

A crucial aspect in the popularity of one-click hosting services is the easy-to-use interfaces. It seems much more convenient to use the conventional web interfaces for uploading files than to run a search for BitTorrent files and using BitTorrent clients in the first place. Although file-sharing systems are popular, users have to be aware of the high occurrence of computer viruses and damaged or false files. In sharing communities, for instance on user forums or boards revolving around a certain topic, an atmosphere of trust encourages the use of posted links to hosting services, because users can assume the posted file is valid and not corrupted. If links refer to corrupted or fraudulent files, other members will issue a warning, and the moderators will remove the post. Although many of the posted film and audio files on hosting services might violate copyright laws, one has to keep in mind that again it is the labour of users that makes these services possible in the first place. Users produce files (either in the form of homemade or ripped content), upload them, and share the links with their peers. There are entire websites dedicated to indexing the contents of the various share-hosting services and organizing them according to the content in links into e-books, audio files, and video files. Indexing and archiving become a key user activity in that respect.[56] The share-hosting provider merely offers the infrastructure for the easy uploading and exchange of files, but they constitute the emergence of an entire socio-technical ecosystem of many different related websites and web forums (Roettgers 2007).

The service provider earns money from paid account fees or from advertising revenues. The design of the web service stimulates users to sign up, because for the free downloads there are annoyingly long waiting times and file limitations, as well as many advertisement pop-ups. It has to be acknowledged that the easy availability of large numbers of copyrighted files is an incentive to use the service. Once again, an infrastructure is provided, and the contents distributed on it draw from the resources of the culture industries. Many file hosting services thrive on the popularity of file exchange, which in many cases infringes upon copyright laws.

Participation as mass commodity

The latest development of technologies (Web 2.0) were celebrated as highly participatory and encouraging, enabling the user to make a difference in cultural production (e.g. Anderson 2006; Tapscott, Williams 2006; Leadbeater, Miller 2004). An overtone of social progress and an expectation of increasing consumer participation in the culture industries are discernible in the enthusiastic accounts on the subject, which often coin or take up metaphors such as 'social bookmarking', 'folksonomies', 'social software', 'collective intelligence', and 'user-led production'. The obvious production of media content by users and their even more profound participation in commenting, remixing, changing, and distributing media content from established production channels led to a plethora of texts praising the enormous rise of creation.

The often neglected point is the role technology plays in assisting the performance of user activities through easy-to-use interfaces and offering handy applications for integrating data created and posted on one platform into another one. Designers seek to implement services from other providers as well by taking advantage of application programming interfaces (APIs). It is possible for users to implement their Flickr photos on the Blogger weblog and to post YouTube videos directly into their weblog articles. This content is then referred from the providing services and the extra traffic for posted videos and photos does not affect the user. As O'Reilly points out 'the value of software is proportional to the scale and dynamism of the data it helps to manage' (O'Reilly 2005). The managed data do not come from company employees anymore, who never succeeded in keeping up with the enormous need for information and the organization of data. Companies like Amazon.com, Google, eBay, and Yahoo already used user activities to extend their information database (O'Reilly 2005). In the case of Amazon, users write reviews, post lists of favourite books, evaluate reviews, and even by simply buying books they are contributing to the information system that can provide better recommendation services to others. They also help to constitute algorithmic analysis of user behaviour. Like Google, Amazon evaluates each buy, each product view and rating in order to analyse a user's interest and to point her to appropriate items to buy (Baker 2008). O'Reilly states that the software design solutions described as Web 2.0 are pushing this goal even further by not only relying on the system-wide database but by incorporating information from other sources as well. Users can literally implement these services by, for instance, adding buttons to their personal weblogs for information services such as Digg, Delicious, and others, thereby offering users the possibility to add this weblog article directly to their personal Delicious profiles or to the Digg.com website. In return, their own visibility will be heightened because the search functions in information management systems will recognize the increased frequency of posting. Again the service provides the infrastructure and will only be attractive when it is adopted by large numbers of users. The requirement of software design to dynamically manage large amounts of data is recursive, since the value of these services is proportional to the amount of data available. This will lead to aggressive competition among service providers, who might have to buy out their competitors or keep them off the market. Only a few of the major providers with efficient APIs for interconnecting their different services will succeed in accumulating the larger user bases.

Increasingly aware of the potential of an 'architecture of participation', media companies seek ways to develop business models around platforms that appeal to large numbers of users. Recognizing users' activities, habits, and needs leads to services that provide opportunities for social interaction in various degrees, and the production of media texts. The rash of enthusiasm in popular and scholarly discourses resulted in the somewhat premature claims of the user becoming a producer, without first examining rather important matters such as ownership structures, compensation for labour, questions of copyright and the intellectual property of users, their cultural freedom, and issues of censorship and privacy. Furthermore, the emphasis on user activities neglected the fact that many platforms for user-created content exceed any community-based project in terms of size, user numbers, and maintenance costs. Many of the services of those platforms respond to user activities developed over the past decade, providing cheap or free storage space, easy-to-use interfaces, and a variety of choices to connect to other users or services. In many of these services, previously developed media practices are simplified for a larger number of less-skilled users. Blogger – purchased by Google in 2003 – offers users the possibility of website publishing free of charge. MySpace – bought by Rupert Murdoch's News Corporation for $580 million – initially provided web presence for artists and musicians but became more generally popular as a provider of weblog-like websites, used mostly for self-presentation and promotion, as well as for social networking. The already-described photo sharing website Flickr facilitates a wide range of user actions by providing an infrastructure for publishing and archiving photos online and engaging in social networking. The service was acquired by Yahoo, which subsequently discontinued its previous photo service Yahoo! Photo. Flickr reportedly stores approximately a billion photos. In online video services, such as YouTube, users upload videos and rate them using comments or the rating system inherent in the web interface, and in social network services like Orkut (developed by Google), Facebook, Friendster, LinkedIn, and hi5, users create personal profiles and refer them to their friends, family, colleagues, and acquaintances. All these platforms provide an infrastructure and an organized information management system, but content and social interaction are completely generated by users, who in return for their labour usually receive little more than limited free accounts. The user numbers attracted to these platforms at the same time increase their value, because as more users contribute to them and create more possibilities for interaction, more value is generated for these platforms, for potential use, advertising purposes, or selling paid accounts.

The mentioned websites are all frequently acclaimed examples of the Web 2.0 and were embraced by the enthusiasts in popular discourse as yet another set of enabling technologies culminating in the nomination of the user by *Time* magazine as 'the hero of the Information Age.' A closer look at these sites reveals another dimension of their success. Each of the sites mentioned belongs to the top 30 websites in the world according to the Alexa ranking and are mostly owned by large corporations.[57] Interestingly, Wikipedia is the only non-profit website among the top-ten in the Alexa Global 500.

Most of the websites are owned by large corporations or otherwise benefit from significant investments from a large corporation. Many require a sophisticated infrastructure for administration, marketing and promotion, and for the technology itself. In the case of websites like Photobucket, Flickr, Rapidshare, and Megashare, and, most significantly, YouTube or Google Video, the scale of the online traffic and the hosting capacity is only affordable for enterprises with significant financial backing. The estimated traffic costs of Google subsidiary YouTube are in the region of $30 million a month, which accounts for only 3 percent of the total operating costs of $11.5 billion that Google spent in 2007.[58] The 'industrial' scale of these services are not only evident in the large user groups and the content generated, which frequently captures the media's attention, but also in their technical capacity for bandwidth, downloads, and uploads, and in their sheer presence on the Internet. YouTube has a Google page ranking of 8 out of 10, thus ranking high and having its service implemented in the websites of a large number of users just by linking to YouTube when posting YouTube videos on their sites or referring to them on YouTube. In quantitative terms, those services attain numbers that by far exceed the audience of broadcast media. YouTube reported 100 million video views per day in 2006, and it is estimated that 79 million users watched 3 billion videos in January 2008.[59] Facebook claims to have over 400 million users, its competitor Orkut, owned by Google and popular in South America, has more than 100 million users, which is close to MySpace's estimated 110 million registered users, and in the relatively small Netherlands, an astonishing 60 percent of the population is registered with the local social networking site Hyves.

Another matter of scale is the capitalization capacity of these sites. In the meantime, major media industry players have acquired most of them for large sums of money, banking on future revenues and synergy effects for vertical industry organization by attracting large communities. One can expect a process of concentration in this domain, and only the big platforms with large user communities and many databases have a chance of successfully retaining their communities and stimulating them to produce content. Google purchased YouTube for a phenomenal $1.65 billion, and Murdoch's News Corporation paid $580 million for MySpace, while Facebook has allegedly turned down a $750 million offer by Google. In 2007, Microsoft acquired a 1.6 percent share of Facebook for $240 million. According to a 2010 Nielsen survey, Web 2.0 applications consume 22 percent of the overall time users spent online.[60] The promise to monetize these services successfully, for instance through targeted advertising, is a primary motivation for media companies to invest. Although many of these deals seem to be a wild bet on a prosperous future, and potential revenue models are still rather unclear, the capitalization leads to an infrastructure and availability of resources that users can benefit from and explore. Google Earth and Google Maps, services providing geographical data, photographic images, and maps of most parts of the planet, allow people to use its data for integration in other websites and applications. Its database forms a resource for many different applications, both commercial and non-profit or even just for fun. They form an important resource that stimulates an astonishing cultural production which would not be possible if the companies' major funding didn't allow them to benefit from their users' activities for trial-and-error research and as an unpaid resource for research and development. It has been a highly neglected fact that the means for these activities draw upon the enormous financial resources these companies have accumulated. A great deal of the participatory culture thrives on this informal availability of technologies and resources.

What Time magazine celebrates as the user's means of production in the Web

2.0 has been described by Tim O'Reilly as an 'architecture of participation' (O'Reilly 2005). In this programmatic text, O'Reilly advocates the rigorous implementation of user activities into software design. This development of what is called participatory design ought in fact to raise questions about power and control. To what extent do mechanisms of control find their way into the back end of the software? One must also ask what the real price of the 'free' playgrounds these companies offer actually is, with regard to the back end politics involved. Invisible and often incomprehensible for the user, the back end of the software application facilitates the exploitation of user data and user activities. After a phase of unquestioned enthusiasm, criticism and doubts have recently been voiced in respect to the brave new Web.[61] The meshed technologies in Web 2.0 applications, the implemented labour of users, and the evaluation of their personal data, social network, and communication through data mining and profiling all raise the issues of privacy and consumer rights (Zimmer 2008; Scholz 2008). The exploitation of user activities on commercial platforms is now criticized as unpaid labour, duping the user in a similar way to the traditional and passive mass media consumer (Bruns 2008:33; Hyde 2006; Petersen 2008; Scholz 2008). The underlying software design is in critical reference to O'Reilly's notion of participation now dubbed as 'architecture of exploitation' (Petersen 2008). Trebor Scholz has pointed out a social dependency these services might create. Since the appeal of most services relies on the number of users contributing to the service and thus facilitating social networks, they make it difficult for individuals to abandon the platform when they are dissatisfied with the service or disagree with a change of policies (Scholz 2008). While it is possible to migrate content from one platform to the other, it is much more difficult to transfer the social interaction. Leaving a platform might imply losing the social connections as well. The implementation in so-called social media is noteworthy for its media specificity. Through implementing user activities into the technical design of platforms the social interaction, communication and cultural production by users becomes inseparably and irreversibly implemented. While messages can be exported from one e-mail client to another, it is practically impossible to download your communication from platforms such as Facebook. For users it is only possible to access this information as long as they have an account, and it is impossible to be in control of this information. Furthermore, Facebook accounts cannot be deleted, only set to 'inactive', which makes it impossible for users to easily leave Facebook and delete their personal data and documented social interaction. When a group of hackers launched the Suicide Machine, a solution to scrap personal data from Facebook and other social networking sites, Facebook immediately sent a cease-and-desist letter, arguing that the software violates Facebook's copyrights.[62]

Socio-technical ecosystems such as the recently emerged Web 2.0 applications are affected by both the user activities and the intelligence in the application's back end. As Tim O'Reilly has pointed out elsewhere, 'Web 2.0 is not about front end technologies. It's precisely about back end, and it's about meaning and intelligence in the back end.'[63] Here, the user-generated data are evaluated and processed and maintained for further use. Connected to various databases and through APIs to many different other applications, the borders of these socio-technical ecosystems are difficult to define. Instead of a black box, the meshed socio-technical ecosystems constitute a black foam, as Bernhard Rieder rightly pointed out with regard to search engines (Rieder 2005). It is unclear to the user where one system ends and the next one starts. The meshed information systems, connected through various API that synchronizing data streams, are difficult to differentiate. Here, the technical design not only appears to implement user activities and their social interaction, it also reveals a concept of 'deep' implementation. The data generated on one platform can be employed elsewhere without users being aware of the depth of this information aggregation. It is not revealed in the application's terms of use what platform owners and their licensed third parties do with the generated information. The meta-information users generate on Flickr or Delicious, for instance, contributes to search requests on Yahoo and helps the company to improve their search engine services (Zimmer 2008). Personal data and private communication users maintain on social networking sites constitute a commodity for the commercial operators of these platforms (Lauer 2008:50). The opaqueness of the underlying structure easily conceals what is actually happening with generated data and for which purposes they are used, and to which other systems these data are streamed. The inscribed regulations and control mechanisms of data streams and the stored content are hardly recognizable to the end users. They constitute an underlying 'protocol of control' (Galloway 2004). User interactions with services that gather personal information in order to increase an alleged convenience have already been warningly acknowledged as 'the proliferation of an increasingly invisible, automated, and autonomous network' (Andrejevic 2002:245).

The connectivity of various data streams is simplified and translated into the graphical user interfaces of mash-up editors, allowing users to combine data streams from various sources. For instance, users who synchronize different data streams by connecting the graphical pipes through the drag-and-drop method in the Yahoo Pipes interface are actually programming. But thanks to the easy-to-use interface, an operation that used to be a complex task for programmers became largely automatized for lay users. Again, the difference between the front end of an application, such as user interface, and the underlying structure is complex. While users are able to relate different data streams to each other, they have much less insight into the regulation of the underlying data structures. Although they can participate in developing and extending the API, the companies have final control over the API specifications and the database. Through simplification, many interfaces become opaque but actually easier to use, thereby lowering the difficulty level of use, and eventually they participate in cultural production. The facility of producing content using these means is what made the Web 2.0 and its applications such a good story to tell. Neglecting the impact of the underlying structures, it has been perceived exclusively as an enabling technology because it allowed larger numbers of users to do something in an interface and produce anything, from uploading videos, editing media texts, generating personalized data, providing meta-information, or merely generating view and click rates.

The aspect of implementation shows that the range of user activity largely surpasses the domain of explicit participation. One could even state that publishing media texts does not turn users into producers as long as they cannot participate in the revenues these produce, and as long as they have no influence over or even insight into the technologies used. Rather, this raises the question to what extent users should actually be perceived as audiences instead.

5.3   Integration: embracing participation

After having described confrontation and implementation as dynamics growing out of the emerging media practice, integration will be discussed as a strategy that arguably aims at responsibly employing user activities. Strategies resulting in confrontation seek to control user activities through a design that prevents appropriation and implementing laws that prohibit appropriation. Policies intending to achieve implementation attempt to control user activities through software design and graphical user interfaces, stimulating users to perform activities on corporate platforms and participate implicitly in generating commercial value. The concept of integration, conversely, describes a logic of cultural production that adapts cultural values developed in the media practice of collaborative work and the sharing of resources. As opposed to the conventional logic of exploiting a copyright by strictly controlling the use and distribution of media texts, integration instead relies on the global dissemination of collaborative work via commonly used resources that are exploited commercially at a local level. The logic of integration ranges from software development and web design to creating and distributing media texts as music, films, or books. It employs many affordances of digital artefacts, such as the modularity of software, the possibility to organize complex programming projects, the collaboration within a globally dispersed community, or the capacity to distribute digitized artefacts at low cost. Integration offers companies the chance to explicitly expand their production into the sphere of consumers and to actively participate in their processes of appropriation. Clearly, Sony missed that chance when Aibopet and a dynamic community of AIBO users started to tweak the little robot dog. Even when Sony withdrew from filing a lawsuit against Aibopet, they never explored the possibility to engage actively with their users. In contrast to this first confrontational and then laissez-faire approach is Google's way of integrating a user community into their software development of Google Maps (Rieder 2007). Google Maps attracted a dynamic community of developers participating in creating mash-ups and developing the Google Maps code. Software frameworks like Django, for building web applications, show how a community that is spread all over the globe collaborates in the development of open-source software that is commercially exploited at a local level where web designers employ the free resource for building customized software solutions. The online music service Last.fm shows how musicians can employ a platform motivated by explicit and implicit participation to promote their music without being part of the major labels marketing and distribution channels. Wikipedia provides another example of integration. Thriving primarily on explicit participation, it developed into a major platform of knowledge creation. Its influential role in the debate on knowledge in the digital age, as well as the controversial appropriation of Wikipedia, requires the Wikimedia Foundation and their diverse community of collaborators to take over responsibility. Integrating an approach to public policy, Wikipedia demonstrates at both the technological and social levels how to maintain a large cultural resource.

Developing software: Google Maps

Like many other Web 2.0 applications, Google Maps offers an API to synchronize data from the Google Maps database to other websites. Google Maps provides satellite images or aerial photography, and geographical data for the visualization of maps and navigation processes. Competing technologies of a similar kind are also provided by *Yahoo Maps* and Microsoft's *Virtual Earth*. The *Google Maps* API is the most popular application programming interface used in mash-up websites.[64] Users can access the satellite picture database and integrate the geographical visualization into their own web applications. As Rieder reports, Google established a close collaboration with various developers near and far, actively engaging in their work and providing platforms for communication (Rieder 2008).[65] The *Google Developers Day* offers them an opportunity to meet with each other in person and to present projects, and a discussion group on Google Groups serves as the main platform for exchange.[66] As a socio-technical ecosystem, Google Maps does not only attract a multitude of lay users, but also communities of expert users and commercial parties employing the resource for their own purposes and building additional infrastructures for development. Independent from Google's corporate structure, many weblogs and platforms dedicated to developing and using the Google Maps API are spread out all across the web.[67] Rieder distinguishes four different layers of expert user participation in the Google API. In terms of database use, users constantly create new definitions and applications for the Google API. On a second level, the user community develops tools and extensions for using the Google API and the database resources. On a third level, expert users engage in the development of the API itself and not only report bugs to the corporate Google development team, but also come up with new solutions and opportunities for future integration and improvement. On the fourth level, that of culture and knowledge, Rieder emphasizes the role of the user community in the creation, administration, and distribution of knowledge, and the shaping of cultural norms and values. Eventually, the participation of a user community will slow down, which might be related to the evolution of the software itself reaching a state of stability that does not require further participation in development.

The first three levels have been acknowledged as crucial for software development (e.g. Raymond 1998; Ciborra 2002; Von Hippel 1988, 2005), and companies increasingly focus on user-centred design (Norman 1988) in software development (e.g. 37Signals 2006).[68]

But what is often underestimated is the dynamic that the extended branches of production can develop. Software alone is already complex, but the social dynamic is of an even greater complexity. Engaging in a large community which itself is not homogeneous but diverse and consisting of a multitude of individual members not committed to a corporate policy, the company is in need of many communication platforms to facilitate debate, to communicate its own policies, and to explain its own point of view on issues such as copyright, fair use, and the collaborative and unpaid labour of its extended developers. The Google Public Policy Blog is something like a hallmark sign of a company acknowledging software development as being a socio-political matter and thus having understood the importance of communicating the company's policy. It serves as a public interface between company and users, explaining the company's decisions concerning its software applications and the collaborative development. Comments posted by users are in fact often critical and offer dissenting points of view on the topics in question.[69] This example demonstrates, in other words, that the logic of integration requires constant renegotiation and mediation between all participants involved. This also creates a socio-political level of interaction where all participants engage in decision-making processes and debates on, for instance, how to deal with new technologies and how to regulate them. Transparency and corporate responsibility thus appear to be crucial aspects for companies in order to interact with dynamic communities, to establish trust and, of even greater importance, to establish a culture of governance relying on discussion and fair policies. As Rieder notes, Google tries to settle many aspects without recourse to legal means, by engaging in discussions and making a case for its own policies. In the case of Google Maps, this is a delicate undertaking, since the use of the database is regulated, and the satellite images are protected by copyright. Even if the collaboration processes of the Google API Group is reminiscent of open-source software development, Google Maps is for a large part not open source at all: the aerial photographs and the cartographic maps remain copyrighted property of Tele Atlas and NavTeq and are only licensed to Google. Furthermore, Google decides to what extent the API will be adapted, and controls the server back end, the code for which remains closed. Nevertheless, Rieder is right to argue for the participation of user communities, which have indeed emerged as crucial partners in producing Google Maps. The user communities benefit from a service providing data (e.g. geographical data), images (e.g. aerial photography), and an infrastructure that user communities could not create or offer. Google benefits from these communities but is also responsible for meeting their expectations and measuring up to their cultural norms and values. With reference to Gilbert Simondon, Rieder emphasizes that a 'technical culture' can emerge in the interactions between the various participants (Simondon 1980). Like Ciborra, Rieder argues in favour of freedom of action and possibilities for appropriation as crucial premises for the synthesis of such a technical culture (Ciborra 2002; Rieder 2007).

Spreading music: Last.fm

While the dominant players of the music industry appear to be reactionary when it comes to the uncontrollable distribution of digitized music, other services start to integrate this practice into new applications and seek new ways of rewarding musicians. The online platform Last.fm presents many aspects of explicit and implicit participation. Musicians can upload their music and create individual artist's sites, similar to MySpace, but on Last.fm, tagging facilitates connections between different genres and musicians, and it provides handy ways of navigating as well as exploring new music. Last.fm streams music from a licensed catalogue of more than 65 million songs, and with 21 million monthly users it has emerged as a major music platform on the web.[70] The company generates undisclosed revenues from advertising and premium subscription fees, commissions from the sales of CDs, and tickets sold through their website.

Users can download the Last.fm player and listen to streamed 'radio stations' that can be personalized by users, or are generated from other users' playlists.[71] Employing user-generated tags for managing songs and genres, Last.fm seeks to deliver music according to search requests. More important is Last.fm's 'audioscrobbler' technology, which requires users to download a plug-in for their media player. After the initial download, the audioscrobbler sends meta-information of any played song to the Last.fm database. The audioscrobbler automates tagging by adding the meta-information attached to MP3 files to a database for further information management. Implicitly, users participate in creating the Last.fm database by streaming meta-information about the songs they listen to automatically to Last.fm. This generates individual music profiles of users, and relates them to other listeners with similar tastes in music. Opportunities for social networking are provided through the weekly updated 'neighbours' who share a similar taste in music, the possibility to look up users, and add them as 'friends', and join 'groups'. If users add their geographical location, the service notifies them about concerts, festivals, and events featuring musicians that match those on the user's profile. Another crucial aspect are the data generated about which songs are played and how often. The audioscrobbler enables Last.fm to establish an exact count, while performance rights organizations can actually only give an estimate. In 2008 Last.fm started a royalty programme for artists who are not affiliated with a major label and therefore do not benefit from performance rights organizations' payments. To emerging and independent artists, the platform is attractive, probably not so much because of the potential royalty revenues, but rather as a vehicle for gaining popularity. The new songs of unknown artists are related through the tagging and audioscrobbling system to groups of a similar genre and are thus communicated to an audience of people who listen to similar bands.

Emerging artists can actively promote their music by searching for listeners of similar bands that might be more popular and leave a message to refer users to their own artist's page on Last.fm. Possibilities for explicit participation in extending Last.fm are created through the API. Similar to Google Maps, Last.fm offers a wide range of possibilities which cannot be provided by the company alone, but which unleash their potential onto a dynamic community of developers. Through the API, the Last.fm database can be synchronized with all other applications providing an API.[72] Users employ the data streams for creating mash-up websites, as well as also develop completely new features, such as exporting the audioscrobbler technology onto mobile telephones.[73] They also develop programs that employ data from the Last.fm database, e.g. an application for developing desktop wallpapers according to personal music charts. Users come up with many ideas for additional features that they think Last.fm should have, and post their suggestions and requests on the development forum at Last.fm. User requests include the possibility to select Creative Commons licensed music only, a service that is also used for photos in Flickr. It enables users to find music they can then use for remixes or other productions. Other user requests include a Last.fm player for game consoles, portable players, and the iPhone.

Like Google, Last.fm also thrives on the creativity of a dynamic and productive community, but it is also challenged by their ideas. This even goes as far as mashing the Last.fm API with their competitors Pandora and Napster.[74] While Google Maps shows a great deal of participation from users, Last.fm could also provide a significant opportunity for the traditional music industry to participate in the digital age. Opening APIs literally unleashes an unimaginable and hardly controllable creativity. The rather hermetically closed music industry with its conservative stance towards digital distribution and the participation of communities can possibly find in Last.fm their connection to the digital age. And indeed, Warner Music and Sony BMG have licensed their catalogues to Last.fm.[75] However, Warner Music retracted its catalogue in June 2008, because the corporation expected Last.fm to introduce a fee-based subscription service for streaming music, a model Last.fm is not supporting aggressively, because those services have not been adopted substantially by consumers.[76] Media giant Bertelsmann also seems to have second thoughts about their chances to earn profits from selling music in the digital age. Their stake in Sony BMG was sold in August 2008 to Sony.[77]

Similar to Google Maps, the Last.fm socio-technical ecosystem oscillates between copyrighted content and the free use of an information system. Last.fm mediates between major players from the music industry and a large number of users who require additional value to just downloading music. This is also true for the Google subsidiary YouTube, which recently even engaged in active confrontation with the media corporation Viacom. YouTube, like Last.fm, provides environments and tools to perform new ways of listening to music or watching videos. This obviously raises the concern of those who control the traditional means of listening to music and watching television.

By opening their database, Last.fm turned into a socio-technical ecosystem of an information management system and their many users. Through widgets and third-party applications, such as streaming Last.fm to Facebook, it mashes with other socio-technical ecosystems. Last.fm is therefore much more than just the homonymous company. It is an ecosystem where the creativity of developing communities meets the intellectual property of the music industry, but where emerging and independent artists can also promote their music, where event organizers can advertise, and retailers can sell their products, and it furthermore serves as a 'third place' where users can meet. Moreover, Last.fm is not limited to the Last.fm website, but spreads out through an API to any other platform. Participation in Last.fm therefore reflects an integrated collaborative effort, which is only concerted to a certain degree and more often than not appears unorganized with regard to its users as well as with regard to its licensing partners from the industry.

Creating knowledge: Wikipedia

The online encyclopaedia Wikipedia received attention due to the explicit participation of a multitude of users creating or contributing to articles (Benkler 2006:70-71). Founded on principles of free access to information by new economy entrepreneur Jimmy Wales, it provides an easily accessible interface enabling lay users to add or change any article. The easy-to-use interface and the free access very much embody the projects mission statement: 'Imagine a world in which every single person is given free access to the sum of all human knowledge. That's what we're doing' (Wales 2005). This approach quickly raised questions concerning authorship, quality control, the fact that lay users were replacing experts, and the danger of possible misinformation. A prominent critic is former Encyclopaedia Britannica editor-in-chief, Robert McHenry, who described Wikipedia as a 'faith-based' encyclopaedia, criticizing its policy with regard to correcting mistakes and the lack of guarantees for facts and truth.[78] Comparing Wikipedia with established encyclopaedias, such as the Encyclopaedia Britannica, triggered arguments from both critics and promoters. Most notable and frequently quoted is the 2005 survey in Nature on the accuracy of scientific entries in both encyclopaedias.[79] The heated debate about Wikipedia demonstrates how public perception of knowledge is changing. This transformation raises utopian expectations as well as dystopian fears. However, comparing Wikipedia to the Encyclopaedia Britannica makes little sense since both are completely different formats which are in fact impossible to compare. Wikipedia is primarily a technical platform and infrastructure facilitated by the wiki software MediaWiki and maintained by the Wikimedia Foundation. The interface design of this software and the quality of a wiki as an editable web page enable the thousands of users to participate actively in the creation of a wide variety of encyclopaedias and other media formats.[80] The different languages Wikipedia appears in do not simply feature translations of articles from one language to another, but differ in their cultural and regional nuances. Wikipedia therefore is by definition more than just an encyclopaedia; it is a socio-technical ecosystem, nourished by utopian ideology as fertilizer. The barrier to participation in Wikipedia is deliberately low. Users do not necessarily have to register in order to participate, which allows less interested users to just participate in correcting spelling mistakes in articles, or quickly start editing or adding one. These anonymous 'good Samaritans' contribute significantly to the quality and scope of Wikipedia, while the registered users maintain and improve the overall resource (Anthony, Smith, Williamson 2007). However, the low barrier to participation has also attracted vandals, spammers, and frauds. In that respect, the Wikipedia project faces even greater challenges than Google Maps or Last.fm. Wikipedia usually deals with an anonymous group of participants and relies on a software design that is easy to employ, even for lay users without any specialized computer skills. With the increasing visibility and the pervasive use of Wikipedia in many countries, the encyclopaedia has become the target for socio-political debates and a 'battlefield for truth'. Articles about politicians have been sugar-coated by their supporters and distorted by opponents, articles about controversial persons or controversial topics are subject to 'edit wars'.[81] Just as the quality of articles on Wikipedia is assured through the process of reviewing and using them, the adaptation of the social and technological structure of Wikipedia by its users is in flux and constantly in the making. All kinds of users are involved in the creation of Wikipedia, and unlike tweaking the Google Maps API or the Last.fm API, changing a Wikipedia article does not need any skills at all, and this expands the group of potential users significantly. They all create Wikipedia, no matter what their motivation or the quality of their contribution. Scientology removes critical references to itself from articles, as does Dow Chemicals, by deleting references to the disaster in Bhopal, and their involvement with Agent Orange and silicone breast implants. The FBI deleted aerial photographs from an article on Guantanamo, and members of the US Republican Party changed the wording from 'occupying' to 'liberating' in an article on Iraq. A user from the Turkish Treasury deleted an article on the Armenian Genocide, and the company Diebold, manufacturer of voting machines that have played an infamous role in recent American elections, removed any critical or controversial references from the Diebold entry.[82] Aside from the participation at the level of creating or changing Wikipedia articles, users participate in maintaining, and often guarding articles, creating policies for article writing and social interaction on Wikipedia as well as creating tools to improve and promote these policies.[83] Researchers at IBM and MIT developed software that allows us to retrace the evolution of individual Wikipedia articles and visualizes the number of changes and the users involved (Viégas, Wattenberg, Dave 2004).[84] Caltech student Virgil Griffith developed the WikiScanner, a tool that traces the IP addresses of users and links them to the owners of related blocks of IP addresses. WikiScanner relates these data to changes made in Wikipedia anonymously, registered in the history only with an IP address, and thus reveals the organizations and institutions from which users accessed and changed Wikipedia entries.[85] The Wikipedia community and the Wikimedia Foundation engage in social processes of quality control and improvement. Disputes on editing and etiquette are delegated either to 'discussion' boards linked directly to the article in question or to 'requests for comments', where a commentary is requested from a third party on an informal platform. In response to the violations of Wikipedia policies by members of the US Congress, for instance, a request for comments was initiated to collect responses from the community. It presented evidence of the violation of Wikipedia's policies and etiquette and advocated the ban of related IP addresses from being able to edit Wikipedia entries.[86] The media's response to the ban of US Congress IP addresses from editing on Wikipedia, as well as the allegations that articles on the free, accessible online encyclopaedia were distorted and vandalized, exposed the cheaters in an embarrassing way. The WikiScanner is a handy tool to enforce Wikipedia policies and reveal potential motivations for changes made to entries. The social control performed through moderators, who can temporarily close articles for further editing in order to avoid editing wars, or the request to delete an article that doesn't meet the quality standards or policies defined by Wikipedia, increase the pressure on editors to contribute quality entries and make it easier to bar vandals. A number of other techniques increase reliability and quality, such as labelling an article as incomplete, as excellent or as supposedly biased. On the level of software design, many features were integrated in the MediaWiki software to enforce the Wikipedia policies. The change log of the various software versions, as displayed in the related Wikipedia article, shows that over the course of time, features have been integrated that allow easy recovering of deleted articles, user tracking, user banning, article protection, and so on.[87] A dynamic practice therefore developed over the years, involving the most divergent parts of society who either engaged in the debate over knowledge production, actively contributed to the creation of a growing resource, developed tools for expanding it, or even found ways to commercially exploit it.[88] Recent research shows that fewer articles are added to Wikipedia, and the encyclopaedia's growth is slowing down (Suh et al. 2009). This might be similar to community participation in API developing, such as in Google Maps, when the software reaches a stable state. As Suh et al. indicate, many topics are covered in Wikipedia, and a growing resistance emerges against new content as well as new changes. An increasing number of entries are therefore protected against new changes (2009:9).

Wikipedia demonstrates how the most divergent parts of society can be involved in a large project that causes controversy, but also generates meaning and constitutes a powerful, extensively used cultural resource. Like Google Maps and Last.fm, it demonstrates a practice of debate and discussion rather than legal confrontations. As opposed to the logic of confrontation, approaches of integration demonstrate the basic affordances of digital technology and take their social use into account when discussing socio-political integration into society. While many examples of implementation thrive on the unacknowledged participation of users, integration by far exceeds an understanding of users as 'handy helping hands', often dubbed 'crowdsourcing'. Instead, it requires a radical rethinking of corporate policies, and even more importantly, a society-wide debate on copyright, patents, and the common use of cultural resources. A culture characterized by the dynamics of integration thrives on free accessibility and the free use of collectively created resources, and could effectively enable a mode of participation that transforms the user's knowledge of technology into a civilization of participatory technology.

Chapter 6

Participatory Culture

Understanding participation

Das Wissen muß ein Können werden (Carl von Clausewitz).

As I have described extensively in previous chapters, the recently emerged media practices that have been labelled participatory culture must be understood as built up from three interrelated components: a) narratives and rhetoric developed and distributed in popular and scholar discourses, b) specific technological qualities, and c) media practices. This book has argued that the emerging media practice and the discourse on information technologies harbour a promise for social progress. In fact, the affordances to fulfil such a promise can be inscribed into technological design, which in return can also stimulate participation. In many aspects, the participatory culture constitutes new formations of cultural production. The intertwined dynamics of design and appropriation in the cultural industries are one of them. It mingles users and producers in processes of producing, modifying and distributing artefacts. While traditional distinctions such as those of user-producer and audience-sender begin to blur, the increasing participation of users in the production of media texts and the appropriation of consumer goods and technology need to be analysed in a way that differentiates the various ways in which what has come to be known as participatory culture takes shape.

The popular discourses and the representation of technology in media have been recognized as crucial for shaping public understanding of participatory culture and labelling new media as enabling technologies. References to past 'media revolutions', as well as employing commonly shared images and associations created awareness and shaped an imagination of possible uses for new technologies. Those discourses often have been overly optimistic regarding social progress through technological advancement, and a revolutionary change in power structures between consumers and producers was hastily announced. However, the framing of these new media was crucial for creating awareness and market capitalization as well as for political agenda setting. Tracing the constituents of participatory culture revealed that dynamic actor networks are transforming the meaning of technologies, affecting discourses, and shaping media practice. As I pointed out earlier in this book, technology matters, and many media practices are directly related to specific technological qualities of computer, software, and the Internet. Furthermore, laying bare these actor networks through various case studies resulted in suggesting the need for a shift in understanding participatory culture.

Understanding user participation as a dynamic unfolding in the shape of an extension of cultural industries adds a critical notion to the concept of participatory culture (Jenkins 2006a, 2006b; Jenkins et al. 2006; Benkler 2006; Bruns 2008). Using a term such as 'extended culture industry' deliberately recalls the Frankfurt School notion of cultural production as a capitalist imperative (Adorno, Horkheimer 1947). It refuses hasty enthusiasm about user participation, and thus questions the power structures unfolding in an interdependence of business and politics. More importantly, a concept of extended cultural industries does not posit the emerging media practice as a radically alternative production, as Bruns and Benkler describe it, but recognizes its mode of productions and media practice as ambiguously useful. Therefore, participation in the extended culture industry has been described without a generalizing positive connotation. This concept emphasizes the ability of the media industry enterprises to employ user activities in a way that clearly questions the acclaimed status of users as producers.

While Jenkins defines participatory culture as a community-driven appropriation of commercial media texts, my approach of extended cultural industries acknowledges production beyond the established channels of corporate product development as well as the ability to incorporate user activities into commercial media production. It furthermore emphasizes potential and actual interrelations between corporate designers and appropriating users, and it points out the overlaps between different areas of accumulation, archiving, and construction. Products that have been developed by users beyond established industries can in turn be implemented into those industries' business models. Further, modified products may be re-implemented by their original vendors as new or further developed design. Other products may remain completely outside the conventional structures, or be released into a public domain in order to be reused and employed for new creations, which in turn can re-enter the sphere of the cultural industries. And the most recent development of the Web 2.0 shows clearly that media enterprises were successfully able to implement user activities into new business models.

The concept of extended cultural industries covers the various user activities (accumulation, archiving, construction) and traces potential collisions with traditional practices as well as possible inclusions in the established channels of production. Instead of homogeneous user communities, collective production seems to be very heterogeneous, as do the participant's motives, their social contexts, technical skills, and individual dedication. Within the various categories of user activities, participation can unfold explicitly or implicitly. Especially the implicit participation became a crucial aspect in employing 'architecture of participation' (O'Reilly 2005) in popular Web 2.0 applications. Participatory culture therefore has to be understood as an extension of the traditional cultural industries into the realm of users. In contrast to the romanticized narratives spread in popular discourses, participatory culture is very heterogeneous and characterized by a plurality of different configurations that are affected by many, often contradictory, interests. It is also not helpful to glorify the 'Davids' battling the industrial 'Goliaths', or to prematurely embrace a pseudo-participation of users on corporate Web 2.0 platforms. Despite the many examples for active user participation in design processes, the MySpace, YouTube, Facebook, Twitter, and other Web 2.0 applications instead bear witness to the emergence of a new form of media consumption and the constitution of audiences, as well as the rise of powerful corporations shaping and controlling cultural production and its preconditions. Here the 'culture industry' proved to successfully implement user activities into new services and business models. Critical to our perception of participatory culture is the ability of the media industry to effectively seize control over processes of cultural production and to establish major platforms of consumer culture that are placed in the very centre of the culture industry.

While diffusion of information technology in general, and the personal computer, software, and the Internet in particular, have resulted in the far-reaching availability of technological knowledge in society, the implications of technological choices for the functioning of participation are hardly brought to the fore in discourses on participatory culture. On the fringes of the cultural industries, users are taking the initiative and creating specific practices of media use. While these practices stand in stark contrast to established business models, modes of perception, and traditions, they simultaneously create the conditions for innovative business opportunities, open new perspectives, and shape new habits. In this very process, users recognize the need for social acceptance and legal protection, the objective being to encourage new forms of social action and interaction through legal means. It has been argued that the blurring of the users and producers has led to a new alignment of consumers and citizens (Uricchio 2004). But where is this going? Was 'Empowering of the Internet Generation' just another empty promise, or will the revolution spread through the BitTorrent networks as decisive instruments in the digital class struggle? Probably neither one of these scenarios is absolutely correct, but what is unfolding in response to user participation is a socio-political process by means of mediating technology.

Shaping society

> First of all, we think the world must be changed (l'International Lettriste, 1957).

The main forms of digital technologies – computer, software, and the Internet – have led to the emergence of widespread technological knowledge and competences, as well as the availability of resources and various communities to develop and master this knowledge. What has been termed participatory culture, however, is to a great extent characterized by emerging new media corporations which conceived ways to provide platforms for user activities embedded in new business models. In addition, there also is the emergence of a socio-political concern for user activities, and the attempts to constitute a collectively shared understanding of the new technologies. This transformation from knowledge about technology to a socio-political regulation of technologies and their related practice is visible in the dynamics that have been described in this book as strategies of confrontation, implementation, and integration.

Legal conflicts are the effect of controversial practices such as unauthorized file downloads, and socio-political debates are unfolding in view of attempts to regulate those and other practices. They develop in society-wide debates, affecting decision-making processes and legal solutions. In 2005, software patents were on the agenda of the European Parliament, which rejected an earlier directive of the European Council of Ministers on copyrights and software patents. In 2008, the International Organization of Standardization (ISO) caused disturbance among its members because Microsoft obviously compromised the process in order to have their format Open XML accepted as the international standard. More recently, the Anti-Counterfeiting Trade Agreement (ACTA) has been causing concern among various actors, including companies that are afraid too much regulation of intellectual resources might stifle innovation. Eagerly, politicians respond to the growing concerns of those many people unfamiliar with, and often scared of, Internet culture and propose inappropriate measures, such as censorship, to deal with phenomena that are explicitly visible in, but not inherently constituted through, digital culture, such as violence, pornography, crime, and racism. Organizations concerned with issues of privacy and citizens' rights object to the measures that are proposed to enforce copyright laws, regulate Internet traffic, monitor and filter media content, control user activities and limit their certified civil rights. They criticize that many political decisions concerning the use of Internet technology are severely influenced by companies and lobbyists. Monetary issues as well as the repressive politician's hope for effective and cheaper control seem to govern many decisions rather than a concern for a truly technologically aware society where new media practices are integrated into innovative means of social interaction and cultural production. The cases in this book show how media practice is accompanied by an increasing concern for public policies and questions of governance. They also demonstrate a public interest in questions of technology regulation, and the definition of technological leitmotifs.

Organizations such as the Electronic Frontier Foundation (EEF), the Internet Society (ISOC), and the Foundation for a Free Information Infrastructure (FFII) represent on a wide and international level civil society's interest in co-shaping the legal integration of information technology and its use into society. The World Summit on the Information Society (WSIS) is a platform for the process of global implementation, use, and legal regulation on the national and the international levels of information technologies. Those platforms and countless other citizen initiatives, activist groups, corporate lobby groups, and public administration institutions are part of a transformation process that eventually will further constitute the information society. What appears on the macro level – presented in chapter 4 as the emergence of a new media practice with regard to the development and diffusion of technological knowledge – is transformed into a socio-political debate and law proposals on a society-wide level (e.g. Lessig 2000, 2006; Biegel 2003). The challenge is to question to what extent a participatory democracy (Bachrach 1967; Pateman 1970) will enable the people who are actually using these technologies to actively take part in this transformation process and affect the decision-making processes that will eventually result in laws. But as yet we understand little of the dynamic and complex interactions unfolding between the many actors involved, not to mention the ways in which this 'participatory practice' could be connected with formalized processes of democratic decision-making.

What can be seen in the dynamics of confrontation, implementation, and integration is that software is indeed politically charged. That has been very visible in the copyright wars and the attempts of old media industries to preserve laws and rules for cultural production dating back to the age of mechanical reproduction. But it is unfolding on a more fundamental level in the dynamics I have labelled as implementation and integration. Here, the interactions of users and producers are fundamentally political. Platforms such as Facebook, MySpace, Google Maps and also virtual worlds such as *Second Life* or the popular game *World of Warcraft* force companies to transform their interaction with their clients from the traditional product and customer support to a sort of 'user and software governance'. It turns companies and users in something more similar to a 'society', where through various processes of interaction both sides try to balance their various interests in a sort of 'agreement'. It requires process-oriented strategies that involve 'public policies', law-like texts that are very much recognizable in 'end user license agreements' and 'terms of use'. It also requires a different way of communicating with users or even integrating them actively in the development process. Another crucial aspect is that some of the mentioned platforms are much more than just simply services or products, they are constituents of public 'space' (Münker 2009). User are therefore less like traditional consumers and become more like citizens. The disturbing aspect about this shift is that it would turn companies into something more similar to governments and public administration without the traditional democratic legitimation.

There clearly is a participatory aspect in the way users seek to transform their knowledge of technology into culturally accepted norms and habits. Extending participation from tinkering with products to socio-political actions is important in view of the challenges facing the emerging information society: copyright enforcement, software patents, surveillance technologies, data retention, privacy, as well as network neutrality are but a few of the urgent issues whose regulation will affect the use and development of information technologies substantially. The ongoing attempts by the copyright industries, in concert with the aim of politicians to control access to information and citizens' communication, seriously threatens the recently developed media practices (Lessig 2001, 2004; Vaidhanathan 2001).

An increasing interest of politicians in surveillance technologies, and the ever-growing need of copyright industries to lock down cultural resources and technologies, could lead to a regulation of Internet technologies and computer use that would immediately abolish user anonymity, free information, and access to resources (Walker 2003). By requesting civil enforcement of copyrights, these corporations ultimately constitute a serious danger to civil rights. Recently, Jonathan Zittrain launched an urgent call for change, to escape from the anticipated restrictions on technology and freedom (2008). These voices are not necessarily a dystopian backlash to the formulated utopia of participation, but again show the social scope of technology use. All this constitutes a reconfiguration of established business models, modes of production, and power structures. As Armand Mattelart has warned, the debates on media practice are not settled yet, and more than a decade after the World Wide Web became a massively used application, users' freedom to communicate is by no means guaranteed (2007).

It is therefore necessary to take a step beyond understanding participatory culture as merely appropriating consumer goods; instead, it can be seen as the constitution of a technologically aware society where new media practices transform many aspects of everyday life, including politics, the economy, and public discourse. The emerging participatory culture describes a profound transformation of cultural production. On many levels it provides exciting opportunities to actively participate in political discussion, collective production, and to interact and communicate in global networks. It is not only changing what it means to be a consumer through the possibilities of participation, it is also changing citizenship. The transformation of citizenship becomes very much explicit in the dynamics of confrontation, implementation, and integration. While confrontation tries to stifle any media practice that threatens old business models, implementation tends to turn users into subjects of corporate platforms. The dynamic of integration shows how consensus and stability – even if they are temporary – can be achieved for communities and technologies. On the level of social interaction, integration provides examples of mutual respect and cooperation; furthermore, it shows extraordinary examples of organization of distributed participants. Although it would be quite inappropriate to label these examples from Wikipedia to Google Maps as 'provisional micro-societies' (Debord 1957), they provide inspiration for ways of integrating new media practices into society. The process of advocating the emerging media practice has already resulted in many requests for constituents of an effective participation in the information society, such as transparency of technologies, free access to information infrastructures, a neutral regulation of web traffic, and the right for private and anonymous communication. Furthermore, policies can formulate a technological leitmotif embracing the innovative value of shared resources.

Participating in this process is possible on several levels. Within scholarly debate, it is important to revisit the affection for active users, and to analyse user activities with regard to the actual socio-political implications they may have for a reconfiguration of power structures. I argued extensively against the rosy picture of user participation, not only because it describes the phenomenon of participation insufficiently, but also because it's illusionary rhetoric neglects the problems at hand and serves 'a self-incurred immaturity'. Providing an analysis of the actor networks involved in shaping our cultural reality through patent laws, regulations, and technological design can contribute significantly to making socio-political dynamics public and comprehensible to a broader audience. In that way, scholars can contribute to an interdisciplinary effort of reflecting the constituents of a participatory culture, and provide insights that can influence the integration of new media practices into society. The humanities must not blindly justify technological development (nor adopt the conservative stance of the techno-pessimists) but instead must become critically involved in the debate and provide the necessary insight and analysis for reflection and decision-making. Instead of letting the humanities become a mere appendix of marketing departments, critical theory has to participate in the process of policy-making. Its aim should be to unveil hidden networks, to 'make things public' and map assemblages and detect alliances to provide arguments in the ongoing and forthcoming debates on our cultural values, our freedom, and our civil rights (Latour 2005a).

Defending the cultural freedom and values of a participatory culture also unfolds on the level of design. The open-source community explicitly discusses socio-political aspects of design. Wikipedia and Google Maps are two other examples of technological design and knowledge creation accompanied by a discourse and decision-making processes that resemble a democratic approach to cultural practice and design, founded on constitutional guidelines. Already a lively discussion is taking place in the domain of open source, as well as in the many grassroots movements, about free information, citizen journalism, and the free culture movement, aiming to amend copyright laws.

An interdisciplinary effort is necessary to bridge the divide between cultural analysis and technical design. Participants from both domains need to develop a shared understanding of technology and socio-political implications. Both sides need to develop a certain form of sensibility: scholars need to comprehend, as students of culture, to what extent design solutions are related to materials, tools, and prior definitions of objectives, while designers can develop a sensibility for the discursive aspects of technology. In some developing communities this is already the practice.

We must not sit on our hands while cultural resources are exploited and chances for enhancing education and civil liberties are at stake. The current debates on copyright, software patents, privacy, and net neutrality are actually affecting questions of principle. Our civil rights and our cultural freedom are more important than monetary revenues or a shallow promise of cost-effective safety. The media practice that emerged in the past two decades consists of many aspects that improve and promote our society. It would be grossly negligent to risk these values by aligning the cultural practice to dubious business objectives and populist politics.

Notes

Introduction

1   The term 'participatory culture' was initially introduced by Henry Jenkins (1991, 2006a; 2006b, Jenkins et al. 2006) to distinguish active user participation in online cultural production from an understanding of consumer culture, where audiences consume corporate media texts without actively shaping, altering, or distributing them.

2   The World Wide Web (WWW) is actually only one of many applications that are executed on the Internet. The term Internet is most often used synonymously for the WWW, which in fact is interfacing many different applications that are all different Internet protocols. In the context of this publication, the term Internet is used to refer to Internet technologies in general. When necessary to differentiate, the individual network, protocol, or application will be named explicitly.

3   The Internet World Stats counted 1.966 billion Internet users in June 2010, <http://www.Internetworldstats.com/stats.htm>.
    The PEW Institute identifies 74% of US American adults as regular Internet users, and within the European Union, overall access to the Internet is an estimated 63.8% of the population. Topping the list are Scandinavian countries, such as Sweden, with over 89%, while new EU members, such as Bulgaria, rank at 36.7% and Romania at 33.4%, respectively, see Lee Rainie, 'Internet, Broadband and Cell Phone Statistics', PEW Internet & American Life Project, January 5, 2010, <http://www.pewinternet.org/Reports/2010/Internet-broadband-and-cell-phone-statistics.aspx>; 'Internet Usage in the European Union', January 2009, <www.InternetWorldstats.com/stats9.htm#eu>.

4   Weblogs in particular serve as a medium to comment on political affairs, media coverage, and a variety of socio-political issues. For an enthusiast's account of the 'grassroots' media, see Dan Gilmore (2006) and, for a critical analysis, Geert Lovink (2008);

5   Fan cultures and the transformation of their activities in the digital age have been extensively analysed by Henry Jenkins (e.g. 1991, 2002, 2004, 2006b).

6   Appropriation describes how consumers use, change, and adapt products. This process often involves uses unintended by the original vendors, and can also include modifications of the technical design. Appropriation has been perceived as a second stage of design, or 'completing design in use' (Carrol 2004). Different levels of

appropriation have been recognized according to the degree of modification and use (Akrich 1998) and considered a crucial aspect in innovation and improvement of design (e.g. Hippel 1988, 2005; Ciborra 2002).

7   Xbox-Linux-Project, <www.xbox-linux.org>.

8   There are a number of musicians using Little Sound DJ, Nanoloop, and Pocketnoise software to produce music on the Game Boy; see Game Boy Music Club Vienna <http://www.gameboymusicclub.org/>.

9   The hacker Aibopet offers a large number of programs on his website <www.aibohack.com>. The program DiscoAibo, which makes Aibo dance, is available there as well.

10 Foucault's dispositif has been translated into English as 'apparatus'. However, with reference to Kessler (2006) the French term dispositif will be used.

11 There is strand of theoretical work in the field of cinema studies which uses the concept of dispositif in order to describe the actual setting in which moving images are screened (e.g. Baudry 1978; Metz 1977; Heath 1981).

12 Often these APIs are openly available for use and further development, so any interested party can start developing an application using an API. An example would be the social networking site Facebook, which offers a huge platform for the developing community to discuss with the Facebook core developing team. Facebook developers can be accessed at <http://developers.facebook.com/>. Additionally, a handbook is available for getting started with Facebook API development, or to learn more about how APIs work, see Wayne Graham, *Facebook API Developers Guide*. New York: Apress, 2008.

13 Xbox Team: <http://blogs.msdn.com/xboxteam/default.aspx. *Ieblog*: http://blogs. msdn.com/ie/>.

14 The *Official Google Blog*, <http://googleblog.blogspot.com/>. The *Google Public Policy Blog*, <http://googlepublicpolicy.blogspot.com/>.

15 Interestingly, these spaces are simultaneously platforms for presenting new trends in the field of digital culture and forums for discussing and reflecting its development. They serve social networking as well as knowledge transformation and public representation. Ars Electronica 1998, 2000, 2001, 2002, 2003, 2004 (Linz); Barcamp Rotterdam 2007 (Rotterdam); [d]vision 2000: Interfaces of Digital Culture, [d]vision 2001: Electronic Kindergarten, [d]vision 2002: Digital Biedermeier (Vienna); Dutch Electronic Art Festival 2002, 2004, 2007 (Rotterdam); Kiev International Media Art Festival 2000, 2001 (Kiev); Media in Transition 5 (Boston, 2007); Parliaments of Art 2005 (Vienna); Paraflows 2006 (Vienna); ReadMe Festival 2004 (Aarhus); Stuttgarter Filmwinter - Festival for Expanded Media 2001, 2002 (Stuttgart); Transmediale 1999, 2000, 2001 (Berlin).

Chapter 1

1   Web 2.0 was coined by Tim O'Reilly to describe a development of the WWW where web designers employ a set of technologies, Asynchronous JavaScript and XML (AJAX),

to provide enhanced services. Web 2.0 commonly describes web applications which enable users to create and share content, and can actively employ data streams for their own websites.

2   *Scientific American: Communications, Computers, and Networks*, 265 (3), September 1991. Alan Kay: 'Computers, networks, and education', (pp. 100-107). Mark Weiser: 'The computer of the 21st century', (pp. 108-111). Al Gore: 'Computers, networks and public policy: Infrastructure for the global village', (pp. 150-153). Mitch Kapor: 'Civil liberties in Cyberspace: When does hacking turn from an exercise of civil liberties into crime?', (pp. 158-164).

3   Gore, Al: Speech delivered at the Information Superhighway Summit at UCLA January 11, 1994. <http://www.uibk.ac.at/voeb/texte/vor9401.html>.

4   In 1995 at the G7 Ministerial Conference on Information Society in Brussels, some basic principles were agreed upon for engaging emerging information infrastructures. At a national level, initiatives were formed in many countries to promote and organize the diffusion of information technology and to adopt the basic principles, which were outlined as *Perspectives on the global information infrastructure*. Online at <http://www.ntia. doc.gov/oiahome/Giiagend.txt>.

5   For a recent account dealing with agenda setting, consult the special edition on the topic in the *Journal of Communication*, Vol. 57 Issue 1 (March 2007).

6   The year 1995 was a turning point in the development of these technologies. Channeling the process of WWW technology developments, the W3 Consortium had already started coordinated activities in 1994; between 1995 and 1996 the number of web servers increased tenfold (from approximately 10,000 to 100,000 and to 1.6 million in 1998) and the WWW was the main theme of the G7 meeting in Brussels in 1995. See a *Little history of the World Wide Web*. Online at <http://www.w3.org/History. html>.

7   Metaphors structure the world we live in and how we talk about it (Lakoff, Johnson 1980) and that is true for our technology as well. See also Marianne van den Boomen, 2009.

8   Vice President Albert Gore, Jr. in President William J. Clinton and Vice President Albert Gore, Jr., 'A Framework for global electronic commerce,' 1997, retrieved via Archive. org: <http://web.archive.org/web/20011212071309/http://www.iitf.nist.gov/ eleccomm/ecomm.htm>.

9   An arbitrary list of digerati would include Nicholas Negroponte, Sherry Turkle, Sadi Plant, Donna Haraway, Howard Rheingold (scholars); Esther Dyson, John Markoff, John Brockmann, Cory Doctorow, Douglas Rushkoff (writers); David Bunnel, Kevin Kelly, Tim O'Reilly (publishers), Bill Gates, Steve Jobs, John Chambers, Scott McNealy, Larry Ellison (entrepreneurs), Richard Stallman, John Perry Barlow, Eric Raymond, Al Gore (activists and politicians), Tim Berners-Lee, Linus Torvalds (engineers).

10   An incomplete list of these texts would include books by Howard Rheingold, *Virtual reality* (1991), *The virtual community* (1993), and *Smart mobs* (2002); Nicholas Negroponte, *Being digital* (1995), Kevin Kelly, *New rules for the new economy* (1998);

Esther Dyson, *Release 2.0: A design for living in the digital age* (1997); Bill Gates, *The road ahead* (1995), *Business @ the speed of thought* (1999); Sherry Turkle, *Life on the screen: Identity in the age of the Internet* (1995); Donna Haraway, *A cyborg manifesto: Science, technology, and socialist-feminism in the late twentieth century* (1991); William J. Mitchell, *City of bits* (1996); Douglas Rushkoff, *Cyberia: Life in the trenches of hyperspace* (1995), *Children of chaos* (1997); Sadie Plant, *Zeroes + ones: Digital women and new technoculture* (1997); and Cory Doctorow, *Down and out in the magic kingdom* (2003).

11 It is noteworthy how the emerging technologies are producing their own branch of special-interest print magazines. Early on, wireless telegraphy had led to publishing of magazines such as *Wireless*; the advent of radio was accompanied by special-interest magazines as well, and the same holds true for computers, the Internet, various game consoles, and the iPhone. Different Linux magazines are also available as publications on Windows and Mac OS. Those media are crucial actors in the popular discourse on new technologies.

12 It is worth mentioning that many of the claims made about the personal computer during the late 1970s and early 1980s are again being used to promote the *One Laptop Per Child* project (OLPC): <http://laptop.org/vision/mission/>.

13 This was not unique to Cisco Systems, but was a recurring phenomenon in promoting technology to mass audiences and can be found in images promoting wireless communication in the early 20th century and in adverts praising the telephone or campaigns for television in the 1950s.

14 Founded in 1984 by Len Bosack and Sandy Lerner, two computer engineers from Stanford University, the company became the market leader in producing multi-protocol routers and, by 2000, Cisco Systems was the world's most valuable company. The legend goes that Bosack and Lerner produced the first router in their living room to facilitate communication between their two computers. In the 1990s, Cisco Systems developed in tandem with the growing World Wide Web by offering products facilitating networked computing. Cisco Systems, as well as other innovative computer and telecommunication companies and online services, was able to exploit the opportunity of transferring business to the World Wide Web (Castells 2001:68). Using the company's website as a key interface between it and its customers, handling most requests, support, and orders online, the company saved money and increased the speed with which it handled customer requests and subsequently expanded its business opportunities. Castells notes that although the success of Cisco Systems is due to good engineering and excellent products, their Internet-focused business administration was the key to their commercial success (2001:69). With their CEO John Chambers, Cisco Systems installed an advocate for electronic commerce and cutting-edge technology development. In countless media appearances, at conferences and business fairs as well as in boardrooms Chambers repeated his mantra 'the Internet will change the way we work, live, and play.' Chambers made the cover of *Fortune Magazine* in May 2000 and was praised as the man who 'has created a company that is nothing less than a money-making machine.' Personalizing an enterprises'

performance and communicating the company's objectives became the major motive for CEOs to make media appearances, who became the equivalent of rock stars during the boom years of the new economy. The leaders of the new economy made the front pages of Wired magazine, Time magazine and Business Week. Andy Serwer, 'There is Something about Cisco', Fortune, May 15, 2000, <http://money.cnn.com/magazines/fortune/fortune_archive/2000/05/15/279729/index.htm>.

However, the bubble of market capitalization had already reached its bursting point by March 9, 2000 (NASDAQ) and a year later in April 2001, Cisco's stocks were devalued by more than 70%, and the company was forced to lay off 8,500 of its 44,000 employees.

15 The two different campaigns discussed here are entitled 'Empowering the Internet Generation' from 1998 and 'The Human Network' from 2006; see the campaign website, which resembles the style of video platforms <http://videolounge.cisco.com/>.

16 New York Times columnist Thomas L. Friedman reiterates this vision in his popular account of the economic and political impact of telecommunication infrastructures in his 2005 book The World is Flat.

17 Another example from the fragmented spoken monologue is: 'Over 17 million people received an education on the Internet this year – Across the world seven out of ten students say they are getting better grades – One day some training for every job on earth will be available on the Internet.'

Wendy Chun points out that viewers confronted with the recurring 'Are you ready?' had to perceive the Internet as a desirable but competitive place (2006:255).

18 For a critical examination of Cisco advertising, see the very convincing account of 'moral landscapes' created in advertising by Robert Goldman, Stephen Papson, Noah Kersey (1998/2003) at <http://www.lclark.edu/~goldman/global/pageslandscapes/ciscoscapes.html>.

19 Analysing over a hundred of these companies' print ads in the UK Financial Times, Christian de Cock, James A. Fitchett, and Matthew Farr recognized a 'discourse construction' that spread the terminology of e-commerce, pushing the lowercase 'e' (as in e-business, or e-commerce) as a signifier for a commercial application on the Internet (2001: 211). IT was thereby actively used to construct the words and terminology used to describe the new technology and what it can be used for. In describing possible ways to use new technology, IT companies pushed the reorganization of business administration in respect to information technology (2001: 213). Using best-practice examples of IT applications, the ads showed how much money a company could save or how new business could be developed by subscribing to the products and services of IT solution providers. On a more semiotic and ideological level, advertisements from the boom years referred to the aspect of revolutionizing the organization of the world in terms of globalization and the speed of transactions.

20 Known as the 'Gang of Four', Microsoft, Yahoo, Cisco Systems, and Google helped to

create the 'Golden Shield', also called the 'Great Firewall of China', which separates the Chinese Internet from the world's information infrastructure. An estimated 40,000 policemen are patrolling the online world and suppressing links to websites critical of the regime and controlling users' communications. Western companies were criticized for collaborating with a dictatorial regime. See *Wired*, <http://www.wired.com/techbiz/media/news/2005/07/68326>, and *Reporters sans Frontiers*, <http://www.rsf.org/article.php3?id_article=10749>.

See also Naomi Klein, 'China's all-seeing eye', *Rolling Stone Magazine*, May 29, 2008, <http://www.rollingstone.com/politics/story/20797485/chinas_allseeing_eye>. Klein describes how US companies collaborate with Chinese enterprises in developing and producing surveillance products. The Chinese industry is eager to serve other market areas, and its products seem to be ready to be exported to democratic societies, where the aftermath of 9-11 and the US 'war on terror' already have created an atmosphere of security paranoia. However, democratic countries are in danger of importing China's repressive political model along with Chinese surveillance equipment.

21 PEW Research Center, 'Internet now major source of campaign news', October 31, 2008, *PEW Research*, <http://pewresearch.org/pubs/1017/internet-now-major-source-of-campaign-news>.

22 Evgeny Morzov, 'Vorsicht, Freund hört mit!' *Frankfurter Allgemeine Zeitung*, March 18, 2010, online: <www.faz.net/-00muws>.

23 An incomplete list would include *The social media bible: Tactics, tools, and strategies for business success* by Lon Safko and David K. Brake (2009); Dan Zarella, *The social media marketing book* (2009); Dave Evans and Susan Bratton, *Social media marketing. An hour a day* (2008); *Twitter power. How to dominate your market one tweet at a time* by Joel Comm (2010); *YouTube marketing. Online video marketing for any business* by Michael Miller (2008); *The Facebook era: Tapping online social networks to build better products, reach new audiences, and sell more stuff* by Clara Sih (2009); *Social media metrics: How to measure and optimize your marketing investment* by Jim Sterne (2010); *Web analytics 2.0: The art of online accountability and science of customer centricity* by Avinash Kaushik (2009); *Socialnomics: How social media transforms the way we live and do business* by Erik Qualman (2009), *Twitterville: How businesses can thrive in the new global neighborhoods* by Shel Israel (2009); and not to forget the '*Whatever 2.0 for dummies*' books, such as *Twitter marketing for dummies* by Kyle Lacy (2009); *Facebook marketing for dummies* by Paul Dunay and Richard Krueger (2009); and *Social media marketing for dummies* by Shiv Singh (2009).

Chapter 2

1 Nettime formulates its mission statement deliberately as an educational project that exceeds the online sphere: 'nettime is not just a mailing list but an effort to formulate an international, networked discourse that neither promotes a dominant euphoria (to sell products) nor continues the cynical pessimism, spread by journalists and intellectuals in the 'old' media who generalize about 'new' media with no clear

understanding of their communication aspects. we have produced, and will continue to produce books, readers, and web sites in various languages so an 'immanent' net critique will circulate both on- and offline.' <http://www.nettime.org/info.html>. *Next 5 Minutes*, <http://www.next5minutes.org/>.

2   Raessens refers to critical games and to modifications of games to point out opportunities to make cultural criticism part of media content itself. An example would be Velvet Strike (Anne-Marie Schleiner, Joan Leandre, Brody Condon 2002), a tool for placing 'graffiti' in the virtual environment of the multiplayer game *Counter-strike*. It is conceived as a playful form of applying critique inside the criticized environment (Schleiner 2005); see Velvet Strike at <http://www.opensorcery.net/velvet-strike/>.

3   The term 'culture studies' is used here as an equivalent to the German term *Kulturwissenschaft* (e.g. Kittler 2001; Böhme et al 2002). Culture studies, influenced by the humanities, forms an interdisciplinary field between disciplines including art history, film, theatre, media studies, and communication studies.

4   4 See also: Jay Rosen, 'The people formerly known as the audience' [sic], online: < http://journalism.nyu.edu/pubzone/weblogs/pressthink/2006/06/27/ppl_frmr.html>.

5   As a fan of comic books himself and a researcher examining fan communities, Jenkins has actually experienced this sense of genuinely shared values and the mutual interest into each other's contributions. He is also aware of the blurred area between independent comic-strip artists and the industry. At conventions, independent comic-strip artists are often contracted by big publishers.

6   An example cited by Jenkins is the anti-Bush campaign contest entitled 'Bush in 30 Seconds'. The users were invited to send in their homemade campaign movies. Six final winners were then selected by a jury (Jenkins 2006b:219); see the website <www.bushin30seconds.org> for the awarded advertisements and the jury's 150 top choices.

7   Using image editors to change a popular motive into a picture with a somewhat political message was not only done by common users or graphic designers killing time, but also by popular magazines such as *MAD Magazine*, which made reference to the movie *Pirates of the Caribbean: Dead Man's Chest* (Gore Verbinski, USA 2006). It changed the title to *Pirates of the Constitution: Head Man's Mess*, presenting George W. Bush, Dick Cheney, and Condoleeza Rice as villains. The tag-line reads: 'Now Subverting a Government Near You'. However, one might mention that Walter Benjamin had already noted that bourgeois media machines are able to produce proletarian propaganda aimed at undermining capitalism without affecting the capitalist system at all.

8   With reference to Clay Shirky, he employs the term 'social software' for applications which enable users to produce and share artefacts and facilitate social interaction. Despite the fact that Bruns pays much more attention to the relationship between cultural production and the socio-technical ecosystem it operates in, the ability to take action is assigned to users only. He underrates the technical design as a crucial actor

for channelling user activities and establishing implicit participation.

9 Bruns acknowledges that 'it also remains possible, of course, that the continuing tendency towards harvesting the outputs of produsage communities for commercial gain, or towards hijacking the communities themselves by locking them into corporate-controlled environments, combined with stronger enforcement of commercial copyrights, will serve to fundamentally undermine participant enthusiasm for taking place in produsage projects' (2008:6). However, labelling the culture industry as a spoilsport for user communities is no substitute for the much-needed critique on the unfolding socio-political dynamics.

10 An example of a Star Wars fan film is The Jedi Who Loved Me (Henry Burrows, Adam Ahmad, Steven McCombe, UK 2000), <http://www.foiled.co.uk/tjwlm/index2.html>.

11 The computer industry noticed the nostalgic need for 'old school' games and recently, several compilations of computer and video games from the late 1970s and early 1980s were released emulated for current platforms like Playstation, Xbox, and Nintendo. See also The Oldskool PC, <www.oldskool.org> and Classic Gaming <www. classicgaming.com>.

12 Supported by media corporation lobbyists, the Digital Millennium Copyright Act (DMCA) was passed by the US Congress in 1998 to adapt traditional copyright to the situation of the digital age.

13 Scene.org is hosted at the Rotterdam University of Professional Education and stores approximately 500 GB of demoscene-related files and facilitates daily traffic of up to 200 GB: <www.scene.org>. The Internet Archive preserves screenshots of a number of websites in order to document the WWW (known as the Wayback Machine) and hosts books, films, and pictures that are in the public domain: <www.archive.org>.

14 Xbins is an ftp server. Its content can be browsed on its website <www.xbins.org>.

15 In 2010, Sourceforge consisted of more than 240,000 projects and more than 2.6 million registered users. <www.sourceforge.net>.

16 Copyleft is similar to copyright, but grants third parties the free use of intellectual labour under certain regulations, e.g. sharing derivatives drawn from the original work according to the licence and making them available as original works. Open-source software is often released under copyleft licences as the GNU General Public License, which was originally written by Richard Stallman. For an overview of the different software licences, see Free Software Foundation, 'Various Licenses and comments about them', online: <http://www.gnu.org/licenses/license-list.html> and Lawrence Liang, Guide to open content licenses. Rotterdam, Piet Zwart Institute, 2004, online: <http://pzwart.wdka.hro.nl/mdr/research/lliang/open_content_guide/index_html/>. Those licences require a user to publish further developed works, or products consisting partly of works released under a copyleft licence to be again released under the same licence. Other free licences that do not require this share-alike policy cannot be labeled as copyleft. This applies to several Creative Commons licences, many open-source software licences such as BSD, MIT, or Apache licences.

For an overview of the different open source software licences, see Open Source

Licenses, <www.opensource.org/licenses/category>.

17 The Creative Commons licence, which appears in different versions, was originally initiated by Lawrence Lessig, who aimed for an enforcement of fair use rights in digital culture, and is mostly used for written texts, music, photos, and movies. Creative Commons covers the traditional copyright and always requires a contribution to be made to the original creator, but provides various possibilities for adapting the original work. Users of Creative Commons licensed works can rely on their fair use rights according to the licence and create derivatives, quote from the original work, or integrate it into new productions. The photo-sharing website Flickr provides a search option for Creative Commons licensed pictures. Other websites refer to Creative Commons-licensed music. This very book is also published under a Creative Commons licence. See Creative Commons, <www.creativecommons.org>.

Chapter 3

1 See also Bernhard Rieder's blog post about the 'moral processing' of participatory culture, 'Moral Processing', The Politics of Systems, April 25 2008, <http://thepoliticsofsystems.net/2008/04/25/moral-preprocessing/>.

2 When this argument is made, often Langdon Winner's example of the low-built Long Island overpasses is cited, indicating how architecture could execute social control. In the above-mentioned case, the lower class were denied access to Long Island beaches by public transport, because buses were not able to pass under the low bridges. Joerges convincingly shows how this argument developed a life of its own and has created a legend of racism traceable to Robert Moses' urban planning (Joerges 1999). Nevertheless, Joerges does not argue against the concept of artefacts being political, but rather emphasizes that politics can develop its own artefacts, such as the legend that Winner allegedly created with his 'well-told story' of the Long Island overpasses. Furthermore, it is important to highlight that politics in artefacts might be even more complex. In the case of the low overpasses on Long Island, they should be examined in light of whether the law prohibiting public transport in parks contributed to what was a cost-effective planning scheme for the low overpasses in the first place. As such, the low overpasses might merely be the result of administrative policies that already excluded the lower classes from accessing certain areas.

3 The aspect of universality goes back to the first attempts of Leibniz to introduce a binary system for accounting (Dotzler 2006). It led eventually to the first automatic calculating machines in the 19th century. Calculating had become an increasingly important task in the 19th-century world of the British Empire and other countries facing the dynamic of the industrial age, in order to calculate pensions, mortality rates, navigation tables, etc. An overview of the 18th and 19th centuries' difference engines is provided by Williams 2003 and Lindgren 1990, who also analyses Babbage's failure.

4 'The computer is like a tool, in that it is brought up for use by people engaged in some domain of action. The use of the tool shapes the potential for what those actions are and how they are conducted' (Winograd; Flores 1986:170).

5   This notion is striking because it refers directly to the transformation from an
    industrial age of mechanics and steam engines to an information age of silicone chips
    and fiber optics. Lovelace recognizes the analytical engine not only as a mere
    difference engine for calculating equations, but as a universal device able to solve any
    mathematical operation which is put to the machine in an appropriate way. Among
    other concepts, prototypes, and finalized difference engines from that era, the
    analytical engine stands out for its universality. Ada Lovelace's notes on the analytical
    engine can be retrieved at: http://www.fourmilab.ch/babbage/sketch.html
    Due to several problems, such as mechanics and personal failure, neither the
    difference engine nor the analytical engine ever became actual devices. However, the
    science fiction writers Gibson and Sterling imagined the successful completion of
    automated information machines in the 19th century (Gibson, Sterling 1990).
6   John von Neumann published the basic principles of electronic computing in the
    widely distributed paper 'First Draft of a Report on the EDVAC' in 1945 (Ceruzzi
    1998:22). The Von Neumann architecture furthermore divides the world of computer
    technology into the two domains of hardware and software (Bolter 1984:49), defining
    the hardware as the physical components (processing unit, hard drive, motherboard,
    power unit, cooling devices, and peripheral devices such as keyboard, mouse, and
    screen) on which the software is executed and represented in an interface.
7   The control unit fetches instructions from the memory by copying them, as well as the
    necessary data for executing instructions. Transferring data from one storage unit to
    another actually means copying them. When a user looks up a website, the actual site
    is copied from a web server to the user's computer where it is displayed in the web
    browser. Sending an e-mail is copying the text and the transmission instructions from
    one computer to another. Even starting a program implies the process of copying;
    instructions and data are copied from memory to the processing unit.
8   The emerging meaning of the copy as an emblematic feature of digital culture is
    excellently demonstrated in contemporary media art: in Virgil Widrich's short film
    Copy Shop (Virgil Widrich, 2001) a copy-shop clerk gets copied himself over and over
    again. Countless clones of him start populating the scene. The media artwork Amazon
    Noir, The Big Book Crime (Ubermorgen.com, Alessandro Ludovico, Paolo Cirio 2006)
    perfectly illustrates the area of conflict between copyright, media practice, and
    technology appropriation; by programming a bot to send 5 to 10,000 requests per
    book to the 'search inside the book function', allegedly 3,000 complete books were
    downloaded from Amazon.com and then distributed through p2p networks. The
    artists claim that Amazon eventually bought the software and settled litigation threats
    outside court. See: <http://www.amazon-noir.com/>. See also: Michael Dieter,
    'Amazon Noir. Piracy, distribution, control', M/C Journal, Vol. 10, No. 5, 2007, <http://
    journal.media-culture.org.au/0710/07-dieter.php>.
9   Although Bush cannot be seen as the first person to propose a system of linking
    documents to each other semantically and storing them accordingly, his text effectively
    stimulated ingenuity. Recent publications show that Bush actually was the last in a row

of thinkers proposing non-digital devices for organizing information (Buckland 2006, Hartmann 2006). Remarkable – but neglected – pioneers were the German chemist and engineer Emanuel Goldberg and the Belgian information scientist Paul Otlet. In 1925, Goldberg, known for his invention of microfilm, demonstrated microphotography as a means of knowledge organization at the international congress of photography in Paris (Buckland 2006). Otlet was not only among the first who exceeded archiving work for libraries from written texts to multimedia, but approached the organization of knowledge on a global scale, developing a structure of meta-information to refer to individually stored files (Hartmann 2006:220, 222). Goldberg fell into oblivion and Otlet died in 1944, badly disappointed by a world at war that seemed to have dismissed the enlightening project of worldwide knowledge organization.

10 In his visionary account, Bush conceives a tool to extend human memory – called the Memex – to organize, store, and comment on texts. He suggested making semantic connections between different texts that would organize them according to associations rather than to alphanumerical classifications (Bush 1945). He further anticipated input and output devices, search technology, and storage and organizing methods. The sketch of the entire apparatus resembled a desktop with screen and a keyboard as interfaces. But in addition to proposing a new invention, Bush more importantly sought to promote a new mindset. As Friedemann convincingly argues, Bush was more affected by the potential role of engineers and scientists in supporting the organization of information with the invention of supportive tools (Friedemann 1999:53). His widely distributed text, which was reprinted in *Life* magazine accompanied with pictures of the proposed apparatus, marks a step in public perception towards the information age (Hartmann 2000:304). Another important notion of the text is the anticipation of a man-machine interface for information processing and the delegation of organizing, storing, and processing information to a machine for individual use and antedates the concept of personal media for everyday use (Friedemann 1999:70). Friedemann emphasizes Bush's functional outline of an information-processing machine that contrasted with the abstract concepts of mathematicians such as Turing or Von Neumann, who brought an application-oriented engineer's approach to computer development that was unfolding in the following decades (1999:71). Although the Memex has never been built, Bush's vision of engineers making a profound difference through their ingenuity inspired many of those who are called computer pioneers today. The text 'As We May Think' remains important as a crucial agent of change promising unknown possibilities by supporting human intelligence and knowledge capabilities with information-processing machines.

11 The long time Engelbart spent working alone and without significant funding attests to the marginal interest for the computer as a medium for intellectual labour (Friedemann 1999:149, 217).

12 Alan Kay's object-oriented programming language SmallTalk was an attempt to

provide a universal language users could use for writing all the applications they need.

13 Not surprisingly the rhetoric used in the project recalls the spirit of the late 1970s when Kay, Goldberg, Papert, and others promoted computers and programming languages as an appropriate means for children's education. Piaget's theory, represented in Papert's constructionist learning, is literally part of the formulated vision, as Papert is on the board of directors and Kay is a member of the advisory board. See One Laptop Per Child, <http://laptop.org/vision/index.shtml>.

14 Nelson proposed a hypertext system called Project Xanadu, which was never realized on a large scale. As opposed to the succeeding hypertext system – the World Wide Web – Nelson's Project Xanadu consisted of an eternal storage system that would retain all uploaded documents and track all changes. It would further facilitate a royalty system of micro-payments, and the individual identification of all users. A rather polemic account of Nelson's 'universal, democratic hypertext library that would help human life evolve' was featured in Wired. See Gary Wolf, 'The Curse of Xanadu', Wired, Vol. 3.06, June 1995. For Project Xanadu, see <http://www.xanadu.net/>.

15 Legend has it that Nelson, who had participated in the development of hypertext systems, sold the book from his trunk because he could not find a publisher. However, it became an influential book anticipating the area of interface design and influencing many computer designers and engineers at the time (Wardrip-Fruin, Montford 2003:301).

16 Similar to Papert, Kay, and Goldberg, he perceives computers as appropriate learning machines, but he emphasizes the concept of hypertext as the key factor and brings to mind Licklider's anticipated learning centres in his vision of a large library in the sky. Again, learning is perceived as the traditional process of enlightenment, but here the interaction of hypertext and computer technology was not only proposed as an effective learning process but also as a means of emancipation.

17 One of the first microcomputers targeted for a mass audience was released in 1977. Most attention is devoted to the Apple II, which had a superior architecture and excellent graphics. However, Commodore's PET (Personal Electric Transactor) was distributed with great success in Europe (Ceruzzi 1998:264). The company continued to sell successfully on the European market. The successor of the PET, the Commodore VIC 20, sold 500,000 units between 1981 and 1985, 200,000 of them in West Germany. Over four million units of the Commodore 64 were sold until 1984, and occasionally the company held a 75% market share. The contribution of Commodore, its CEO Jack Tramiel, and computer designer Chuck Peddle, and the PET is somehow committed from publications on computer history. A popular account of the history of Commodore was provided by Brian Bagnell, On the edge: The spectacular rise and fall of Commodore (2005).

18 For a differentiation of software and related aspects and terms, such as algorithm, source code, code, programming, object-orientation, etc., see Matthew Fuller, Software Studies. A Lexicon, 2008.

19 Friedrich Kittler argues that a clear distinction between hardware and software is

rather difficult to make, since software always relies on hardware and cannot be defined independently from the hardware it is supposed to operate on (1996:332). His critique discusses the inscription of program routines into hardware and the protected mode of processors as introduced by Intel. How software and hardware are intertwined becomes explicit in the increasing hardware requirements for software. Furthermore, producers of electronic consumergoods increasingly use firmware to control the way consumers use a device. The functioning of hardware is inseparably connected to proprietary software.

20 Software certainly has more affordances, but the three affordances mentioned here appear to be the crucial ones with respect to participatory culture.

21 Toby Miller, for instance, emphasizes the emergence of a globally spread division of cultural labour equivalent to the division of labour in the industrial age (Miller 2006). This refers to the emerging critique about a new proletariat and a precarious labour situation, a 'cybertariat' (Huws 2003), as discussed recently in the mailing lists of the Institute for Distributed Creativity, or My Creative Industry (my-ci). See also the *Fibreculture Journal* on precarious labour, *Fibreculture Journal* 5, 2005, online: <http://journal.fibreculture.org/issue5/index.html>.

A discourse on creative labour and precarious conditions is emerging in Europe among what's been called the 'creative class' (Richard Florida 2002). The Institute for Network Cultures organized the conference MyCreativity in 2006, see the accompanying publication *The Creativity*, <http://networkcultures.org/wpmu/portal/publications/newspapers/the-creativity/>.

See also Rosalind Gill. 2007. 'Technobohemians or the new cybertariat? New media work in Amsterdam a decade after the web', *Network Notebooks* 01, Institute of Network Cultures: Amsterdam <http://www.networkcultures.org/_uploads/17.pdf>.

22 Andreas Leo Findeisen (2003:74) describes constructed languages, such as Esperanto or Volapück, as the missing link between 'human' or 'natural' languages and 'machine' languages.

23 These metaphors were discussed in the field of software design in order to differentiate software design from software engineering. For an introduction, see Winograd 1996. The most notable early contribution to the debate was made by Mitch Kapor, who raised the issue of software design in his 1990 talk 'A Software Design Manifesto' (reprinted in Winograd 1996).

24 Perl poetry can be found in the poetry section on the Perl community website PerlMonks, <http://www.perlmonks.org/>.

25 See Damian Conway, Lingua Romana Perligata, 'Perl for the XXI-imum Century' (2000), online: <http://www.csse.monash.edu.au/~damian/papers/HTML/Perligata.html>.

26 An interesting phenomenon is the reverse use of language as a comment on software programming. The Linux Kernel Swear Count lists the number of words, such as 'fuck', 'shit', 'bastard', and 'penguin' attached to lines of code in the different Linux kernel versions, see: Linux Kernel Swear Count, <http://www.vidarholen.net/contents/

wordcount/>. The Linux Kernel Fuck Count notes a significant decrease in the use of the word 'fuck', while commenting code with the word 'love' increases in the version 2.2 of the Linux kernel (1999).

When the source code of Microsoft's Windows 2000 leaked in 2004, many embarrassing comments by programmers were found in the programming code, see: Selznak, 'We are morons! A quick look at the Win2k source', Kuro5hin, February 16, 2004, <http://www.kuro5hin.org/story/2004/2/15/71552/7795>.

27 However, Latour points out that this is true for technology in general, which is an argument he developed in 'Technology is society made durable' (1991).

28 To enhance the discussion of enabling and preventing artefacts, one could argue the opposite, namely that structures of software as well as of language not only enable but also restrict. See Judith Butler's response to the criticism that her writing is inaccessible: 'It's not that I'm in favour of difficulty for difficulty's sake; it's that I think there is a lot in ordinary language and in received grammar that constrains our thinking – indeed, about what a person is, what a subject is, what sexuality is, what politics can be – and that I'm not sure we're going to be able to struggle effectively against those constraints or work within them in a productive way unless we see the ways in which grammar is both producing and constraining our sense of what the world is' (2004: 327-8). With reference to Kenneth Burke's concept of the 'terministic screen', one could also argue that software not only reflects but also deflects reality. Especially in view of interfaces, e.g. GUIs, it has been argued that user actions are confined and determinate (Fuller 2003b:99-120).

29 German philosopher Max Bense saw technology as a new modality, a combination of potentiality, reality, and necessity: 'Für den geistigen Menschen der technischen Intelligenz ist die Technik eine neue, vierte Modalität neben Möglichkeit, Wirklichkeit und Notwendigkeit - es ist gewissermaßen die komplexe Modalität aus allen drei anderen' (1999:126).

30 In the 1980s, computer programs were often exchanged as a printout of all lines of code and then distributed by 'snail mail'. Novice users would then type those programs line by line into their Atari or Commodore computers and thus enhance their knowledge of programming.

31 A very pleasant account of sampling and remixing is the book Rhythm Science by Paul D. Miller (2004), who works as a DJ under the name DJ Spooky That Subliminal Kid. The book is accompanied by a CD demonstrating sampling and the use of found footage. The cultural dimension of remixing as a deconstructive and intertextual process is excellently demonstrated by his performance Rebirth of a Nation (Paul D. Miller aka DJ Spooky 2004). By remixing the controversial film Birth of a Nation (D.W. Griffith, USA 1915) and compiling a soundtrack, Miller actually revisits parts of the United States' cultural heritage and creates a new ways of reading it. To use a term from the work of Bolter and Gruisin (1999), one could argue that Birth of a Nation is 'remediated' in the media practice of the DJ remixing culture. For an account of remixing as 'cultural intertwining', see Hartmann (2000:329-333).

32 In that sense, media studies has to accept software and program code as new media texts and develop hermeneutics and methods of analysis in order to provide interpretation and critique accordingly. Software cannot only be used in ways similar to media texts, in its production or re-arranging, but as in the encoding of texts, the encoding of program code subject to inscribing ideology and dominant modes of reception.

33 There is another analogy with music here: synthesizers come with many preset sounds and sound effects which are used as modules for new compositions.

34 A valuable insight in the Python community is provided by Aspeli (2005) and by Findeisen (2005).

35 That this process is anything but an easy task, even for smaller teams, is demonstrated excellently in Scott Rosenberg's *Dreaming in Code* (2008). Rosenberg followed a group of developers over a period of three years and observed the process of developing a software application.

36 The web platform Sourceforge.net, for instance, provides the means for hosting software projects. It provides users with a source code repository in order to develop code collaboratively, the possibility to present their project on a website, and the means to organize the project management and the team communication.

37 The sequential character of software is already recognizable in the early programming process. Attempts to formalize software design in development models, like the waterfall model, integrated programming and debugging into the process of testing and improving.

38 Recent Internet applications (Web 2.0), make the aspect of permanent development visible by emphasizing their beta status in the logos, like 'Google Mail beta' or 'Plazes still beta'. Flickr acknowledges the extent of their beta status by adding the word 'gamma' to the logo. Recently they replaced the 'gamma' with 'loves you', i.e. 'Flickr loves you', to indicate the constant care and passion developers provide their applications and users with.

39 Attempts have been introduced to implement this aspect into formal structures of software development models, such as the waterfall model, the spiral model, or other iterative software development processes (Royce 1970). The continuous flow of simultaneously planning and programming, testing and debugging, is formalized in the development steps. Royce argued that programming and developing a prototype should precede testing and documenting in order to continue with the development of the actual software system under iterative connections in each programming phase, and also to maintain proper documentation (1970:3). Programming methods like Extreme Programming (EP) seek to involve this aspect in the way an application is programmed (Wake 2000). Often, a rough beta version is presented to the actual users who rapidly send their feedback to developers. Their feedback on the program's advantages, needs, and specifications is then integrated into the next step of programming.

40 Both Reeves and Kapor therefore emphasize the importance of software design, the

process of conceptualizing the software in view of its future use and its users, and its compatibility with other software systems (Kapor 1991/1996; Reeves 1992).

41 A similar picture was sketched of young radio amateurs in the 1920s, who were also depicted as an astonishing source of innovation in the development of radio by amateurs, see *Inventing American Broadcasting, 1899-1922* by Susan J. Douglas 1987. For a critique of gender representations of hackers in popular culture, see *Sexing Code. Subversion, Theory and Representation* by Claudia Herbst (2008).

42 Ellen Ullman depicts a thrilling imagination of a 'bug hunt' in her excellent novel *The Bug*. The painful process of tracing a programming error in complex code is shown in detail and shapes the image of the bug as a living organism that tries to evade the programmers whose lives are profoundly affected by the bug's perpetual emergence.

43 See the case studies in section 4.1. Another bug, discovered by accident, is a feature used by players for what is called 'trick jumping'. When a player aims at the floor in a first-person-shooter game and fires a gun while jumping simultaneously, the engine adds the power of the backstroke to the movement of jumping, causing a far higher movement. As a result, players can reach places in a level they could never reach before and move significantly faster. An entire branch of gaming is dedicated to trick jumping.

44 The practice of hiding features in a game or any other software application is often deliberately executed and referred to as an 'easter egg'. In the first-person-shooter game *Doom II* (iD Software 1994), an 'entrance' was hidden to two levels resembling the popular iD Software game *Wolfenstein 3D*. Therefore, a playful hide-and-seek game exists between developers and users, which is used to explore all the functions of a software 'environment'.

45 The Internet and the World Wide Web (WWW) represent a technology where accessing stored information is just as easy as sending and receiving data. The process of sending does not distinguish between voice, text, moving images, pictures, or programming codes, as anything that is encoded in digital format can be sent and received. Transportation, communication, and accessing stored information therefore finally converge. With a computer hooked up to the Internet, the terminal becomes a sender and receiver simultaneously.

46 Imagining computers as a communication device immediately evokes an association in any media scholar's mind with Brecht's programmatic essay of the radio as a communication device. The concept was also anticipated by Licklider and Taylor in 1968. A participatory approach is already recognizable in their choice of tool for facilitating computer networking: 'Creative, interactive communication requires a plastic or moldable medium that can be modelled, a dynamic medium in which premises will flow into consequences, and above all a common medium that can be contributed to and experimented with by all' (Licklider, Taylor. 1968:22).

47 The dream of universal access to information as an impelling force behind the Internet and the World Wide Web has been eloquently formulated by Tim Berners-Lee: 'The dream behind the Web is of a common information space in which we communicate

by sharing information. Its universality is essential: the fact that a hypertext link can point to anything, be it personal, local or global, be it draft or highly polished. There was a second part of the dream, too, dependent on the Web being so generally used that it became a realistic mirror (or in fact the primary embodiment) of the ways in which we work and play and socialize. That was that once the state of our interactions was on line, we could then use computers to help us analyse it, make sense of what we are doing, where we individually fit in, and how we can better work together' (Berners-Lee, 1998).

48 For an overview of important Internet engineers and participating designers, see G. Malkin: 'Who is Who in the Internet', RFC 1336, May 1992, <http://datatracker.ietf.org/doc/rfc1336/>, which consists of biographies of members of the Internet Architecture Board (IAB), Internet Engineering Steering Group (IESG), and the Internet Research Steering Group (IRSG).

49 A historical account of the Internet is available in Abbet (1999), and an account focusing more on the WWW is available in Castells (2002). A popular account of the pioneers involved in the creation of the Internet is provided in Hafner, Lyon (1996); for a history of the World Wide Web, see an 'autobiographical account' by Berners-Lee, Fischetti (1999), and Gillies, Cailliau (2000).
For a list of people involved in the early development of the World Wide Web, see <http://www.w3.org/History/19921103-hypertext/hypertext/WWW/People.html>.

50 Paul Vixie, 'Why I am participating in the ORSN Project', October 1, 2005, <http://www.circleid.com/posts/why_i_am_participating_in_the_orsn_project/>.

51 In an RFC for the 30th anniversary of requests for comments, Vint Cerf reflects: 'When the RFCs were first produced, they had an almost 19th century character to them - letters exchanged in public debating the merits of various design choices for protocols in the ARPANET. As email and bulletin boards emerged from the fertile fabric of the network, the far-flung participants in this historic dialog began to make increasing use of the online medium to carry out the discussion - reducing the need for documenting the debate in the RFCs and, in some respects, leaving historians somewhat impoverished in the process. RFCs slowly became conclusions rather than debates' (RFC 2555, 7 April 1999). See RFC 2555, April 7, 1999, by Robert Braden, Joyce K. Reynolds, Steve Crocker, Vint Cerf, and Jake Feinler, online: <http://www.ietf.org/rfc/rfc2555>.

52 The first website of the WWW is archived at <http://www.w3.org/History/19921103-hypertext/hypertext/WWW/>.

53 See <http://www.w3.org/History/19921103-hypertext/hypertext/WWW/Helping.html>. A call for participation is attached to many collaborative work projects. Offering low barriers to participation increases the number of contributions from volunteering developers.

54 Another standard for the WWW was a universal address syntax, which was created with the universal resource identifiers (URI) that became known as URLs (uniform resource locaters). It assigned universally valid, individual addresses to websites and

files (RFC 1630, June 1994). Due to its universal nature, the principle of hypertext that links one document to another was taken to a global scale. No matter from where, a user could retrieve specific documents, and the URL was valid throughout the entire WWW, which ensured that every user would be able to read the same document or connect to it by placing a link to the URL in a web document (Berners-Lee, Fischetti 1999:42). Many incompatibility problems in file exchanging have been solved by this, and it became possible to connect to already-existing archives, such as Telnet, FTP, and WAIS resources, and newsgroups (Krol 1992:232).

55 The core protocol of the World Wide Web, hypertext transfer protocol (HTTP), was published in RFC 1945 as version 1.0 in 1996 (further versions were published in RFC 2068 in 1997 and RFC 2616 in 1999). The WWW itself was already operating on the existing infrastructure of the Internet. It benefited from an existing, globally expandable communication system by using the newly developed HTTP for the Internet protocol suite.

56 At the 1991 ACM Hypertext Conference '91 in San Antonio, Berners-Lee and Cailliau were only granted a poster presentation slot. Apparently, large and expansive hypertext systems didn't seem to attract much attention. A year later, the World Wide Web already counted 50 web servers. See Robert Cailliau, 'A Short History of the Web'. Keynote delivered at the launching of the European branch of the W3, November 2, 1995, Paris.
<http://www.netvalley.com/archives/mirrors/robert_cailliau_speech.htm>.

57 An interesting analogy for providing innovations to the public domain in order to stimulate its wide diffusion can be found in Findeisen (2003). Findeisen dates the birth of open-source codes back to the first release of the constructed language Esperanto in 1887. Its inventor Ludwig Zamenhof declared the language as public domain. According to Findeisen, this move was intended to facilitate swift diffusion of the language in order to win many users. A differently constructed language, called Volapück, failed due to the tight control of its inventor, J.M. Schleyer, who stifled any further development of the language by executing his copyright.

58 See the policy of the WWW project at: <http://www.w3.org/History/19921103-hypertext/hypertext/WWW/Policy.html>.

Chapter 4

1 Christophe Lécuyer draws a direct line from the radio amateurs of the 1920s to computer hobbyists in the 1970s by demonstrating how their technological knowledge shaped the economic development in the San Francisco Bay area and especially Silicon Valley (Lécuyer 2005).

2 *Half Life* was developed by Valve Software and published by Sierra Studios and Electronic Arts in 1998. A main motivation for modification was to create a multi-player mode. Initially developed by two university students, Jeff Cliffe and Minh Le, the game benefited from a large community called *Planet Half Life* at Gamespy <http://planethalflife.gamespy.com/>. *Counter-Strike* illustrates perfectly how industry and user

appropriation can intertwine. Both Minh Le and Jeff Cliffe joined Valve Software and *Counter-strike* was officially released in 2000.

3   Self-acclaimed Web flâneur Karen Eliot vents her anger about male dominance tellingly by asking 'Do I need a dick to participate in participatory culture?', See Monty Cantsin, 'Searching the XX in Geekdom. Interview with Karen Eliot', February 2, 2008, online at <http://www.archive.org/details/InternetMemes>.

4   In a talk at Barcamp Rotterdam, Femke Snelting from the Belgian organization *Constant* <www.constantvzw.org> emphasized that male dominance in 'alternative' software development communities, which embrace open-source software, is even more visible than in the corporate structures for developing proprietary software. Snelting pointed out that the sector of open-source software development is gender-biased in terms of a majority of male participants, and the existence of a mindset affected very much by gender essentialism. The lively discussion following her talk in order to seek explanations for this phenomenon and the related problems only confirmed her point and revealed a noteworthy amount of arguments merely based on an anachronistic gender essentialism. Barcamp Rotterdam, November 9, 2007.

5   The Genderchangers organize the Eclectic Tech Carnival, an annual festival for women interested in technology, <www.genderchangers.org>. Heacksen is an association of the female members of the German hacker collective Computer Chaos Club, <www.haecksen.org>. The Old Boys Network <www.obn.org> is a collective of 'cyberfeminists' founded in 1997.
More recently, the initiative of Girl Geek Dinner regularly invites woman speakers and provides possibilities for women (and men) to meet. Girl Geek Dinners are organized in various cities such as Amsterdam <www.girlgeekdinner.nl>.

6   Cornelia Sollfrank's art project *Female Extension* (1997) approaches the unbalance of male and female artists by generating virtual female artists and production, as well as generating individual art works for each fake artist. Those productions were sent to the first netart exhibition at the prestigious art museum Hamburger Kunsthalle, which did not notice the fake and initially released a press statement that more than two thirds of the contributing net-artists are women. <http://artwarez.org/femext/index.html>.

7   Claudia Herbst analysed the representation of the female hacker in popular films and compared it to the actual role of women is software development (2008). Game researcher Tanja Sihvonen analysed the role of women in the appropriation of computer games, in particular in modifying of *The Sims* (2010).

8   For an account of feminist concerns with regard to women's access to computer education and the effects of computers on women's' lives, see Ruth Perry and Lisa Greber (1990). Paul Edwards provides an historical analysis of gender issues embedded into computer technology and its use (1990). For an analysis of gender relations and a discussion of gender equity in technology use, see Cynthia Carter Ching et al. (2000), Alan Bain et al. (1999). An analysis of Internet use with focus on information research from a gender perspective is provided by Annbritt Enochsson (2005).

9   The term 'homebrew software' refers to software that was not programmed by a regular company but by members of user communities. Very active platforms for homebrew software are PSP Hacks, <www.psp-hacks.com/>, PSP-Scene <http://pspscene.net/forums/> for the Playstation Portable, and DS-Scene, <www.ds-scene.net/>, for the Nintendo DS.

10 Executing software such as DS Organize or Moonshell on a Nintendo DS requires a modchip, such as the R4 card from which an alternative operating system is booted and which allows executing other codes than those approved by Nintendo. This card replaces the original operating system. It enables users not only to play unlicensed copies of games, but also to run software developed within the homebrew scene. Those applications range from file browsers to organize stored content over media players (such as Moonshell) to web browsers, e-mail clients, picture viewers, text readers, homebrew games, and emulated games from different gaming platforms. DS Organize is a software suite consisting of calendar, e-mail client, web browser, and a file browser.

11 Roomba Community, <http://www.roombacommunity.com/>, see also Tod E. Kurt *Hacking Roomba*, 2006

12 iPod Linux, <http://ipodlinux.org/Main_Page>.

13 Interviews have been conducted by students of the Department for Media and Culture Studies at Utrecht University, who participated in a research group on the appropriation of game consoles. Over a span of almost two years, the project focused on the homebrew software scene and user communities related to the gaming devices Playstation 2, Playstation 3, Xbox, Xbox 360, Playstation Portable, and the Nintendo DS. Results have been presented at the CRESC Conference in Oxford 2006 (Schäfer 2006b).

14 As will be explained later in this chapter, homebrew software for the Xbox is produced using the official Microsoft Xbox Development Kit (XDK). In contrast to software produced by Microsoft's licensed third-party developers, homebrew software consists of unlicensed code, and is therefore not approved. An original Xbox is not able to execute such programming code, and therefore needs to be modified. A wide choice of software for hacked Xboxes is programmed and distributed within these communities.

15 Xbox Media Center, <http://xbmc.org/>.

16 For the Playstation, Sony released the development kit Net Yaroze, which any user can purchase. Due to various specifications, Playstation 2 never became as popular a platform as the Xbox. A problem might have been the community aspect; there was not enough challenge involved in hacking the Playstation, which would have been necessary to draw individuals in to share this interest and build a community. Playstation attracted a group of Linux coders which claims to have more than 20,000 users: Playstation 2 Linux Community, <http://playstation2-linux.com/>.

17 The modchip consists of a modified version of the original devices' BIOS. When booting the game console or any other device with a modchip, the modified chip injects its BIOS into the system so that the original version will not be executed. The

modified operating system then allows software to execute that would not be approved by the original version. In response to that practice vendors made online updates for the devices firmware necessary. Replacing the original version through a modchip therefore became an insufficient practice.

18 Lik Sang, a Hong Kong-based outlet operated by the Austrian Alex Kampl, became the target of copyright infringement claims and had to shut down its service.

19 The problem of the game console business is the subsidized hardware, which is sold below its actual price. The revenues are generated by selling games and peripheral devices, like a remote control for the Xbox and game controllers, as well as online services which were specially introduced for the next generation consoles Xbox 360 and Playstation 3.

20 See Hamptitampti's statement on the SmartXX website, which has been reproduced on several other community pages: 'Zur Seite von Microsoft möchte ich nur sagen: Klar, ihr werdet sicher wieder alles dementieren, wie immer. Aber unter der Hand auf der X05 jedem Reporter zu erzählen, dass der Täter schon gefunden ist ... Ist jedenfalls toll, auch weil in der internen Anweisung auf bezug auf den Fall 'Stillschweigen' ausgerufen wurde. Dann dementiert mal, warum Ihr meinen Rechtsanwalt bezahlt? Bankbelege kann man schwer abstreiten oder handelt es sich hierbei möglicherweise um gefälschte Unterlagen?' Source: <http://www.smartxx.com/forum/thread.php?threadid=4808> (June 2007, spelling in original text).

Translation as posted on XB360info.com: 'To Microsoft I'd like to say: Sure, you're going to deny everything again, as always. But to tell every journalist at X05 that you've already found the perpetrators... that's amazing, since in the internal memo [at Microsoft] everyone was asked to keep quiet about it. Why don't you deny that you're paying my lawyer? It's going to be hard to explain my bank statements, or are these possibly falsified documents?' <http://www.xb360info.com/xbox/news/168>.

21 Prevent AG was involved in investigating the leaked Xbox development kits, but also made media headlines by their engagement in finding the Sasser Worm author <http://www.prevent.ag/>.

22 Xbins website: <www.xbins.org>.

23 Internet relay chat (IRC) is a popular communication channel for hackers, software developers, and members of the game console communities to debate, organize software development, and exchange information.

24 Furthermore, this code consisted of proprietary code from the DVD player producer STMicrosystems for the DVD player's firmware. The complete DVD player code and everything needed for making the 'DVD-Dongle' (for playing copied games) including the DVD menu became available for hackers and other DVD player producers.

25 Alfred Hermida, 'Microsoft aims for hack-proof 360', in BBC News, September 9, 2005, <http://news.bbc.co.uk/2/hi/technology/4218670.stm>.

26 See his posting on his weblog Ozymandias, 'The problem with modchips', June 31, 2006 <http://ozymandias.com/archive/2006/07/31/The-Problem-with-Modchips.aspx>.

27 XNA Creator's Club, <http://creators.xna.com/>.

28 The Xbox Media Center (XBMC) started to focus on platform-independent application development and Linux systems and Mac OS. See Joel Johnson, 'Q&A: The Xbox Media Center team on the future of XBMC for linux', Interview posted on *BoingBoing*, August 28, 2007. <http://gadgets.boingboing.net/2007/08/qa-the-xbox-media-ce.html>.The Free60 project operates more in the tradition of the Xbox-Linux-Project. The former aims to hack the recent Microsoft game console in order to execute Linux on it; so far, booting Linux on the Xbox 360 is only possible with devices produced before January 2007 with kernel versions 4532 and 4548. See Free60, <http://www.free60.org/>.

29 It was possible to hack an Xbox360 by exploiting a security hole in the DVD player of an early version. Those devices are able to play unlicensed copies.

30 Xbox-Linux-Project: <www.xbox-linux.org>.

31 Reverse engineering describes the process of following design steps backwards in order to comprehend the technical design. A great deal of the hacking of the Xbox was accomplished and documented by Andrew 'bunnie' Huang (2003). The Xbox-Linux-Project analysed the mistakes Microsoft designers made with the Xbox security design and summarized their findings in a paper; see Michael Steil, '17 mistakes Microsoft made in the Xbox security system', 22nd Computer Chaos Club Conference, 2005, online:
<http://www.xbox-linux.org/wiki/17_Mistakes_Microsoft_Made_in_the_{^}
Xbox_Security_System>.

32 The anonymous sponsor turned out to be Michael Robertson, former MP3.com CEO, self-appointed and long-time Microsoft enemy, and founder and CEO of Lindows OS, a Linux-based operating and office system for desktop computers. Robertson's sponsorship, which totalled $200,000, does not only reiterate the existing ties between hacker communities and commercial enterprises but also confirms the Linux concept of promotion behind the venture, and has a crucial effect on the project's media appearance. Robertson's involvement gave the project an even more anti-Microsoft slant since the entrepreneur was in conflict with the software corporation in several lawsuits about the brand name of his Linux distribution, initially called Lindows. More information on Michael Robertson's MP3.com enterprise can be obtained at Alderman (2001:46-55).

33 However, their emphasis might also be a pragmatic choice to meet the expectations of Linux enthusiasts, since the project quickly received attention from Linux communities and was invited to exhibit at the German Linuxtag and other occasions. As pointed out by project member Ed in an interview, there was suddenly a need to communicate the project to a broad range of people and media, and many choices made in the style of communication benefited from the overall narrative of Microsoft versus Linux.

34 This is a reason why Ed is not interested in working on Playstation 3, which allows installation of Linux. 'I saw Linux booting on the Playstation 3 and knew enough; there was no reason to deal with it further.'

35 Michael Steil, 'Linux successfully operating on Xbox for first time', Xbox-Linux-

Project, press release, August 16, 2002, online: <http://xbox-linux.sourceforge.net/docs/prlinuxoperating.html> (June 2007).

36 David Becker, 'Hacker cracks Xbox challenge,' News.com, March 31, 2003, <http://news.com.com/2100-1043-994794.html>.

37 There have been other games with an exploitable software bug as well, such as the classic game *Frogger* (Konami 1981) that has been released for the Xbox in the US. A member of Team Habibi, which is responsible for the '007 hack', points out that they tried to find a game that was widespread. *James Bond 007. Agent Under Fire*, was not only popular, it also featured a 'cool title'. Furthermore the exploit was fascinating, because it demonstrated how to circumvent what are known as 'trusted computing' technologies, such as embedded cryptography keys. The disadvantage of *James Bond 007. Agent Under Fire* was its region code, which required the use of four different hacks to disable. Another possibility to hack the Xbox in order to circumvent the vendor's control of executable code, was found in the Xbox dashboard.

38 Xbox-Linux-Project, Getting Started:
<http://www.xbox-linux.org/wiki/Getting_Started>.

39 The heterogeneity of the members is perfectly illustrated in the 'user help user' section of the project's website. The 'Chocolate Project' provides installation services for those who felt uncomfortable using the step-by-step guide to modify their console. A table lists users who are willing to help other users installing Linux on the Xbox. The table also differentiates their skills, assigns profiles from hobbyist to hacker or electric engineer and identifies what users would like to have in return for the favour. The name 'Chocolate Project' refers to the custom of compensating the volunteers with candy or chocolate. A code indicates constraints on personal visits for reasons like '*3: with appointment, I'm 13 years old got homework and school and social life, and i gotta ask my parents'. Some users link to their personal section in the project's website where they introduce themselves and describe their motivation, skills, and interests. Such member sites are also common at Wikipedia, where a large number of registered users present themselves to the community. The user help pages can be found at: <http://www.xbox-linux.org/wiki/Users_Help_Users>.

40 The name is a play on words derived from the abbreviation Artificial Intelligence RoBOt and means 'love' or 'partner' in Japanese. See Sony, *Basic Manual for AIBO*, (2004).

41 Those specifications apply to AIBO models ERS-110 and ERS-111. The later released ERS-210 series came with 32 MB RAM.

42 Aibopet claims that many people who have purchased an AIBO were actually not robot enthusiasts or technically advanced users. However, in using the AIBO and installing homebrew software their knowledge has been extended substantially. It has to be mentioned that AIBO also became a popular gadget and a frequently used platform for artificial intelligence and robotic technologies researchers.

43 AiboHack, 'First letter', April 20, 2001 The letter was published on Aibopet's website AiboHack, <www.aibohack.com/legal/letter1.htm>.

44 For a discussion of the DMCA and Sony's actions against Aibopet, see Lessig (2004:153-154).

45 Aibo-Life, 'Open Letter to Sony ERA', October 27, 2001, Aibo-Life.org: <http://www.aibo-life.org/forums/cgi-bin/ultimatebb.cgi?ubb=get_topic&f=1&t=000390#000000> (September 2010).

46 Slashdot, 'Sony uses DMCA to shut down Aibo hack site', Slashdot.org, October 27, 2001, <http://yro.slashdot.org/article.pl?sid=01/10/28/005233> (September 2010).

47 Dave Wilson and Alex Pham, 'Sony dogs Aibo enthusiast's site', LA Times, November 1, 2001; online version <http://articles.latimes.com/2001/nov/01/business/fi-64041>. Heise News, 'Aibo Hacker gibt auf,' Heise online, October 29, 2001, <http://www.heise.de/newsticker/data/wst-29.10.01-003/>, (September 2010).

48 Graeme Wearden, 'Robotics enthusiast forced to pull Aibo-altering code', ZDNet UK, November 1, 2001, <http://www.zdnet.co.uk/news/it-strategy/2001/11/01/robotics-enthusiast-forced-to-pull-aibo-altering-code-2098461/>; Farhad Manjoo, 'Aibo owners biting mad at Sony', Wired News, November 2, 2001, <www.wired.com/news/business/0,1367,48088,00.html>, (September 2010); Amy Harmon, 'Put off by disco dancing, Sony tightens leash on its robotic dog', New York Times, November 5, 2007, < http://www.nytimes.com/2001/11/05/technology/05AIBO.htmlex=1182139200&en=a560e9496e3151a1&ei=5070> (September 2010).

49 In June 2001, the case of the Russian PhD student Dmitry Sklyarov, who was arrested at the behest of Adobe at the hacker convention Defcon, made worldwide news and alerted programmers and activists alike. As early as April that year, Princeton University professor Edward Felten was threatened with legal action by the Recording Industry Association of America (RIAA) were he to publish his research on copyright protection mechanisms.

50 Sony repeated its mistake. When in 2005 software security expert Mark Russinovich found a rootkit hiding in music a CD released by Sony subsidiary BMG, the news reached an audience already alert to digital restriction management systems. In this case, Slashdot spread the news again, and it hit mainstream news and turned into a major scandal followed by lawsuits against BMG and a damaging loss of reputation.

51 Posted by Dale to Aibosite, October 28, 2001, Aibosite.com <http://bbs.aibosite.com/index.cgi?read=33840> (September 2010).

52 The stunning similarity of the GUIs and the features are documented at AiboHack, <http://www.aibohack.com/copyme/editor.htm>.

53 An example of active participation by both company and users developing and appropriating software would be Google Maps (Rieder 2007). Another example is the computer game industry. Here users are appreciated as constituents of credibility, improvement, and the expansion and maintenance of communities. By creating game modifications, users actually create new business opportunities for the copyright-owning industry. By building and maintaining communities related to games, users create an active and enthusiastic base of users and bring them closer to the product, to the game.

54 Aibopet's significance for the AIBO user communities is evident from the amount of postings on bbs.aibosite.com, where more than 10% of all messages are either written by Aibopet or refer to him and Aibohack.com (5,851 of 48,249 messages by June 14, 2007). Source: <http://bbs.aibosite.com>, search string 'Aibopet' or 'Aibohack' between January 1, 1999 and June 14, 2007.

55 Interview by members of my Utrecht research team with user Xwarrior conducted on IRC, October 9, 2005.

56 See Aftershock Development, <http://aftershock.xbox-scene.com/>.

57 Users' appropriation can be perceived as a mode of improving design. This perception supports the argument for an understanding of technology developing through continuous improvement rather than through revolutionary inventions. For an account of the history of technology as an improvement of design, see Robert Friedel, *A Culture of Improvement. Technology and the Western Millennium.* Cambridge, MA: MIT Press, 2007.

58 The underlying technology of Asynchronous Javascript and XML (AJAX), which is the core feature of the web design in Web 2.0 media, in fact turns websites into dynamic applications rather than just displaying an HTML site. This technology enhances interactive web-based applications and allows continuous reloading of data without having to refresh the entire website. It increases the speed and functionality of websites and enables complex interactions to take place between users adding or changing data, as well as interoperability between various databases streaming data to the web application.

59 Lev Manovich has identified the database as a key aspect of the new media (2001:218), and he emphasizes its effect on creating media texts. In relation to the Web 2.0 this line of reasoning becomes very much evident in the creation of mash-up websites. But in addition the database forms complex constellations with an indefinite number of other databases. It raises questions of data integrity, control of personal data and privacy, and it should raise questions about the unstoppable fluidity of data streams.

60 A popular mash-up editor is Yahoo Pipes, <http://pipes.yahoo.com>.

61 Plazes, <www.plazes.com>; there are several similar services using not only the network addresses but also GPS data provided through smartphones, e.g. Bliin, < http://bliin.com/>, Foursquare, <http://foursquare.com/>.

62 Flightwait, <www.flightwait.com>.

63 Flickrvision, <www.flickrvision.com>.

64 Trendsmap, <http://trendsmap.com/>.

65 The concept of organizing information by classifying, attaching, and organizing meta-information goes back to the work of Melvil Dewey, inventor of the Dewey Decimal Classification for organizing books in libraries in 1876, and the work of information science pioneer Pault Otlet and his attempt to organize the world's accumulated knowledge in an archive named the 'Mundaneum', which he conceived in 1910.

66 This expectation is formulated in rather utopian terms by Clay Shirky, 'Ontology is overrated, categories, links and tags', Shirky.com, <http://www.shirky.com/writings/ontology_overrated.html>.

67 See *Smashing Magazine*, 'Tag clouds gallery. Examples and good practices', November 7, 2007, <http://www.smashingmagazine.com/2007/11/07/tag-clouds-gallery-examples-and-good-practices>.

68 Flickr, <www.flickr.com> is an accidental spin-off of an online game community and became a fast-growing and successful platform for sharing photos. It was bought by *Yahoo* in March 2005. As of August 2009, 4 billion photos were stored on Flickr.

69 The camera statistics can be retrieved at <http://flickr.com/cameras/brands>.

70 The Viralvideochart website is an example of the representation of data indicating the viewing numbers of the most popular videos on YouTube. Through Application Programming Interfaces from the YouTube database the videos, as well as viewing numbers, are routed to Viralvideochart and generate the Internet's top-hundred list of popular videos, <http://viralvideochart.unrulymedia.com/>.

71 URLs attached to www.flickr.com have been saved by 79,756 users (July 2010), <http://del.icio.us/url/fed5c26047551a2705952dbe9912fc57>.

72 Reference is to the lecture Lev Manovich gave on November 15, 2005, at the Piet Zwart Institute in Rotterdam. Manovich kindly provided the author with the lecture notes.

73 On the level of legal authority, the post-compression condition is evident in an unstoppable voracity to collect as much information on citizens' personal lives, their communication, travel data, biometric data, medical and employment history, social networks, and consumption behaviour. DARPA's Information Awareness Office (IOA) started the controversial Total Information Awareness (TIA) programme to monitor as many citizens as possible and search the data with pattern recognition technologies for finding alleged terrorist activities. The project's data collecting and data mining would of course harm the privacy of all citizens, because it aims to store as much information about any given individual as possible and then filter it to define who is likely to fit the profile of whatever has been declared criminal.
Besides the socio-political issues of privacy and democracy, programmes such as the TIA are challenged by the quality of data and interoperability which can mislead data-mining actions, see Jeffrey W. Seifert, 'Data mining and the search for security: Challenges for connecting the dots and databases', in *Government Information Quarterly*, Vol 21, Issue 4, 2004, 461-480.
For privacy concerns and security relevance, see also Kim Taipale, 'Data Mining and domestic security. Connecting the dots to make sense of data', in *Columbia Science and Technology Law Review*, Vol. 5, No. 2, December 2003.

74 The MyLifeBits project was developed at Microsoft Research by Gordon Bell, and is described on its website as 'MyLifeBits is a lifetime store of everything. It is the fulfilment of Vannevar Bush's 1945 Memex vision including full-text search, text & audio annotations, and hyperlinks. There are two parts to MyLifeBits: an experiment in lifetime storage, and a software research effort.' <http://research.microsoft.com/barc/mediapresence/MyLifeBits.aspx>.

75 Bag Lady 2.0, Nancy Mauro-Flude aka sister0, 2008. Project website, <http://sistero.org/baglady2_0/magic/index.php>.

76 The *Internet Archive*, founded in 1996, consists of the Wayback Machine and a collection of audio, text, and movie files. The archive exceeds 2 petabytes and is growing by 20 terabytes per month. The entire archive is mirrored, that means stored redundantly on a different sever, by the Bibliotheca Alexandrina in Egypt, <www.archive.org>.

77 Scene.org is a non-profit organization mainly sponsored by the animation studio Pixar, the Austrian Internet platform for computer hardware prices Geizhals, the Rotterdam University of Professional Education, and the Dutch computer game studio Guerilla Games. The stored data are redundantly stored on several mirror sites.

78 Project Gutenberg was founded in 1971 by Michael Hart and operates as a non-profit organization, <www.gutenberg.org>. Affiliated projects continue to provide access to public-domain books in different languages, such as the German Projekt Gutenberg <http://gutenberg.spiegel.de/>, hosted by the weekly magazine *Der Spiegel*, the Project Gutenberg of the Philippines, focusing on national literature, or Project Gutenberg Australia, which benefits from differences in copyright law between the US and Australia and is therefore able to publish books that are not yet in public domain in the US. See also Michael Hart, 'Gutenberg: The history and philosophy of Project Gutenberg', 1992, Gutenberg.org, <http://www.gutenberg.org/wiki/Gutenberg: The_History_and_Philosophy_of_Project_Gutenberg_by_Michael_Hart>.

79 Alexa Internet generates its web traffic statistics in a similar way. People can download a plug-in or a toolbar for their browsers (by default only for the Internet Explorer, third parties offer tools for Mozilla Firefox and Safari) that reports visited sites back. Alexa Internet estimates the projected web traffic using these data. The tool can only provide an indication of user statistics, since it cannot be accurate: The toolbar gathers data from people who voluntarily installed it, and does not compute a representative sample; it furthermore is confined to the activities of those using Internet Explorer. It might be also a disincentive to potential users that several anti-virus programs report the Alexa toolbar as spyware.

80 An example of a personal archiving tool is Zotero, a client-based tool enabling the archiving of visited websites and stored files. It works as a Firefox plug-in and is even able to grab certain types of information, such as bibliographical notes from library websites and online bookstores, and reproduce them according to different academic annotation styles. By adding tags to each item, users can organize their personal archive according to association and various topics rather than following a hierarchical filing system.

81 The phenomenon has been also described as 'voluntaristic' and 'non-voluntaristic' inclusion. Rogers emphasizes the blurring between voluntaristic participation and non-voluntaristic participation, a fine line that cannot always be drawn accurately (Rogers 2003:15). He explicitly refers to the indexing of Google as a non-voluntaristic approach, because the Google crawler affects most content without explicit 'permission', while an open directory relies on voluntary contributions. The fine line between voluntaristic and non-voluntaristic is evident in the Alexa plug-in and the

Wayback Machine index, which rely on users to download a plug-in to report back visited websites.

82 Another project would be Folding@home, currently the most extensively distributed computing project, where the idle time of computers is used for simulations of protein-folding. Sony features the Folding@home client on its recent game console Playstation 3. In January 2008, one million PS3 consoles contributing to the project accumulated an estimated 74% of the overall performance, although the consoles' processing power could not be fully exploited due to technical problems. See weblog *Folding@home*, <http://folding.typepad.com/news/2008/02/ps-issues-updat.html>.

83 E.g. the online mini-series *The Scene*, revolving around a release group that rips and publishes DVDs on the Internet, is not only offered as a download on its website in various formats, but is also available as a BitTorrent file. The series' story and style, and its distribution, targeted an audience that was familiar with the use of P2P file-sharing systems and aware of its socio-political issues, <http://www.welcometothescene.com>.

84 The *Internet Archive* is stimulating this by providing a manual on how to digitize an LP, which is a process of transforming information stored on a vinyl data carrier into a digital format. *Internet Archive*, 'How to digitize an LP', June 19, 2008, <http://Internetarchive.wordpress.com/2008/06/19/how-to-digitize-a-lp>.

85 A political component is added by the controversy about file sharing by piracy and the alleged revenue losses in the music, movie, and software industries. Indeed, the society-wide debate leads to explicit participation in the form of media campaigning against the legal actions undertaken by copyright holders and their representatives. Section 5.1 will discuss this as a mode of confrontation, which is typical of the extension of the cultural industries, where established business models are challenged by new technologies.

86 Michael Wesch's short YouTube clip *Web 2.0... The Machine is Us/ing Us* (2007) demonstrates perfectly how users and software design are interrelated and interdependent: <www.youtube.com/watch?v=6gmP4nk0EOE>.

87 Good examples of the labour of enthusiasts and fans in documenting and archiving their favourite subjects online are mentioned in: 8 bit Museum, an online museum for vintage computer systems from the 1980s, <http://www.8bit-museum.de>. *The Netlabel Catalogue*, on the other hand, is more of an index than an archive, but constructs an encyclopaedic collection of existing netlabels and their websites, where users can download music legally for free, <http://www.phlow.de/netlabels/index.php/Main_Page>. Transforming Freedom is an initiative funded by the City of Vienna to archive, index, and tag audio files of interviews and lectures in the field of open-source software, copyright, and freedom of information, <www.transformingfreedom.org>. Similar to the Gutenberg Project is the work of volunteers who create audio books from public domain books, and publish them as free downloads on various websites, and in different languages: LibriVox (English), <http://librivox.org>; Vorleser

(German), <www.vorleser.net>; Voorlezer (Dutch), <www.voorlezer.net>; LivresAudio (French), <http://www.livresaudio.net>.

88 Atari History Museum, <http://www.atarimuseum.com/>.

89 As the county court of the city of Düsseldorf in Germany stated in its finding (file reference: Az. 12 O 246/07) on January 23, 2007, the majority of services provided by Rapidshare are not used for legal purposes and very convenient for the distribution of copyright-protected content. The court emphasized that the company benefits not insubstantially from this aspect, and is therefore required to take measures to avoid illegal file sharing and copyright infringement. See, 'GEMA sieht sich erneut gegen Sharehoster Rapidshare siegen', *Heise News*, January 29, 2007, <http://www.heise.de/newsticker/meldung/102599>.

It has to be mentioned that Rapidshare, one of the biggest hosting services online, has been banned from most forums that revolve around the sharing of content, due to its policy of deleting questionable files quickly. The service is commonly dubbed as 'RapidShit'.

Chapter 5

1 One of the most prominent opponents of Wikipedia is Andrew Keen (2007). Keen's position, however, is rather a symptom of the changing social perception of knowledge and its creation. Keen's critique focuses on the process of creating an encyclopaedia. Claiming that Wikipedia is an unreliable source because anyone could just publish anything, he praises the *Encyclopaedia Britannica* as reliable. However, while *Encyclopaedia Britannica* relies on a process of expert knowledge through selection in academic discourse, Wikipedia filters through discussion and peer control after publication. This process is made explicitly visible in Wikipedia and can be traced through the 'history' and 'discussion' options that are linked to all articles, revealing the entire process of creation for each entry. Assuming that texts produced by individuals who are not institutionally recognized and professional experts are amateurish and mediocre, Keen perfectly represents the need for 'guaranteed' and 'safe' knowledge.

2 Stephen Siwek, a consultant at Economists Incorporated and an author of copyright industry association-financed surveys for the Institute for Policy Innovation, is also the author of a survey claiming that copyright infringement and 'piracy' would cost $12.5 billion and threaten over 71,000 jobs (Siwek 2007). This point of view is based on the assumption that all 'illegally' copied songs would have been purchased in stores if file sharing did not exist. The survey has been criticized for not using official data from the US Census Bureau; instead, it is founded on estimates provided by the related industries. As Gehring points out in the German technology magazine *Golem*, the US Census Bureau data indicate a growth of the music business. Robert A. Gehring, 'Neue Studie zu Folgen der Musikpiraterie', *Golem*, August 23, 2007, <http://www.golem.

de/0708/54301.html>. This perspective is confirmed in a Price Waterhouse Coopers survey forecasting a annual 6.6% growth for entertainment and media industry to an estimated 1.8-trillion-dollar market by 2010; see PWC press release, <www.pwc.com/extweb/ncpressrelease.nsf/docid/283F75E5D932C00385257194004DDD0A>.

3   There are various understandings of how open access works, some involving a fee to compensate the publishing house for providing the platform and process for publication, whereas some are not monetary based (for a detailed view on the different kinds of open access, see Willinsky 2005:212-216). However, the publishing industry is challenged by the increasing interest of the scientific and scholarly community in free open-access publications that lead to counter-activities, such as PR activities, to lobby against a concept of open access. See Jim Giles, 'PR's "pit bull" takes on open access', Nature, Vol. 445, No. 347; 2007.!

4   Downhill Battle is a pressure group promoting file sharing and copying that mobilizes support to fight the music and film industries. To protest censorship by the music industry of DJ Dangermouse's record The Grey Album, a remix of the Beatle's The White Album and Jay Z's The Black Album, Downhill Battle initiated 'Grey Tuesday', a day of demonstrating people's objections to current copyright law. Participating websites appear in grey, feature banners, and provide downloads of The Grey Album.
     Steal That Film is a documentary on file sharing and the legal actions undertaken by copyright-holding industries and their representatives; Steal This Film I (The Noble League of Peers, 2006) and Steal This Film II (The Noble League of Peers, 2007), <http://www.stealthisfilm.com/Part1>; <http://www.stealthisfilm.com/Part2/>.
     R.I.P. A Remix Manifesto is a documentary film by Brett Gaylor on the practice of remixing in digital visual and music culture. The film itself is provided online in fragments inviting viewers to produce their own remix of the film <http://ripremix.com/>.

5   'Mehr Linux, mehr Freiheit', interview with Monika Fischer-Lochner by Peter Riedlberger and Peter Mühlbauer, Telepolis July 17, 2003, <http://www.heise.de/tp/r4/artikel/15/15239/1.html>.

6   Pirate parties include the Swedish party Piratpartiet, <www.piratpartiet.se>, the Austrian Piratenpartei, <www.ppoe.or.at>, the German Piratenpartei <www.piratenpartei.de>, the Dutch Piratenpartij <www.piratenpartij.nl>, the French Parti Pirate <www.partipirate.fr>, as well as pirate parties in Argentina, Australia, Brazil, Canada, Finland, Ireland, Italy, New Zealand, Norway, Spain, Switzerland, and other countries. The international platform is Pirate Party International, <www.pp-international.net>.

7   Weblog entry 'The Problem with modchips', by Andre Vrignaud, Ozymandias, <http://www.ozymandias.com/the-problem-with-modchips>.

8   Jonathan Fildes, 'Microsoft disconnects Xbox Gamers', BBC News, November 11, 2009, online: <http://news.bbc.co.uk/2/hi/technology/8354166.stm>.

9   'Crack down on US modchip sellers', BBC News, August 2, 2007, <http://news.bbc.co.uk/2/hi/technology/6928177.stm>.

10 'Cal State Student Arrested for Playing with Video Games', NBC *Los Angeles*, August 3, 2009; online, <http://www.nbclosangeles.com/news/local-beat/Cal-State-Student-Faces-10-Year-Prison-Term-for-Playing-with-Video-Games-52386872.html>.

11 Known teams of Xbox modchip producers are: Aladdin Chip Team, Duo X2, OzChip Team, SmartXX, Team Omega, Team OzXodus, Team SpiderXS, Team Xecuter, Team X-Changer, Team X-Chip, and Team Xodus. Well-known teams of Playstation 2 modchip producers include: Infinity Team, Matrix Infinity, Messiah Team, Modbo Team, MXL2 Team, Ninja Team, and Ripper Team.

12 Surprisingly, modchip development and production have been organized in a primarily Europe-based scene. However, 'cloners' have copies of chips or modchips produced at low cost in Asia. Due to cloning, modchip producers are also forced to protect their product with cryptography.

13 Bill Gates, 'Open Letter to Hobbyists', February 3, 1976; the letter is posted online at Blinkenlights, <http://www.blinkenlights.com/classiccmp/gateswhine.html> [sic]. Of course, the software industry is more than just Microsoft. But Microsoft's Windows represents not only a software monopoly, it completely shapes perceptions of personal computing, and strongly affects the use of computers by common end-users (for a more balanced and historic overview on the development of the software industry, see Campbell-Kelly, 2003).

14 The Halloween documents are a series of internal Microsoft memos, the first of which dates back to October 1998, that were disclosed to open-source promoter Eric S. Raymond who published them, unveiling Microsoft's intentions to possibly fight Linux. The documents are available at: <http://www.catb.org/~esr/halloween/>.

15 Bill Gates in an interview with *Cnet* author Michael Kanellos, 'Gates taking a seat in your den', January 5, 2005, *News.com*, <http://news.com.com/Gates+taking+a+seat+in+your+den/2008-1041_3-5514121.html>.

16 The SCO-Microsoft connection was made public in 2003 when investor BayStar Capital admitted that Microsoft had secured a $50 million investment on the condition that it could execute intellectual property claims.

17 One of the most famous commentators on the Microsoft-SCO affair is Pamela Jones' weblog *Groklaw*, <http://www.groklaw.net>. *Groklaw* covers lawsuits in the field of open-source software and software patents with the goal of explaining and commenting on the legal aspects for an audience not familiar with law.

18 After the hack, the site displayed the slogan 'We own all Your code, Pay us all your Money' as part of the corporate identity. Matt Hines, 'Hackers deface SCO website', 29 November 2004, Cnet, <http://news.cnet.com/Hackers-deface-SCO-site/2100-7344_3-5469486.html?hhTest=1>.

19 An anti-Microsoft attitude is also expressed in countless pictures posted on websites showing the Windows logo photoshopped as a swastika, Bill Gates as a fascist, or pictures mocking the flamboyant Microsoft Word interface.

20 Novell is a software company most known for its GNU/Linux operating system, SUSE Linux.

21 Open-source software promoter Eric Raymond represents a business-oriented and capitalist approach to open-source software, and the entrepreneurial success of enterprises such as Red Hat or Novell – leading companies in distributing GNU/Linux operating systems and related services – shows that open-source software can be implemented into business models. However, a strong ideological connotation is recognizable in many open-source software projects. Rastasoft's software Dynebolic, a GNU/Linux based multi-media production centre, is explicitly aimed at activists < www.dynebolic.org>. The software is consequently dedicated to the memory of famous activists, such as Patrice Lumumba, Martin Luther King, and Malcom X as well as to 'all those who still resist slavery, racism, and oppression, who still fight imperialism and seek an alternative to the hegemony of capitalism in our world' (Jaromil 2005:203).

22 Quoted in M.A. Anastasi, 'Sony exec. We will beat Napster', August 17, 2000. New York Fair Use, <http://www.nyfairuse.org/sony.xhtml>.

23 The phenomenon of mash-up music became popular in 2001 under the name 'Bastard Pop'. Artists would mix several hits together to create a new one. Other synonymously used terms were 'bootleg', 'bootys', and 'blends'. The music was spread over the Internet on websites such as Boomselection (now discontinued). It became a centre for publishing and creating bootlegs, inviting the extensive community to upload their best blends of various pop songs. Since the production existed in a grey area from the outset, bootleg sales were not possible, and commercial benefits were only possible through the many Bastard Pop or mash-up parties. Nevertheless, mainstream media like the BBC and other radio stations quickly started hosting their own sessions, featuring Bastard Pop, and a major label, Rough Trade, released a CD compilation on the subject. Major-label artist Madonna offered audio files for downloading from her website and organized a remix contest.

The Hip Hop artist Jay Z released the vocals of his album *The Black Album* for remix. DJ Dangermouse's *The Grey Album*, a blend of *The Black Album* and The Beatles' *The White Album*, received worldwide attention. The Kleptones' album *A Night at the Hip Hopera* tells the story of rock music using countless samples from well-known rock bands such as Queen. The album *As Heard on Radio Soulwax, Part 2*, released by the Belgian brothers David and Stephen Dewaele as *2ManyDJs*, is considered a landmark production in mash-up music and DJ culture. The examples of Bastard Pop or Bootleg Music show how a phenomenon that already has been part of music culture can spread into new communities of listeners, but they also present new, actively contributing participants. Due to copyright regulations, it inevitably landed in a gray market and could only be distributed in small vinyl editions, radio shows, and dance events in the club culture. Pete Rojas, 'Bootleg Culture', Salon.com, August 1, 2002, <http://dir.salon.com/story/tech/feature/2002/08/01/bootlegs/index.html>.

See also Paul D. Miller, *Rhythm Science*, Cambridge, MA: MIT Press, 2004.

24 In the early 1990s the Software Publishers Association launched the video *Don't Copy That Floppy* to raise awareness about copyright infringement. The metaphor of theft

206

was already used then, and the video calls for fairness towards programmers and advocates their right to get paid for their work. The video appeals to users' fairness and honesty, asking them not to copy or distribute programs, because otherwise they would actually commit theft, exploit the programmers' creativity, and eventually destroy the computer industry. *Don't Copy That Floppy* (Software Publishers Association, 1992), online, <http://www.archive.org/details/dontcopythatfloppy>.

25 The metaphor of piracy used for copyright infringement is an interesting discursive actor itself. It seems to provide a rather unclear understanding of what piracy is. Is piracy a danger of seafaring, is it the commercial infringement of intellectual copyrights, or does it describe users downloading files from the Internet? Furthermore, piracy, and to a far greater extent pirates, commonly carry a connotation of adventure and romantic legend, which was recently emphasized in the popular trilogy *Pirates of the Caribbean* (Gore Verbinski USA 2003, 2006, 2007). The file-sharing scene itself embraced the connotation and uses logos and names referring to piracy, as the name and logo of the website Pirate Bay attests to, as does the T-shirt design featuring a music tape as skull and crossbones which reads 'Hometaping kills the music industry and is fun'. Such imagery has been used since the 1980s. One indication of how confusing the meaning of the skull and crossbones symbol has become is the replacement of the widely recognized 'Mr. Yuk' warning sign for poisonous substances that had been used in the US since the 1970s: it has been changed because children perceived the skull and crossbones as something funny and interesting, and associated it with pirates instead of poison; see 'Mr. Yuk', Washington Poison Center, <http://www.wapc.org/resources/mryuk.htm>.

26 Popular media mock the anti-piracy campaigns as well. In the British TV comedy series *The IT Crowd* (Ben Fuller, UK 2006), the common anti-piracy clip is exaggerated with depictions of brutal violence and an FBI agent shooting a girl who downloads a video. A poster in one of the character's flat, Roy, reads: 'Home sewing is killing fashion', and later in that episode, while Roy and Moss visit an alleged German cannibal, police raid the house. Not because of the cannibal, but to find a copied DVD; *The IT Crowd*, season 2, episode 3 (for the complex relationship between legislation and the common sense perception of copying, see Halpern, 2003, and Patry, 2009).

27 See e.g. the supporting statement by a group of distinguished economists (Georg Akerlof, Kenneth Arrow, James M. Buchanan, Ronald Coase, Milton Friedman, et al.) to the US Supreme Court in the case 'Eldred vs. Ashcroft' on an extension of copyright; the economists do not see a significant increase of economic benefit by extending copyright terms, but rather a decrease in innovation through limiting the use of existing material; see the statement of the amici curiae in support of petitioners, May 20, 2002, <http://cyber.law.harvard.edu/openlaw/eldredvashcroft/supct/amici/economists.pdf>; on Eldred v Ashcroft, see Lawrence Lessig, How I lost the big one, in *Legal Affairs*, March/April 2004, <http://www.legalaffairs.org/issues/March-April-2004/story_lessig_marapr04.msp>.

In 2005 Andrew Gowers conducted a review of intellectual property rights in the UK.

The report argues for 'reforming copyright law to allow individuals and institutions to use content in ways consistent with the digital age', see *Gower's Review of Intellectual Property*, <http://www.hm-treasury.gov.uk/media/6/E/pbr06_gowers_report_755.pdf>.

28 See also the programmatic text of record industry executive John Snyder, who teamed up with his son Ben Snyder to promote new ways of dealing with the emerging media practice of distributing files online, John Snyder, and Ben Snyder, 'Embrace file-sharing or die', *Salon.com*, February 1, 2003, <http://dir.salon.com/story/tech/feature/2003/02/01/file_trading_manifesto/index.html>.

29 Julian Sanchez, '750,000 lost jobs? The dodgy digits behind the war on piracy, *Ars Technica*, October 7, 2008, <http://arstechnica.com/tech-policy/news/2008/10/dodgy-digits-behind-the-war-on-piracy.ars>.
Ben Goldacre: 'Illegal downloads and dodgy figures', *The Guardian*, June 5, 2009, online <http://www.guardian.co.uk/commentisfree/2009/jun/05/ben-goldacre-bad-science-music-downloads>.

30 In Germany, Microsoft sponsored the publication of teaching material on copyright law in the digital age, presenting an unbalanced and inaccurate view on copyright issues and open-source software, a disparaging description of file sharing and open-source developers, as well as praise for digital rights management. *Rerum. Copyrights im digitalen Zeitalter*, Zeitbild Verlag, 2003, <http://zeitbild-de.academy4.com/files/de/downloads/Copyrights/Lehrermappe_31KopVo.pdf>. A critical review of the teaching material can be found at Thomas Schiller, *Kritik über Rerum Copyrights im digitalen Zeitalter*,
<http://www.thomas.xmmx.de/atcpa/pp/Kritik_ueber_RERUM_Copyrights.pdf>.

31 Former German minister for education and research, Edelgard Buhlmann, emphasizes in the preface to the above-mentioned teaching material that instructing students on the complex issues of copyright is of the utmost importance. She expresses her hope that the teaching material will increase the conscientious use of media.

32 However, the Motion Picture Association of America (MPAA) came to an understanding with BitTorrent.com to prevent the unlicensed distribution of intellectual property produced by member companies of the MPAA. BitTorrent.com agreed to filter files that might infringe copyright law. In general, the distribution method of peer-to-peer file sharing can also be used for commercial and legal distribution. Burt Helm, 'BitTorrent goes Hollywood. Once the choice of movie pirates, BitTorrent will now help Warner Bros. sell its films and TV shows', *Business Week*, May 9, 2006, <www.businessweek.com/technology/content/may2006/tc20060508_693082.htm>.

33 The Berlin-based project Pirate Cinema organizes film screenings of hard-to-find pictures or films that violate copyrights. As Sebastian Lütgert points out, the main objective of these screenings is 'not quality but availability'. Consequently the organizers provide on location the opportunity to download the screened films to a USB stick or a portable hard drive. <http://piratecinema.org/>.

34 See also the Electronic Frontier Foundation's evaluation of the DMCA: *Unintended*

Consequences, 7 Years under the DMCA, April 2006, <http://www.eff.org/wp/unintended-consequences-seven-years-under-dmca>.

35 As Thomas Mennecke argues, these efforts consequently led to the development of safer, less corruptible file-sharing protocols, such as BitTorrent and eDonkey. Due to its inefficiency, Overpeer was discontinued in 2005 after three years of anti-P2P activities. Thomas Mennecke, 'End of the road for Overpeer', *Slyck News*, December 10, 2005, <http://www.slyck.com/story1019.html>.

36 Ashlee Vance, 'Like A Virgin – Madonna hacked for the first time', *The Register*, April 22, 2003, <www.theregister.co.uk/2003/04/22/like_a_virgin_madonna_hacked>. Other acts in response to the industry's attempt to fight online sharing and the remixing of movie and music files include several hackings of the RIAA's website and defacing it with pro-file-sharing statements.

37 Initiated by Miriam Rainsford, aka iriXx, the Madonna Remix project protested 'against the lockdown of digital technology', see the 'Madonna Remix project', press release, April 30, 2003, <http://www.irixx.org/madonna/pressrelease.txt>; the remixes are hosted online, *WTF? The Madonna Remix Project*, <http://www.archive.org/details/wtf_mrp_mp3>.

38 An eyewitness account of the inner working mechanisms of FXP groups and ftp fillers and the involvement of the German Federation against Copyright Theft (Gesellschaft zur Verfolgung von Urheberrechtsverletzungen, GVU) is provided by Oliver Dierks, *Undercover. Einblicke in die Arbeit eines verdeckten Ermittlers der Gesellschaft zur Verfolgung von Urheberrechtsverletzungen e.V.* (GVU), 2005. Dierks infiltrated the scene of release groups and FXP communities. By order of the GVU, he collected evidence and set up 'honeypot servers' on which he stored content provided by the GVU. In 2006 the GVU received some media attention when authorities raided their offices, and prosecutors accused the federation of having actively participated in copyright infringement and the distribution of copyrighted material. See 'GVU soll Raubkopierer gesponsert haben', *Heise News*, January 24, 2006, online: <http://www.heise.de/newsticker/meldung/68760>.

39 Holger Bleich: 'Vorverurteilt. Staatsanwaltschaft glaubt Urheberrechtsvertretern blind', *c't* 2006, No. 22:102. Holger Bleich, and Volker Briegleb, 'Die Hilfssheriffs als heimliche Komplizen. Fahnder der GVU sponserten Film-Raubkopierer', *c't* no. 4:18, 2006. Holger Bleich, 'Warez vom Staatsanwalt. Mit dubiosen Methoden gegen Releasegroups', *c't* no. 24:52, 2007.

40 'Digital rights management' describes the regulation and use of media content as applied by copyright holders in order to control and limit distribution and frequency of use of digital artifacts. DRM systems can imply digital watermarks to identify individual copies, product activation, encryption, and copy protection. 'Trusted computing' describes the attempt to identify individual computer users. The concept involves product activation, personalization of hardware and operating system, and an individual IP address.

41 A list with CDs containing the rootkit was provided by the Electronic Frontier

Foundation, online at <http://www.eff.org/deeplinks/2005/11/are-you-infected-sony-bmgs-rootkit>.

42 For Mark Russinovich's blog entry disclosing the rootkit, 'Sony and rootkits: Digital rights management gone too far', October 31, 2005, <http://blogs.technet.com/markrussinovich/archive/2005/10/31/sony-rootkits-and-digital-rights-management-gone-too-far.aspx>.
    For the blog entry concerning the uninstaller, 'Sony: You don't reeeeaaaally want to uninstall, do you?', <http://blogs.technet.com/markrussinovich/archive/2005/11/09/sony-you-don-t-reeeeaaaally-want-to-uninstall-do-you.aspx>.

43 The news appeared initially on the Dutch website Webwereld. Brenno de Winter, 'Spyware Sony lijkt auteursrechten te schenden', Webwereld, November 10, 2005, < http://webwereld.nl/articles/38285>. An English translation was also posted to Slashdot.org, <http://yro.slashdot.org/yro/05/11/15/1250229.shtml?tid=117&tid=188&tid=17>.

44 In March 2008, Sony BMG again made news as a copyright thief when a small software company called Point Dev filed a lawsuit for using an unlicensed version of their administration software tools. Allegedly the Business Software Alliance estimates that there is a percentage of 47% pirated software at Sony BMG. See 'Sony BMG sued for using pirated software', Slashdot.org, March 30, 2008, <http://yro.slashdot.org/article.pl?sid=08/03/30/1856232&from=rss>.

45 Lawrence Lessig, 'How creativity is being strangled by the law', TED Talks, 2007, <http://www.ted.com/talks/view/id/187>.

46 The website of the netlabel Ideology says: 'So, why record-stores? Why collecting-societies and distributors? Why the n-th copy of your average pop-trash? Why launch-parties with champagne and caviar-appetizers? Does music need an industry? Or does an industry merely use music? Start the download ... and decide for yourselves.' Never Mind The Industry, <http://www.ideology.de/archives/audio000121.php>.

47 The terms of use and end-user license agreements are not negotiable. By default, the user has either to accept the overall 'agreement'' or to abstain from installing the software or using the services.

48 TheForce.net is probably the biggest unofficial Star Wars fan site with over 244,000 registered members and close to 20.5 million postings on the forums. The forum is the most frequently visited section of the website, attracting 66% of the users. Sources: Big-Boards.com and Alexa.com as of September 1, 2010.

49 Sarah McBride, 'Make-it-Yourself Star Wars', Wall Street Journal, May 24, 2007, <http://online.wsj.com/article/SB117997273760812981.html>.

50 Eyespot's relations with Tremor Media, an in-streaming-media advertiser, and Audible Magic, a company specialized in copyright protection, might explain why content is not allowed on sites other than the Star Wars platform. LucasFilm can only advertise and apply copyright protection if they have complete control over the user-generated content. Eyespot's own media platform offers a very different model, and its terms of use are in marked contrast to those of the Star Wars platform, <www.eyspot.com>.

51 Lawrence Lessig, 'Lucasfilm's phantom menace', *The Washington Post*, July 12, 2007, < http://www.washingtonpost.com/wp-dyn/content/article/2007/07/11/ AR2007071101996_pf.html>.

52 Section c) and e) of Lucasfilm's *Star Wars Mash-ups'* terms of service, <http://web. archive.org/web/20080623042924/http://www.starwars.com/welcome/about/mashup-copyright>.

53 These services have become very popular since 2005. An incomplete list on the 110mb forum lists over 200 different file-hosting sites as of July 2010, <http://www.110mb. com/forum/biggest-list-of-free-file-hosting-sites-updated-monthly-t1428.0.html>.

54 Due to a lawsuit filed by a German organization to maintain and protect copyrights, Rapidshare implemented an extremely strict policy and is immediately deleting files that may violate copyrights.

55 According to the Rapidshare website news section as of August 6, 2007, <http://web. archive.org/web/20070814115534/rapidshare.com/en/news.html> (retrieved from Archive.org). A year later, Rapidshare provided a 240 GB/s Internet bandwidth and a storage capacity of 4.5 petabytes <http://rapidshare.com/en/news.html>.

56 Websites providing search engines for files posted to various file-hosting services include: Filefield <www.filefield.net>; Filestube <www.filestube.com>; Filesbot < www.filesbot.com>; Rapidsharefilms.com <http://rapidsharefilms.com/>; Rsdown < www.rsdown.com>; Rapidsharefilms.com <http://rapidsharefilms.com/>; and search. jrfreelancer.com, <http://search.jrfreelancer.com>.

57 Alexa is one of the leading companies measuring Internet traffic. Although their service has been criticized for its methodology and the lack of accuracy of its sample group, the Alexa results indicate to a certain extent the popularity of a website.

58 Yi-Win Yen, 'YouTube looks for the money clip', Fortune, March 25, 2008, <http:// techland.blogs.fortune.cnn.com/2008/03/25/youtube-looks-for-the-money-clip>.

59 Michael Arrington, 'YouTube's magic number - $ 1.5 million', *TechCrunch*, September 21, 2006, <http://www.techcrunch.com/2006/09/21/youtubes-magic-number-15-billion>.

60 'Social networks/blogs now account for one in every four and a half minutes online', *Nielsen Wire*, <http://blog.nielsen.com/nielsenwire/online_mobile/social-media-accounts-for-22-percent-of-time-online/>.

61 The online journal *First Monday* published a special issue on 'Critical perspectives on Web 2.0' in March 2008, edited by Michael Zimmer (2008).

62 The Suicide Machine was built by the Rotterdam-based hacker group Moddr_, <www.suicidemachine.org>.

63 Tim O'Reilly, in a comment on the article 'Web 3.0, the best official definition imaginable', *Novaspivack*, October 4, 2007, <http://novaspivack.typepad.com/ nova_spivacks_weblog/2007/10/web-30----the-a.html>.

64 On the website The Programmable Web, a ranking of 823 different APIs lists the Google Maps API as most popular among 2,071 mash-up websites, followed by Flickr with 546 mash-ups, YouTube with 500, and Twitter with 464 mash-ups as of

September 2010, <http://www.programmableweb.com/apis/directory/1?sort=mashups>.

65 I draw here from the research conducted by Bernhard Rieder in 2007 on the Google Maps API Group, see Rieder (2007, 2008). Rieder kindly provided his research notes to me.

66 The Google Developer Day 2007 took place at various locations around the globe: <http://code.google.com/events/developerday/2010/index.html>. The Google Maps API group numbers 43,905 members as of September 22, 2010, <http://groups-beta.google.com/group/Google-Maps-API>.

67 Google Maps <http://maps.google.com> and the API <http://code.google.com/apis/maps/index.html> are connected to websites in the developing community such as the Unofficial Documentation http://mapki.com/wiki/Main_Page and numerous weblogs on Google mash-ups such as Google Maps Mania http://mapki.com/wiki/Main_Page. Additionally, it is also connected to many commercial services such as Maps24 <http://mapki.com/wiki/Main_Page> and institutional sites such as the United Nations Cartographic Section <http://www.un.org/Depts/Cartographic/english/htmain.htm> and the NASA Worldwind website <http://worldwind.arc.nasa.gov>. Furthermore, Google Maps is connected to the official Google Blog and from there to many online technology magazines and other media websites. Here, a single service such as Google Maps stimulates the emergence of an entire ecosystem of related and interconnected applications and services.

68 The web application design company 37Signals promotes its approach to web design as a way of dealing with the complexity of software better by integrating the user into the production process. In addition to several web applications for project management and document-sharing, the company developed the open-source web application framework, Ruby on Rails. Like many other web design companies, 37Signals's business model relies on collectively built and constantly improved resources that can be used by anyone, and on the creation of commercial applications. Its design approach is published as *Getting real*, 2006, <http://gettingreal.37signals.com>.

69 The *Google Public Policy Blog* is hosted at Google subsidiary Blogspot, <http://googlepublicpolicy.blogspot.com>.

70 In 2008, 21 million users per month were reported, but Last.fm claims that the service is used by an estimated additional 19 million users listening in through third-party applications; see Jeremy Kiss: 'Last.fm widgets boost user numbers', *Guardian.co.uk*, February 28, 2008, <http://www.guardian.co.uk/media/2008/feb/28/web20.digitalmedia>, and Dan Carlin, 'Last.fm, mashing to the music', *Business Week*, November 13, 2006, <http://www.businessweek.com/technology/content/nov2006/tc20061113_604776.htm>

71 By clicking a 'Love' or 'Ban' button in the Last.fm music player, users create individual profiles.

72 The use of the Last.fm API is licensed under the Creative Commons 'Attribution-

NonCommercial-ShareAlike License', and limited to one request per second. For more information on the Last.fm API, available data are 'user profile data', 'artist data', 'album data', 'track data', 'tag data', 'group data', 'forum data', and 'geo-aware data', see <http://www.audioscrobbler.net/data/webservices>.

Last.fm subscriber Tomsky007 developed an 'audioscrobbler' for Napster, streaming the meta-information to the user's Last.fm profile <http://napscrob.sourceforge.net>.

73 A list of Last.fm mash-ups can be found at The Programmable Web, <http://www.programmableweb.com/api/last.fm/mashups>. A mobile audioscrobbler, called Mobbler, for Nokia smartphones has been developed by Last.fm subscriber Eartle, and can be found at: <http://code.google.com/p/mobbler>.

74 Pandora.fm uses the streaming service of online music provider Pandora but streams the metadata directly into the Last.fm user profile, <http://pandorafm.real-ity.com/login.php>.

75 See blog entry of Last.fm co-founder and audioscrobble programmer Richard Jones, 'Free the music', January 23, 2008, <http://blog.last.fm/2008/01/23/free-the-music>.

76 Saul Hansel, 'Warner Music ends at Last.fm', New York Times, June 6, 2008, <http://bits.blogs.nytimes.com/2008/06/06/the-warner-music-ends-at-lastfm>.

77 Eliot van Buskirk, 'Sony buys Bertelsmann's Sony BMG stake for $ 1.2 billion', Wired, August 5, 2008, <http://blog.wired.com/music/2008/08/bertelsmann-bai.html>.

78 Robert McHenry, 'The faith-based encyclopedia', TCS Daily, November 15, 2004, <http://www.tcsdaily.com/article.aspx?id=111504A>. A popular account of the debate on the question of truth and Wikipedia can be found in the documentary The Truth according to Wikipedia, VPRO, April 7, 2008, <http://www.youtube.com/watch?v=WMSinyx_Ab0>.

79 Jim Giles, 'Internet encyclopedias go head to head', Nature, Vol. 438, No. 7070, 2005.

80 Wikipedia appears in 272 different languages (as of July 2010), all of them constituting an independent encyclopaedia featuring different articles on the same topic in the different languages; they also differ significantly in scope and number. Other media formats on the infrastructure of the Wikimedia Foundation are among others, Wikiquote, a collection of quotations, Wiktionary, an online dictionary, Wikibooks, a collection of public domain learning materials, and Wikisource, a platform for translating public domain texts. See Wikimedia Foundation <http://wikimediafoundation.org/wiki/Our_projects>.

81 In January 2006, Wikipedia noticed changes made by members of the US Congress to articles on politicians. See Matthew Davis, 'Congress "made Wikipedia changes"', BBC News, February 6, 2006, <http://news.bbc.co.uk/2/hi/technology/4695376.stm>. An 'edit war' describes the conflict between different editing parties over the content of an article. Frequently subject to edit wars are controversial topics and people, such as the 'Yugoslavian Civil War', the 'Armenian Genocide', 'George W. Bush', 'Open Source', etc. Many companies and PR firms attempt to manipulate Wikipedia articles as well.

82 All examples are taken from the Wikidgame website hosted by Wired magazine and collect the 'most shameful Wikipedia spin jobs', <http://wired.reddit.com/

wikidgame/?s=top>. See also Kevin Poulsen, 'Vote on the most shameful Wikipedia spin jobs', *Wired Blog*, August 13, 2007, <http://blog.wired.com/27bstroke6/2007/08/vote-on-the-top.html>.

83 Policies for writing articles in Wikipedia include the 'neutral point of view' (NPoV) that requires each article to be written without bias and with a balanced presentation of controversies, see the official 'Wikipedia neutral point of view policy', <http://en.wikipedia.org/wiki/Wikipedia:Neutral_point_of_view>. See also Wikipedia, 'List of policies', <http://en.wikipedia.org/wiki/Wikipedia:List_of_policies>, and Wikipedia, 'List of guidelines', <http://en.wikipedia.org/wiki/Wikipedia:List_of_guidelines>.

84 History Flow can be found at <http://www.research.ibm.com/visual/projects/history_flow>.

85 The WikiScanner is hosted at <http://wikiscanner.virgil.gr/>. See also John Borland, 'See who is editing', *Wired*, August 14, 2007, <http://www.wired.com/politics/onlinerights/news/2007/08/wiki_tracker>.

86 Wikipedia, 'Request for comments/United States Congress' <http://en.wikipedia.org/wiki/Wikipedia:Requests_for_comment/United_States_Congress>.

87 See release history of the MediaWiki software, Wikipedia.org/MediaWiki <http://en.wikipedia.org/wiki/Mediawiki#Release_history>.

88 The search engine Powerset seeks to address requests formulated in natural language, and uses Wikipedia to retrieve answers. This is possible because Wikipedia's content is accessible and, more importantly, can be read by machines. Powerset <http://www.powerset.com>.
The German publisher Directmedia issued a DVD with selected articles from the German Wikipedia, as well as a book on the evolution of Wikipedia.

Resources

Background interviews and e-mail exchanges with:

Aibopet (Aibohack), Hans Bernhard (Ubermorgen.com), Canphaz, Florian Cramer, Andreas Leo Findeisen (TransformingFreedom.org), Hamtitampti (SmartXX), Edgar Hucek (Xbox-Linux), Dr. Helmut Kolba (Sony Austria), Christian Kausch (Broque), Franz Lehner (Xbox-Linux), Sebastian Lütgert (Pirate Cinema), Moritz 'mo' Sauer (Netlabel Catalogue, Phlow.de), Rnd0m; Denis Jaromil Rojo (Rastasoft), Audrey Samson (Genderchangers), Michael Steil (Xbox-Linux), Thomas Thurner (Team Teichenberg), Xwarrior.

In addition to the above interviews, two collections of interviews conducted by Andreas Leo Findeisen were used in this book:
1) Interviews with the Plone Community at Plone Conference 2005, **Semper DVD 1.0**, edited by Leo Andreas Findeisen, unpublished.
2) Interviews with the NetzNetz Community, Mana Sprint 2005, unpublished.

Websites, forums, weblogs

Aibohack <www.aibohack.com>
AIBO-Life <www.aibo-life.org>
Aibosite <http://bbs.aibosite.com>
Alexa, Web traffic statistics <www.alexa.com>
Big Boards <www.big-boards.com>
Ars Technica <www.arstechnica.com>
Fibreculture <www.fibreculture.org/>
First Monday <www.firstmonday.org>
Heise.de <www.heise.de>
Internet Archive <www.archive.org>
Internet Spec List <www.graphcomp.com/info/specs>
Nintendo DS-Scene <www.ds-scene.net>
NDSS.NL <www.ndss.nl>
PEW Internet & American Life Project <www.pewinternet.org>

PEW Internet & American Life Project, Trend Data <www.pewinternet.org/Trend-Data.aspx>
Requests for Comments <www.ietf.org/rfc.html>
Slashdot <www.slashdot.org>
Sourceforge <www.sourceforge.net>
Touchgraph Google Browser <www.touchgraph.com>
Transforming Freedom <www.transformingfreedom.org>
Wikipedia <www.wikipedia.org>
Xbox-Scene <www.xbox-scene.com>
YouTube <www.youtube.com>

Mailing lists

AIR-L, Association of Internet Researchers <http://aoir.org>
iDC List, Institute for Distributive Creativity <http://distributedcreativity.org/>
my-ci, creative industries research network <http://idash.org/mailman/listinfo/my-ci>

Literature

Abbate, Janet. 1999. *Inventing the Internet*. MIT Press: Cambridge, MA.

Adorno, Theodor W., and Max Horkheimer. 1987 [1944/47] Die Dialektik der Aufklärung. In Gesammelte Schriften, Band 5: *Die Dialektik der Aufklärung*, Horkheimer, Max. Fischer: Frankfurt a.M.

Akrich, Madeleine. 1991. The de-scription of technical objects. In *Shaping Technology/Building Society. Studies in Sociotechnological Change*, eds. Bijker, Wiebe, and John Law, 205-224. MIT Press: Cambridge.

— 1998. Les utilisateurs, acteurs de l'innovation (Users as agents of innovation), *Education permanente*, No 134: 79-89.

Alderman, John. 2001. *Sonic boom. Napster, MP3 and the new pioneers of music*. Perseus: Cambridge, MA.

Andrejevic, Mark. 2002. The work of being watched. Interactive media and the exploitation of self-disclosure. *Critical Studies in Communication*, Vol. 19, No. 2:230-248.

Aspeli, Martin. 2005. *Plone. A model of a mature open source project*. Master thesis, London School of Economics: London.

Austin, J.L. 1990 [1955]. *How to do things with words*. Oxford University Press: Oxford.

Bachrach, Peter. 1967. *The theory of democratic elitism: A critique*. Little, Brown and Company: Boston.

Bagdikian, Ben H. 2004. *The new media monopoly*. Beacon Press: Boston.

Bain, Alan, Peter T. Hess, Gerard Jones, and Carl Berelowitz. 1999. Gender differences and computer competency. The effects of a high computer access program on the computer competence of women. *International Journal of Educational Technology*. Vol. 1, No. 1, no pages.

Baker, Stephen. 2008. *The Numerati*. Houghton Mifflin Harcourt: New York

Barbrook, Richard. 1997. The digital economy: Commodities or gifts? *Nettime* mailing list, 17 June 1997 <http://subsol.c3.hu/subsol_2/contributors3/barbrooktext.html>.

— 2007. *Imaginary futures. From thinking machines to the intergalactic network*, Pluto Press: London, Ann Arbor.

Barbrook, Richard, and Piet Schultz. 1997. The digital artisan manifesto. Nettime <http://www.ljudmila.org/nettime/zkp4/72.htm>.

Bardini, Thierry, and Michael Friedewald. 2002. Chronicle of a death of a laboratory: Douglas Engelbart and the failure of he knowledge workshop. *History of Technology*, Vol. 23: 191-212.

Barlow, Perry. 1996. A declaration of the independence of cyberspace. EFF <http://homes.eff.org/~barlow/Declaration-Final.html>

Barthes, Roland. 1967. Death of the author, *Aspen* 5 and 6, <http://www.ubu.com/aspen/aspen5and6/index.html>.

Baudry, Jean-Louis. 1978. *L'Effet cinéma*. Albatros: Paris.

Bell, Gordon, and Jim Gemmel. 2007. A digital life, *Scientific American*, February 18, 2007 < http://www.sciam.com/article.cfm?id=a-digital-life>.

Beniger, James R. 1986. *The control revolution. Technological and economist origins of the information society*. Harvard University Press: Cambridge, MA.

Benjamin, Walter. 1971. *Versuche über Brecht*. Suhrkamp: Frankfurt a.M.

— 1983. The author as producer. In Walter Benjamin. *Reflections: Essays, aphorisms, autobiographical writings*, ed. Peter Demetz, 220-238. Schocken Books: New York.

Benjamin, Walter. 2003. *Medienästhetische Schriften*. Fischer: Frankfurt a.M.

— [1934] 2003. Der Autor als Produzent. In *Medienästhetische Schriften*, Walter Benjamin, 231-147. Fischer: Frankfurt a.M.

Benkler, Yochai. 2006. *Wealth of networks. How social production transforms markets and freedom*. Yale University Press: New Haven, London.

Bense, Max. 1999. Technische Existenz. In Max Bense. *Ausgewählte Schriften*, ed. Elisabeth Walter, 122-146. Metzler: Stuttgart.

Berg, Marc. 1997. Formal tools and medical practices: Getting computer-based decision techniques to work. In *Social science, technical Systems, and cooperative work. Beyond the great divide*, Berger, Peter L, and Thomas Luckmann. 1967. *The social construction of reality: a treatise in the sociology of knowledge*. Anchor: Garden City, NY.

Berners-Lee, Tim. 1989/1990. Information management. A proposal, *W3.org* <http://www.w3.org/History/1989/proposal.html>.

— 1998. The World Wide Web: A very short personal history. World Wide Web Consortium. <www.w3.org/People/Berners-Lee/ShortHistory.html>.

Berners-Lee, Tim, and Mark Fischetti. 1999. *Weaving the Web. The past, present and future of the World Wide Web by its inventor*. Orion Business: London.

Bey, Hakim. 1985, 1991. The temporary autonomous zone, ontological anarchy, poetic terrorism. *Hermetic* <http://www.hermetic.com/bey/taz_cont.html>.

Biegel, Stuart. 2003. *Beyond our control. Confronting the limits of our legal system in the age of cyberspace*. MIT Press: Cambridge, MA.

Bijker, Wiebe, and John Law, John, eds. 1992. *Shaping technology/building society. Studies in sociotechnological change*. MIT Press: Cambridge, MA.

Bijker, Wiebe, and Trevor Pinch, eds. 1987. *The social construction of technology*. MIT Press: Cambridge, MA.

Blossom, John. 2009. *Content nation. Surviving and thriving as social media changes our work, our lives and our future*. Wiley Publishing: Indianapolis.

Böhme, Hartmut; Peter Matussek, and Lothar Müller. 2002. *Orientierung Kulturwissenschaft*. Hamburg: Rohwolt.

Bolter, David J. 1984. *Turing's man. Western culture in the computer age*. The University of North Carolina Press: Chapel Hill.

Boomen, Marianne van den. 2009. Interfacing by material metaphors. How your mail box may fool you. In *Digital material: Tracing new media in everyday life and technology*, eds. Marianne van den Boomen et al. eds, 253-266. Amsterdam University Press: Amsterdam.

— forthcoming. Transcoding the Internet. How metaphors matter in digital praxis. PhD Thesis, University of Utrecht: Utrecht.

Boomen, Marianne van den, and Mirko Tobias Schäfer. 2005. Will the revolution be open sourced.? How open source travels through society. In *How Open Is the Future? Economic, Social and Cultural Scenarios inspired by Free & Open Source Software*, eds. Marleen Wynants, and Jan Cornelis, 31-68. VUB Press: Brussels.

Borgman, Christine L. 2000. From Gutenberg to the global information infrastructure. Access to information in the networked world. MIT Press: Cambridge, MA.

Bowker, Geoffrey. 1992. What's in a Patent. In Shaping technology/building society. Studies in sociotechnological change, eds. Wiebe Bijker, John Law, 53-74. MIT Press: Cambridge, MA.

Bowker, Geoffrey C. et al. eds. 1997. Social science, technical systems, and cooperative work. Beyond the great divide. LEA: Mahwah, New Jersey; London.

Brecht, Bertolt. 1999 [1932]. Der Rundfunk als Kommunikationsapparat. In Medienkultur. Die maßgeblichen Theorien von Brecht bis Baudrillard, eds. Engell, Lorenz et al., 259-263. DVA: Stuttgart.

Brockmann, John. 1996. Digerati: Encounters with the cyber elite. HardWired: San Francisco.

Bruns, Axel. 2005. Gatewatching. Collaborative online news production. Peter Lang: New York.

— 2006. Towards produsage. Futures for user-led content production. In Proceedings: Cultural Attitudes towards Communication and Technology, eds. Charles Ess, Fay Sudweeks, Herbert Hrachovec, 275-284. Murdoch: Murdoch University.

— 2007. Produsage, Generation C, and Their Effects on the Democratic Process. Conference paper at Media in Transition 5, 27-29 April 2007, MIT, Boston, <http://citeseerx.ist.psu.edu/viewdoc/download?doi10.1.1.71.2436&reprep1&typepdf>.

— 2008. Blogs, Wikipedia, Second Life, and beyond. From production to produsage. New York: Peter Lang.

Buckland, Michael. 2006. Emanuel Goldberg and his knowledge machine. Information, invention, and political forces. Westport, CT: Libraries Unlimited.

Burroughs, William S. 1961. The Cut-Up Method of Brion Gysin. In The new media reader, eds. Noah Wardrip-Fruin, and Nick Montford, 90-91. MIT Press: Cambridge, MA.

Butler, Judith, and Sara Salih. 2004. The Judith Butler reader. Blackwell Publishing: Malden, MA.

Campbell-Kelly, Martin. 2003. From Airline reservations to Sonic the Hedgehog. A History of the software industry. MIT Press: Cambridge MA.

Campbell-Kelly, Martin et al. eds. 2003. The History of mathematical tables. From Sumer to spreadsheets. Oxford: Oxford University Press.

Carpentier, Nico, and Benjamin de Cleen, eds. 2008. Participation and media production: Critical reflections on content creation. Cambridge Scholars Publishing: Newcastle.

Carroll, Jennie. 2004. Completing design in use. Closing the appropriation cycle. Proceedings of the 12th European Conference on Information Systems (ECIS 2004) <http://is2.lse.ac.uk/asp/aspecis/20040031.pdf>.

Carter Ching, Cynthia, Yasmin B. Kafai, and Sue K. Marshall. 2000 Spaces for change: Gender and technology access in collaborative software design. Journal for Science and Education Technology, Vol. 9, No. 1: 67-78.

Castells, Manuell. 2001. The Internet galaxy. Reflections on the Internet, business, and society. Oxford University Press: Oxford, New York.

Certeau, Michel de. 2003 [1980]. The practice of every day life. University of California Press: Berkley, Los Angeles, London.

Ceruzzi, Paul E. 1998. A history of modern computing. MIT Press: Cambridge, MA.

Chun, Wendy Hui Kyong. 2006. Control and freedom. Power and paranoia in the age of fiber optics. Cambridge, MA: MIT Press.

Ciborra, Claudio. 2002. The labyrinths of information. Challenging the wisdom of systems. Oxford University Press . Oxford, New York.

Cock, Christian de, James A. Fitchett, Matthew Farr. 2001. Myth of a near future. Advertising the new economy. *Ephemera*, Vol. 1, No. 3:201-228.

Copeland, Jack B. ed. 2004. *The essential Turing. The ideas that gave birth to the computer age.* Oxford University Press: Oxford, New York.

Cox, Geoff, and Joasia Krysa. 2005. *DATA browser 02. Engineering culture.* Autonomedia: Brooklyn.

Cox, Geoff, and Adrian Ward. 2008. Perl. In *Software studies: A lexicon*, ed. Matthew Fuller, 207-213. MIT Press: Cambridge, MA.

Cox, Geoff, Joasia Krysa, and Anya Lewin. 2004. *DATA browser 01. Economising culture.* Autonomedia: Brooklyn.

Cramer, Florian. 2005. *Words made flesh.* Piet Zwart Institute: Rotterdam, online <http://pzwart.wdka.hro.nl/mdr/research/fcramer/wordsmadeflesh/wordsmadeflesh.pdf>.
— 2008. Language, In *Software studies: A lexicon*, Matthew Fuller, ed, 168-174. MIT Press: Cambridge, MA.

Daniels, Dieter. 2002. *Kunst als Sendung. Von der Telegrafie zum Internet.* Beck: München.

Deibert, Ronald, John Palfrey, Rafael Rohozinski and Jonathan Zittrain (eds). 2008. *Access denied. The practice and policy of global Internet filtering.* MIT Press: Cambridge, MA.

Dierks, Oliver. 2005. *Undercover. Ein verdeckter Ermittler enthüllt Aktionen und Methoden seiner Arbeit für die Gesellschaft zur Verfolgung von Urheberrechtsverletzungen e.V. (GVU).* M-V Verlag: Münster.

Dijck, José van. 2007. Video sharing as cultural practice and peer production, *Proceedings MIT Media in Transition Conference 2007*, Boston, MA, online: <http://web.mit.edu/comm-forum/mit5/papers/vanDijck_Television2.0.article.MiT5.pdf>.

Dijck, José van, and David Nieborg. 2009. Wikinomics and its discontents. A critical analysis of collobative cultural manifestos. *New Media Society*, Vol. 11 no. 5 855-874.

Dijk, Jan van. 2006. *The network society. Social aspects of new media.* Sage: London, Thousand Oaks, CA.

Dix, Alan. 2007. Designing for Appropriation, *Proceedings of the 21st BCS HCI Group Conference 2007, British Computer Society*, Volume 2. <http://www.hcibook.com/alan/papers/HCI2007-appropriation/>.

Doctorow, Cory. 2003. *Down and out in the magic kingdom.* Tor: New York.
— 2008. *Little Brother.* Tor: New York.

Dotzler, Bernhard. 2006. *Diskurs und Medium. Zur Archäologie der Computerkultur.* Fink: München.

Douglas, Susan Jeanne. 1987. *Inventing American broadcasting, 1899-1922.* John Hopkins University Press: Baltimore, London.

Dyson, Esther. 1997. *Release 2.0: a design for living in the digital age.* Broadway: New York.

Dyson, Freeman J. 1998. Science as craft Industry. *Science*, Vol. 280. No. 5366: 1014-1015 < http://www.sciencemag.org/cgi/content/full/280/5366/1014?view=full#Dyson>.

Edwards, Paul S. 1990. The army and the microworld: Computers and the politics of gender identity. *Signs: Journal of Women in Society*, Vol 16, No. 1: 02-127.

Electronic Frontier Foundation (EFF). 2006. *Unintended consequences. Seven years under the DMCA.* EFF, <http://www.eff.org/wp/unintended-consequences-seven-years-under-dmca>.

Ellul, Jaques. 1964. *The technological society.* Vintage: New York.

Engelbart, Douglas. 1962. *Augmenting human intellect: A conceptual framework*, Stanford Research Park, Menlo Park, CA.

Enochsson, Annbritt. 2005. A gender perspective on Internet use: Consequences for information seeking on the net. *Information Research*, Vol. 10 No. 4, <http://informationr. net/ir/10-4/paper237.html>.

Enzensberger, Hans Magnus. 1999 [1970] Baukasten zu einer Theorie der Medien, In *Medienkultur. Die maßgeblichen Theorien von Brecht bis Baudrillard*, eds. Engell, Lorenz et al., 264-278. DVA: Stuttgart.

Ernst, Wolfgang. 2007. *Das Gesetz des Gedächtnisses. Medien und Archive am Ende (des 20. Jahrhunderts)*. Kadmos: Berlin.

Feenberg, Andrew. 1999. *Questioning technology*, London. Routledge: London, New York.

Fickers, Andreas. 2007. Design als 'mediating interface'. Zur Zeugen- und Zeichenhaftigkeit des Radioapparates. *Symposium der Gesellschaft für Wisenschaftsgeschichte*, No. 43, Vol. 30, No 3: 199-213.

Findeisen, Andreas Leo. 2003. Some code to die for. In *Ars Electronica. Code. The language of our time*, eds. Gerfried Stocker, and Christine Schöpf, 73-87. Hatje Cantz: Ostfildern.

Fiske, John. 1995 [1987]. *Television Culture*, London, Routledge: London, New York.

Flichy, Patrice. 1999. The Construction of New Digital Media, *New Media Society*, Vol. 1, No. 1: 33-39.

— 2002. New media history. In *The handbook of new media*, eds. Leah A. Lievrouw, and Sonja Livingstone, eds, 187-204. Sage Publications: Thousand Oaks.

— 2007. *The Internet imaginaire*. MIT Press: Cambridge, MA.

Florida, Richard. 2002. *The rise of the creative class*. Basic Books: New York.

Foucault, Michel. 1977. What is an author? In *Language, counter-memory, practice*, ed. Donald F. Bouchard, 113-138. Cornell University Press: New York.

Freiberger, Paul; Swaine, Michael. 2000. *Fire in the valley. The making of the personal computer*. McGraw-Hills: New York.

Friedewald, Michael. 1999. *Der Computer als Werkzeug und Medium*. GNT Verlag: Berlin, Diepholz.

Friedman, Batya ed. 1997. *Human values and the design of computer technology*. Cambridge University Press: Cambridge.

Fuchs, Christian. 2009. Social networking sites and the surveillance society. *ICT&S Center Research Report*, Salzburg, Vienna. <http://fuchs.icts.sbg.ac.at/SNS_Surveillance_Fuchs>.pdf.

Fuller, Matthew. 2003a. *Behind the blip. Essays on the culture of software*. Autonomedia: Brooklyn.

— 2003b. *The impossibility of interface*. Piet Zwart Institute: Rotterdam.

— 2005. *Media ecologies. Materialist energies in art and technoculture*. MIT Press: Cambridge, MA.

— ed. 2008. *Software studies: A lexicon*. MIT Press: Cambridge, MA.

Galloway, Alex. 2004. *Protocol: How control exists after decentralization*. MIT Press: Cambridge, MA.

Gates, Bill, Nathan Myhrvold and Peter Rinearson. 1995. *The road ahead*. Viking: New York.

— 1999. *Business @ the speed of thought : using a digital nervous system*. Warner books: New York.

Gemmell, Jim, Gordon Bell, and Roger Lueder. 2006. MyLifeBits: a personal database for everything. Communications of the ACM, Vol. 49, No. 1. 88-95.

Gemmel, Jim et al. 2002. *MyLifeBits: Fulfilling the Memex vision.* Proceedings ACM Multimedia '02: 235-238. http://research.microsoft.com/~jgemmell/pubs/MyLifeBitsMM02.pdf.

Gibson, William. [1982] 2003. Burning chrome. In *Burning Chrome*, William Gibson, 179-204. Eos: New York.

Gibson, William. 1984. *Neuromancer.* Ace Books: New York.

Gibson, William, and Bruce Sterling. 1990. *The difference engine.* Gollancz: London.

Gillies, James, and Robert Cailliau. 2000. *How the web was born: The story of the World Wide Web.* Oxford University Press: Oxford, New York.

Gilmore, Dan. 2006. *We the media: Grassroots journalism, by the people, for the people.* O'Reilly Media: Sebastopol, CA.

Golder, Scott, and Huberman, Bernardo A. 2006. Usage patterns of collaborative tagging systems. *Journal of Information Science,* Vol. 32, No. 2: 198-208, <www.hpl.hp.com/research/idl/papers/tags/tags.pdf.>.

Goldman, Robert, Stephen Papson, and Noah Kersey. 1998/2003. *Landscapes of global capital. Moral landscapes. Representations of global capital,* <www.lclark.edu/~goldman/global/pageslandscapes/ciscoscapes.htm>.

Gosh, Rishab Aiyer. 1998. Cooking pot markets: An economic model for the trade in free goods and services on the Internet. *First Monday,* Vol. 3, No. 3 <www.uic.edu/htbin/cgiwrap/bin/ojs/index.php/fm/article/view/580/501>.

Gosh, Rishab Aiyer ed. 2005. *Code. Collaborative ownership and the digital economy.* MIT Press: Cambridge.

Gosh, Rishab Aiyer, et al. 2002. FLOSS: Free/libre/open source software study. Final report, Part IV, *International Institute of Infonomics/MERIT,* <http://flossproject.org/report/>.

Green, Shoshanna, Cynthia Jenkins, and Henry Jenkins. 1998. Normal female interest in men bonking: Selections from 'The Terra Nostra Underground' and 'Strange Bedfellows'. In *Theorizing fandom: Fans, subculture and identity,* eds. Cheryl Harris, and Alison Alexander, 9-38. Hampton: New Jersey: Hampton.

Habermas, Jürgen. 1990 [1962]. *Strukturwandel der Öffentlichkeit.* Suhrkamp: Frankfurt a.M.

Hall, Stuart. 1980. Encoding/decoding. In *Culture, media, language,* ed. Stuart Hall, 128-138. Routledge: London, 128-138.

Hally, Mike. 2005. *Electronic brains. Stories from the dawn of the computer age.* Granta Books: London.

Halpern, Sheldon. 2003. Copyright Law and the challenge of digital technology. In *Image ethics in the digital age,* eds. Larry Gross, John Stuart Katz, and Jay Ruby, 143-170, University of Minnesota Press: Minneapolis, London.

Hammond, Tony et al. 2005. Social bookmarking tools I. A general review. *D-Lib Magazine* <http://www.dlib.org/dlib/april05/hammond/04hammond.html>.

Haraway, Donna J. 1991. A cyborg manifesto: Science, technology, and socialist-feminism in the late twentieth century. In *Simians, cyborgs and women: the reinvention of nature,* ed. D. J. Haraway. Routledge: New York.

Hardt, Michael, and Antonio Negri. 2001. *Empire.* Harvard University Press. Cambridge, MA.

— *Multitude. War and democracy in the age of empire,* Penguin Books: New York.

Hartmann, Frank. 2000. *Medienphilosophie.* Facultas/WUV: Wien.

— 2006. *Globale Medienkultur.* Facultas/WUV: Wien.

Hayles, N. Katherine. 2007. Intermediation: The pursuit of a vision. *New Literary History*, Vol. 38, No 1: 99-125.

Heath, Stephen. 1981. *Questions of cinema*. Macmillan: London.

Hebdige, Dick. 1981 [1978]. *Subculture. The meaning of style*. Routledge: London, New York.

Heidegger, Martin. 2002. [1962]. *Die Technik und die Kehre*. Klett-Cotta: Stuttgart.

Herbst, Claudia. 2008. *Sexing code. Subversion, theory, and representation*. Cambridge Scholars Publishing: Newcastle.

Hesmondhalgh, David. 2002. *The Culture Industries*, Sage: Thousand Oaks, London.

Hippel, Eric von. 2005. *Democratizing innovation*, MIT Press: Cambridge, MA.

— 1988. *The sources of innovation*. Oxford University Press: Oxford, New York.

Hobart, Michael E., and Zachary S. Schiffman. 2000. *Information ages. Literacy, numeracy and the computer revolution*. John Hopkins University Press: Baltimore, MD.

Horkheimer, Max. 1987. *Gesammelte Schriften, Band 5: Die Dialektik der Aufklärung*. Fischer: Frankfurt a.M.

Huang, Andrew. 2002. *Keeping secrets in hardware: The Microsoft Xbox case study*. MIT AI Lab Memo. <http://web.mit.edu/bunnie/www/proj/anatak/AIM-2002-008.pdf>.

— 2003. *Hacking the Xbox: An introduction to reverse engineering*. No Starch Press: San Francisco, CA.

Hughes, Jerald, Karl Lang. 2006. Transmutability. Digital decontextualization, manipulation, and recontextualization as a new source of value in the production and consumption of culture products. *Proceedings of the 39th Annual Hawaii International Conference on System Sciences* (HICSS'06). <http://doi.ieeecomputersociety.org/10.1109/HICSS.2006.511>.

Huws, Ursula. 2003. *The making of a cybertariat. Virtual work in a real world*. Monthly Review Press: New York.

Hyde, Adam. 2006. Against Web 2.0. *Institute for Distributed Creativity*, mailing list, May 30 2006 <https://lists.thing.net/pipermail/idc/2006-May/001535.html>.

Jaromil. 2005. Rasta Software. In *DATA browser 02. Engineering culture*, eds. Geoff Cox, and Joasia Krysa, 203-208. Autonomedia: Brooklyn.

Jenkins, Henry. 1991. *Textual poachers. Television fans and participatory culture*, London, New York: Routeledge.

— 2002. Interactive audiences? The collective intelligence of media fans. In *The new media book*, ed. Dan Harries, BFI: London. <http://web.mit.edu/21fms/www/faculty/henry3/collective%20intelligence.html>.

— 2006a. *Fans, bloggers, and gamers: Exploring participatory culture*, NYU Press: New York.

— 2006b. *Convergence culture. Where old and new media collide*, NYU Press: New York.

Jenkins, Henry, Katie Clinton, Ravi Purushotma, Alice J. Robison, and Margaret Weigel. 2006. *Confronting the challenges of participatory culture: media education for the 21st century*. MacArthur Foundation. <http://www.digitallearning.macfound.org/atf/cf/%7B7E45C7E0-A3E0-4B89-AC9C-E807E1B0AE4E%7D/JENKINS_WHITE_PAPER. PDF>.

Joerges, Bernward. 1999. Do politics have artifacts? *Social Studies of Science*, Vol. 29, No. 3: 411-431.

Kay, Alan. 1990. User interface: A personal view. In *The Art of Human-Computer Interface Design*, ed. Laurel, Brenda, 191-207. Addison-Wesley: Reading, MA.

Kay, Alan C. 1972. A personal computer for children of all ages. *Xerox Palo Alto Research Cen-*

ter: *Proceedings of the ACM National Conference*. Palo Alto.

— Personal computing. *Proceedings meeting on 20 years of computer science*, Instituto Elaborazione della Informazione, Pisa, Italy.

Kay, Alan, and Adele Goldberg, 2003 [1977]. Personal dynamic media. In *The new media reader*, eds. Noah Wardrip-Fruin, and Nick Montfort, 393-404. MIT Press: Cambridge, MA: MIT Press.

Keen, Andrew. 2007. *The cult of the amateur. How today's Internet is killing our culture and assaulting our economy*. Doubleday: New York, London.

Keif, Tine, and Wendy Faulkner, Wendy. 2003. 'I'm no athlete [but] I can make this thing dance!' Men's pleasures in technology. *Science, Technology and Human Values*, Vol. 28, No. 2: 296-325.

Kelly, Kevin. 1998. *New rules for the new economy*. Viking: New York.

Kessler, Frank. 2002. *Het idee van vooruitgang in de mediageschiedschrijving*, University of Utrecht.

— 2006. *Notes on the Dispositif*, unpublished paper, <http://www.let.uu.nl/~Frank. Kessler/personal/notes%20on%20dispositif.pdf>.

Kittler, Friedrich.1996. There is no software. In *Electronic culture. Technology and visual representation*, ed. Timothy Druckery, 331-337. Aperture: New York.

— 2001. Eine Geschichte der Kulturwissenschaft. München: Fink.

Kow, Yong Ming and Bonnie Nardi (eds). 2010. User creativity, governance, and the new media. *First Monday*, Vol. 15, No. 5.

Kristeva, Julia. [1969] 1986. *Word, dialog, novel. The Kristeva reader*, ed. Toril Moi, 34-61. Columbia University Press: New York.

Krol, Ed. 1992. *The whole Internet catalogue and user's guide*. O'Reilly: Sebastopol, CA.

Kurt, Tod E. 2006. *Hacking Roomba*. Wiley: Indianapolis.

Kustritzt, Anne. 2003. Slashing the romance narrative. *Journal of American Culture*, Vol. 26, No. 3: p371-384.

Lakoff, George, and Mark Johnson. 1980. *Metaphors we live by*. University of Chicago Press: Chicago, London.

Lanier, Jaron. 2006. Digital Maoism. The hazards of the new online collectivism, *Edge* < http://www.edge.org/3rd_culture/lanier06/lanier06_index.html>.

— 2010. *You are not a gadget*. Alfred A. Knopf: New York.

Latour, Bruno. 1987. *Science in action*. Harvard University Press: Cambridge, MA.

— 1991. Technology is society made durable. In *A Sociology of Monsters. Essays on Power, Technology and Domination*, ed. John Law, 103-131. Routledge: London.

— 1992. Where are the missing masses. A sociology of mundane artifacts. In *Shaping technology/building society. Studies in sociotechnological change*, eds. Wiebe Bijker, and John Law, 225-258. MIT Press: Cambridge, MA.

— 1993. *We have never been modern*. Harvester Wheatsheaf: New York.

— 1999. *Pandora's hope*. Cambridge, MA: Harvard University Press.

— 2005a. From realpolitik to dingpolitik. In *Making things public*, eds. Bruno Latour, and Peter Weibel, 14-43. MIT Press: Cambridge, MA.

— 2005b. *Reassembling the social*. Oxford University Press: Oxford, New York.

Lauer, Josh. 2008. Alienation in the information economy: Toward a Marxist critique of consumer surveillance. In *Participation and media production: Critical reflections on content creation*, eds. Nico Carpentier, and Benjamin de Cleen, 41-53. Cambridge Scholars Publishing: Newcastle.

Law, John, ed. 1991. *A Sociology of monsters. Essays on power, technology and domination.* Routledge: London.

Leadbeater, Charles and Paul Miller. 2004. *The pro-am revolution.* Demos: London.

Leadbeater, Charles. 2008. *We think. Mass innovation, not mass production.* Profile Books: London.

Lécuyer, Christophe. 2005. *Making Silicon Valley: Innovation and the growth of high tech, 1930-1970.* MIT Press: Cambridge, MA.

Lenhardt, Amanda and Mary Madden. 2007. Social Networking Websites and Teens. An Overview, *PEW Internet & American Life Project*, January 7, 2007, online: <http://www.pewInternet.org/PPF/r/198/report_display.asp>.

Lenhart, Amanda, Kristen Purcell, Aaron Smith, Kathryn Zickuhr. 2010. Social media and young adults. *PEW Internet & American Life Project*, February 3, 2010, online: <http://www.pewinternet.org/Reports/2010/Social-Media-and-Young-Adults.aspx>.

Lessig, Lawrence. 2000. *Code and other laws of cyberspace.* Basic Books: New York.

— 2001. *The future of ideas. The fate of the commons in a connected world.* Random House: New York.

— 2004. *Free culture. How big media uses technology and the law to lock down culture and control creativity.* Penguin Press: New York.

— 2008. *Remix.* Penguin Press: New York.

Lévy, Pierre. 1999. *Collective intelligence. Mankind's emerging world in cyberspace.* Perseus Books: Cambridge, MA.

Licklider, Joseph C.R. 1965. *Libraries of the future.* Cambridge, MA: MIT Press.

Licklider, Joseph C.R., and Robert Taylor. 1968. The computer as communication device. Reprint from *Science and Technology*, April 1968, <http://gatekeeper.dec.com/pub/DEC/SRC/publications/taylor/licklider-taylor.pdf>.

Lindgren, Michael. 1990. *Glory and failure: The difference engines of Johann Müller, Charles Babbage, and Georg and Edvard Sheutz.* MIT Press: Cambridge, MA.

Lovink, Geert. 2003a. *Dark fiber: Tracking critical Internet culture.* MIT Press: Cambridge, MA.

— 2003b. *My first recession. Critical Internet culture in transition.* V2_/NAI Publishers: Rotterdam.

— 2008. *Zero comments. Blogging and critical Internet culture.* Routledge: London, New York.

Malkin, Gary. 1992. Who's who in the Internet: Biographies of IAB, IESG and IRSG members. RFC 1336, FYI 9, May 1992.

Manovich, Lev. 2001. *The language of new media.* MIT Press: Cambridge, MA.

Marwick, Alice. 2007. I can make you a (net) celebrity overnight: Fan production and participatory culture in online reality shows. *Proceedings MIT Media in Transition Conference 2007.* Cambridge, MA.

Mattelart, Armand. 2007. Für eine neue Internet-Regierung. *Le Monde Diplomatique*, August 2007: 4.

McLuhan, Marshall. 1951: *The mechanical bride.* Ginko Press: Corte Madera,CA.

— 1962. The Gutenberg galaxy. The making of typographic man. Toronto University Press: Toronto.

— 1964. Understanding media. The extension of men. Routledge: London, New York.

— 2001 [1967]. The medium is the massage. Gingko Press: Corte Madera, CA.

Metz, Christian. 1977. Le signifiant imaginaire. UGE, Vol.10, No 18, Paris.

Meyrowitz, Norman. 1991. Hypertext - does it reduce cholesterol, too? In *From Memex to hypertext. Vannevar Bush and the mind's machine*, eds. James M.. Nyce, and Paul Kahn, 287-318. Academic Press: San Diego.

Miller, Toby. 2006. The international division of cultural labour. *Proceedings CRESC Conference 2006*. Oxford.

Mitchell, William J. 1996. *City of bits: space, place, and the infobahn*. Mit Press: Cambridge, MA.

Monarch, Ira A. Et al. 1997. Mapping sociotechnical networks in the making, In *Social science, technical systems, and cooperative work. Beyond the great divide*, eds. Geoffrey Bowker et al., 331-354. LEA: Mahwah, New Jersey; London.

Morozov, Evgeny. 2010a. The Digital Dictatorship. *Wall Street Journal*, February 20, 2010, <http://online.wsj.com/article/SB10001424052748703983004575073911147404540. html>.

Morozov, Evgeny, 2010b. Vorsicht, Freund hört mit! *Frankfurter Allgemeine Zeitung*, March 18, 2010, online: <www.faz.net/-00muws>.

Müller, Eggo. 2009. Formatted spaces of participation. In *Digital material: Tracing new media in everyday life and technology*, eds. Marianne van den Boomen et al., 49-64. Amsterdam University Press: Amsterdam.

Münker, Stefan. 2009. *Emergenz digitaler Öffentlichkeiten. Die Sozialen Medien im Web 2.0*. Suhrkamp: Frankfurt a.M.

Negroponte, Nicholas. 1995. *Being digital*. Vintage Books: New York.

Nelson, Ted. 1965. A file structure for the complex, The changing and the indeterminate. *Proceedings ACM 20th National Conference*. 84-100.

— 1987 [1974]. *Computer lib/dream machines*. Revised edition. Tempus Books, Microsoft Press: Redmond.

— 2003. From computer lib/dream machines. In *The new media reader*, eds. Noah Wardrip-Fruin, and Nick Montfort, 301-340. MIT Press: Cambridge, MA.

Nieborg, David B. 2005. Am I mod or not? - An analysis of first person shooter modification culture. *Creative Gamers Seminar - Exploring Participatory Culture in Gaming*. Hypermedia Laboratory, University of Tampere http://www.gamespace.nl/content/ DBNieborg2005_CreativeGamers.pdf.

Norman, Donald. 1998. *The design of everyday things*. MIT Press: Cambridge, MA.

Oberholzer, Felix, and Koleman Strumpf. 2004. The effect of filesharing on record sales. An empirical analysis. *Journal of Political Economy*. Vol. 115, No.1:1-42.

OECD. 2007. Working Party on the Information Economy. Participative Web, User Created Content. OECD, Directorate Science, Technology and Industry, *Committee for Information, Computer and Communications Policy*, online <http://www.oecd.org/ dataoecd/57/14/38393115.pdf>.

O'Reilly, Tim. 2005. What is Web 2.0. *O'Reilly Media*, <http://www.oreillynet.com/pub/a/ oreilly/tim/news/2005/09/30/what-is-web-20.html>.

O'Reilly, Tim, and John Battelle. 2009. Web squared. Web 2.0 five years on. *Web 2.0 Summit 2009*, San Francisco, <http://assets.en.oreilly.com/1/event/28/web2009_web-squared-whitepaper.pdf>.

Oudshoorn, Nelly and Trevor Pinch. *How users matter*. MIT Press: Cambridge, MA.

Pacey, Arnold. 1983. *The culture of technology*. MIT Press: Cambridge, MA.

Papert, Seymour. 1980. *Mindstorms: Children, computers, and powerful ideas*. Basic Books: New York.

Parikka, Jussi. 2008. Copy. In *Software studies: A lexicon*, ed. Matthew Fuller, 70-78. MIT Press: Cambridge, MA.

Pateman, Carole. 1970. *Participation and democratic theory*. Cambridge University Press: Cambridge.

Peeters, Hugues and Philippe Charlier. 1999. Contributions à une théorie du dispositif. *Hermès*, No. 25:15-23.

Perry, Ruth, and Lisa Greber. 1990. Women and computers: An introduction. Signs: Journal of Women in Society and Culture. Vol 16, No. 1:74-101.

Peters, John Durham. 1999. *Speaking into the air. A history of the idea of communication*. Chicago University Press: Chicago.

Petersen, Søren, Mørk. 2008. Loser generated content. From participation to exploitation. In *First Monday*, Vol. 13, No. 3, <http://firstmonday.org/htbin/cgiwrap/bin/ojs/index.php/fm/article/view/2141/1948>.

Plant, Sadie. 1997. *Zeroes + ones: Digital women and the new technoculture*. Doubleday: New York.

Polgar, Tamás. 2008. *Freax. The brief history of the computer demoscene*. CSW Verlag: Winnenden.

Prieur, Christophe, Dominique Cardon, Jean-Samuel Beuscart, Nicolas Pissard, and Pascal Pons. 2008. The strength of weak cooperation: A case study on Flickr, *Arxiv.org*, < http://arxiv.org/abs/0802.2317>.

Rainie, Lee. 2007. Tagging, *PEW Internet & American Life Project*, <http://www.pewInternet.org/PPF/r/201/report_display.asp>.

Raymond, E.S. 1998. The cathedral and the bazaar. First Monday, Vol 3, No 3, <http://www.firstmonday.org/issues/issue3_3/raymond/>.

Reeves, Jack W. 1992. What is Software Design? *C++ Journal*, <http://www.bleading-edge.com/Publications/C++Journal/Cpjour2.htm>.

Renner, Tim. 2004. *Kinder, der Tod ist gar nicht so schlimm. Über die Zukunft der Musikindustrie*. Campus: Frankfurt a.M.

Reunanen, Markku. 2010. *Computer demos. Whate makes them tick?* Dissertation. Aalto University: Helsinki.

Rheingold, Howard. 1991. *Virtual reality*. Summit Books: New York.

— 1993. *The virtual community. Homesteading on the electronic frontier*. Addison Wesley. <http://www.rheingold.com/vc/book/intro.html>.

— 2002. *Smart mobs. The next social revolution*. Perseus Books: Cambridge, MA.

Rieder, Bernhard. 2005. Networked control. Search engines and symmetry of confidence. *International Review of Information Ethics*, Vol. 3, No. 06: 26-32.

— 2006. *Métatechnologies et délégation. Pour un design orienté-société dans l'ère du Web 2.0*. Dissertation. Université Paris 8: Paris, <http://tel.archives-ouvertes.fr/docs/00/17/99/80/PDF/THESE_rieder.pdf>.

— 2007. Teilhaben am Objekt. Adaptierbarkeit als Knotenpunkt von Kultur und Technik. *Proceedings Kongress Kulturwissenschaftliche Technikforschung '07*, Universität Hamburg: Hamburg.

— 2008. Entre marché et communauté : une discussion de la culture participative à l'exemple de Google Maps. In *Actes de la conférence Ludovia 2008*, Ludovia 2008: Do it yourself 2.0, <http://archivesic.ccsd.cnrs.fr/sic_00329899/en/>.

Rifkin, Jeremy. 2001. *The age of access: The new culture of hypercapitalism, where all of life is a paid-for experience*. Tarcher: New York.

Roettgers, Janko. 2007. Piracy beyond P2P, *NewTeeVee*, June 17, 2007, <http://newteevee.com/2007/06/17/one-click-hosters>.

Rosenberg, Scott. 2007. *Dreaming in code: two dozen programmers, three years, 4,732 bugs, and one quest for transcendent software*. Crown Publishers.

Royce, Winston W. 1970. Managing the development of large software systems: concepts and techniques. *RW Software Series*, SS-70-01.

Rushkoff, Douglas.1995. *Cyberia: life in the trenches of hyperspace*. HarperCollins: New York.
— 1996. *Children of Chaos*. Harper Collins: New York.

Schäfer, Mirko Tobias. 2004a. Made by users. How users improve things, provide innovation and change our idea of culture. In *Read_Me. Software art and cultures*, eds. Olga Goriunova, and Alexei Shulgin, 62-77. Aarhus University Press.
— 2004b. Homework. The extension of the culture industry. In *DATA Browser 01. Economising culture*, eds. Geoff Cox, Joasia Krysa, and Anya Lewin, 191-199. Autonomedia: Brooklyn.
— 2006. Spielen jenseits der Gebrauchsanweisung. Partizipation als Output des Konsums softwarebasierter Produkte. In *Das Spiel mit dem Medium. Partizipation – Immersion – Interaktion*, eds. Britta Neitzel, Britta, and Rolf Nohr, 296-310. Schüren: Marburg.
— 2006b. Agency matters! The in-between of software, hardware and user communities. Paper presented at *CRESC Conference 2006*, Oxford.

Schäfer, Mirko Tobias, and Patrick Kranzlmüller. 2007. RTFM! Teach-yourself culture in open source software projects. In *Didactics of microlearning*, ed. Theo Hug, 324-240. Waxman: Berlin, New York.

Schäfer, Mirko Tobias, and Bernhard Rieder. 2008. Beyond engineering. Software design as bridge over the culture/technology dichotomy. In *Philosophy and design: From engineering to architecture*, eds. Pieter E. Vermaas et al, 152-164. Springer: Dordrecht.

Schäfer, Mirko Tobias. 2009. Participation inside? User activities between design and appropriation. In Marianne van den Boomen, Sybille Lammes, Ann-Sophie Lehmann, Joost Raessens, Mirko Tobias Schäfer: *Digital material. Tracing new media in everday life and technology*, Amsterdam: Amsterdam University Press, 2009, 147-158.

Scholz, Trebor. 2007a. A history of the social web. *Collectivate.net*, <http://www.collectivate.net/journalisms/2007/9/26/a-history-of-the-social-web.html>.
— 2007b. What the MySpace generation should know about working for free. *Collectivate.net*, <http://www.collectivate.net/journalisms/2007/4/3/what-the-myspace-generation-should-know-about-working-for-free.html>.
— 2008. Market ideology and the myths of Web 2.0. First Monday, Vol 13. No 3 < http://www.uic.edu/htbin/cgiwrap/bin/ojs/index.php/fm/article/view/2138/1945>.
— 2009. Post.mortem conference mashup. The Internet as playground and factory. December 18, 2009, *Collectivate.net*, <http://molodiez.org/ipf_report_pdf12202009.doc>.

Schleiner, Ann-Marie. 2005. Game reconstruction workshop: Demolishing and evolving PC games and gamer culture. In *Handbook of computer game studies*, eds. Joost Raessens, and Jeffrey Goldberg, 405-414. MIT Press: Cambridge, MA.

Sennett, Richard. 2006. *The culture of the new capitalism*. Yale University Press: New Haven, London.

Shaw, Donald L., and Maxwell McCombs, eds. 1977. *The emergence of American political issues*. West: St. Paul, MN.

Shirky, Clay. 2008. *Here comes everybody. The power of organizing without organizations*. Penguin Press: London, New York.

Shirky, Clay. 2010. *Cognitive surplus: Creativity and generosity in a connected age*. Penguin Press: London, New York.

Sihvonen, Tanja. 2010. *Players unleashed! Modding the Sims and game culture*. Amsterdam University Press: Amsterdam.

Simondon, Gilbert. 1980 [1958].*On the mode of existence of technical objects*, trans. Ninian Mellamphy, unpublished. University of Western Ontario: London, Ontario.

Siwek, Stephen E. 2007. The true cost of sound recording piracy to the U.S. economy. *Institute for Policy Innovation, Policy Report*, No. 188.

Sloterdijk, Peter. 2004. *Sphären III, Schäume*. Suhrkamp: Frankfurt a.M.: Suhrkamp.

Smith, Bradford L. 2005. The Future of software. Enabling the market place to decide. In *How open is the future? Economic, social and cultural scenarios inspired by free and open source software*, eds. Marleen Wynants and Jan Cornelis, 461-477. Brussels University Press: Brussels.

Stalder, Felix, and Jesse Hirsh, Jesse. 2002. Open source intelligence. *First Monday*, Vol. 7, No. 6, <http://firstmonday.org/issues/issue7_6/stalder/index.html>.

Stallman, Richard. 2002. *Free software, free society*. GNU Press: Boston, MA.

Sterling, Bruce. 1993. *The hacker crackdown. Law and disorder on the electronic frontier*. Bantam: New York.

Stocker, Gerfried, and Christine Schöpf, eds. 2003. *Ars Electronica. Code. The language of our time*. Hatje Cantz: Ostfildern.

Sturgeon, Timothy J. 2000. How Silicon Valley came to be. In *Understanding Silicon Valley: Anatomy of an entrepreneurial region*, Martin Kenney, ed. Stanford University Press: Stanford.

Takahashi, Dean. 2006. *The Xbox 360 uncloaked. The real story behind Microsoft's next-generation video game console*. Spiderworks: No place.

Tapscott, Don, Anthony D. Williams. 2006. *Wkinomics. How mass collaboration changes everything*. Portfolio: New York.

Tasajärvi, Lassi. 2004. *Demoscene. The art of the realtime*. Even Lake Studios: Helsinki.

Terranova, Tiziana. 2004. *Network culture. Politics for the information age*, Pluto Press: London, Ann Arbor.

Timmers, Bram. 2005. *Netlabels and open content. Making the next step towards extended cultural production*. Master Thesis. Utrecht University: Utrecht.

Toffler, Alvin. 1980. *The third wave*. William Morrow: New York.

Turing, Alan M. 1948. Intelligent machinery. National Physical Laboratory Report, 1948, Turing Archive <http://www.alanturing.net/turing_archive/archive/l/l32/L32-001.html>.

— 2004 [1936]. On computable numbers, with an application to the Entscheidungsproblem. In *The essential Turing. The ideas that gave birth to the computer age*, ed. Jack B. Copeland, 58-90. Oxford University Press: Oxford, New York.

— 1948. Intelligent Machinery. National Physical Laboratory Report. *Turing Archive* <www.alanturing.net/turing_archive/archive/l/l32/L32-001.html>.

Turkle, Sherry. 1997. *Life on the screen*. Phoenix: London.

Ullman, Ellen. 2003. The bug: a novel. Random House: New York.

Uricchio, William. 2004a. Cultural Citizenship in the Age of P2P Networks. In European Culture and the Media, eds. Ib Bondebjerg, and Peter Golding, 139-164. Bristol. Intellect Books.

— 2004b. Beyond the great divide. Collaborative networks and the challenge to dominant conceptions of creative industries. *The International Journal of Cultural Studies*, Vol 7, No. 1:79-90.

— 2007. The culture of creative convergence. Lecture at Royal Netherlands Academy of Arts and Sciences. January 24, 2007.

— 2009. Moving beyond the artefact. lessons from participatory culture. In *Digital material: Tracing new media in everyday life and technology*, eds. Marianne van den Boomen et al., 135-146. Amsterdam University Press: Amsterdam.

Vaidhynathan, Siva. 2001. *Copyrights and copywrongs. The rise of intellectual property and how it threatens creativity*. New York University Press: New York, London.

Viégas, Fernanda B., Martin Wattenberg, and Kushal Dave. 2004. Studying cooperation and conflict between authors with History Flow visualisations, *Proceedings Conference on Human Factors in Computing Systems (CHI)*, 575-582. ACM: Vienna, <http://web.media.mit.edu/~fviegas/papers/history_flow.pdf>.

Vigh, David, and Tamás Polgar. 2006. *Freax. The brief history of the computer demoscene. The art album*. CSW Verlag: Winnenden.

Virno, Paolo. 2004. *A Grammar of the multitude*. Semiotexte. Los Angeles.

Vries, Imar de. 2008. *Tantalizingly close. An archeology of communication desires in discourses of mobile wireless media*. Dissertation. Utrecht University: Utrecht.

Wales, Jimmy. 2005. Free the Encyclopedia, *Lessig.org*, August 7 2005, <http://lessig.org/blog/2005/08/free_the_encyclopedia.html>.

Walker, John. 2003. The digital imprimatur. Knowledge, Technology and Policy, Vol.16, No.3: 24–77, <http://www.fourmilab.ch/documents/digital-imprimatur/>.

Wardrip-Fruin, Noah; and Nick Montfort. 2003. *The new media reader*. MIT Press: Cambridge, MA.

Weber, Steven. 2005. *The success of open source*. Harvard University Press: Cambridge, MA.

Williams, Michael R. 2003. Difference engines: From Müller to Comrie. In *The History of mathematical tables. From sumer to spreadsheets*, eds. Martin Campbell-Kelly et al., 123-142. Oxford: Oxford University Press.

Williams, Raymond. 2003 [1974]. *Television. Technology and cultural form*. Routledge: London, New York.

Willinsky, John. 2005. *The access principle. The case for open access to research and scholarship*. MIT Press: Cambridge, MA.

Winner, Langdon. 1986. *The whale and the reactor: a search for limits in an age of high technology*. University of Chicago Press: Chicago.

Winograd, Terry. 1996. *Bringing design to software*. Addison-Wesley: New York.

Winograd, Terry, and Fernando Flores. 1986. *Understanding computers and cognition*. Alex Publishing: Norwood.

Wynants, Marleen. 2005. Free as in freedom, not gratis. An interview with Richard Stallman. In *How open is the future? Economic, social and cultural scenarios inspired by free and open Source software*, eds. Marleen Wynants, and Jan Cornelis, 69-84. Brussels University Press: Brussels.

Wynants, Marleen, and Jan Cornelis, eds. 2005. *How open is the future? Economic, social and cultural scenarios inspired by free and open source software.* Brussels University Press: Brussels.

Zimmer, Michael. 2007. The panoptic gaze of Web 2.0. How Web 2.0 platforms act as infrastructures of dataveillance. Paper presented at *Social Software and Web 2.0: Critical Perspectives and Challenges for Research and Business,* October 6, 2007, Aarhus, http://michaelzimmer.org/files/Zimmer%20Aalborg%20talk.pdf.

Zimmer, Michael. 2008. The externalities of search 2.0: The emerging privacy threats when the drive for the perfect search engine meets Web 2.0. *First Monday,* Vol 13, No. 3, <http://www.uic.edu/htbin/cgiwrap/bin/ojs/index.php/fm/article/view/2136/1944>.

Zittrain, Jonathan. 2008. *The future of the Internet, and how to stop it.* Yale University Press: New Haven, London.

Appendix A
Abbreviations

ACTA	Anti-Counterfeiting Trade Agreement
ANT	Actor-Network Theory
AJAX	Asynchronous Javascript and XML
API	Application Programming Interface
CC	Creative Commons
CPU	Central Processing Unit
DIY	Do-It-Yourself
DMCA	Digital Millennium Copyright Act
DRM	Digital Rights Management
EFF	Electronic Frontier Foundation
EXIF	Exchangeable Image File Format
EULA	End User License Agreement
FAQ	Frequently Asked Questions
FLOSS	Free/Libre Open Source Software
FTP	File Transfer Protocol
GPL	GNU Public Licence
GUI	Graphical User Interface
HTML	Hypertext Markup Language
HTTP	Hypertext Transfer Protocol
IP	Internet Protocol
IRC	Internet Relay Chat
P2	Playstation 2
P3	Playstation 3
P2P	Peer-to-Peer
PSP	Playstation Portable
MPAA	Motion Picture Association of America
RFC	Request for Comments
RIAA	Recording Industry Association of America
SDK	Software Development Kit

SMTP	Simple Mail Transfer Protocol
SNS	Social Networking Site
UGC	User-Generated Content
WLAN	Wireless Local Area Network
XDK	Xbox Development Kit

Appendix B
Glossary

AIBO (Artificial Intelligence roBOt), a robotic toy dog with limited learning capabilities developed by Sony from 1999 to 2006.

AiboSite, an AIBO user community forum.

API (Application Programming Interface), enables a software application to interact with other applications. Many Web 2.0 services provide access to their APIs in order to allow users to employ the platform's data for the creation of new services.

Bastard Pop, also called mash-up music, bootlegs, bootys, or blends, a practice of mixing or meshing different pop songs.

BitTorrent, a P2P file-sharing protocol.

Blogosphere, describes the plurality of weblogs often commenting on current politics, popular media, and actual events. The blogosphere has been recognized as a public sphere with reference to Habermas. It is in fact the equalizing of the editorial common to established media.

Case Modding, describes the appropriation of the case of an electronic consumer good, most often a personal computer, a cell phone or the case of a computer game console.

Delicious (Del.icio.us), a Web 2.0 service to index and share bookmarks of websites <www. delicious.com>.

Demo, audio-visual file, comparable to an animated video. It is compiled in real time and mostly written in assembler code. The name demo goes back to the roots of the demoscene in the software cracker world of the early 1980s, and refers to the tradition of adding animated graphics to cracked software to show off programming skills and send shout-outs to fellow scene members.

Digital Rights Management (DRM), technologies to enforce and facilitate the use of copyrighted content. DRM systems often come bundled with digital commodities such as movies, music, games, or electronic books.

Dreamcast, a game console introduced by SEGA in 1998 and due to market failure discontinued in 2001. An active community kept developing applications for the Dreamcast. In 2006 the console was relaunched (main forum: <www.dreamcast-scene.com>).

Electronic Frontier Foundation, EFF, a non-profit advocacy group engaging in preserving civil rights. The EFF is known for their criticism of the DMCA, software patents, and DRM.

Fan Culture, a term widely used to describe activities of fans and fan communities. Henry Jenkins employed the term for describing media productions by fans.

Flickr, a popular photo sharing and hosting website, and subsidiary of Yahoo <www.flickr.com>

Friend Tech, a Taiwan-based CPU upgrading company. It became recognized for its modification of the Microsoft Xbox as DreamX <www.friendtech.com>.

Hack, with reference to the original understanding of hacker, a creative solution to any technical problem.

Hacker, initially the term for a person with a remarkable interest in problem solving, most often related to technology. Hacker became synonymous for cracker, which is someone who does actually the same, but in bad faith.

Hardmodding, hardmod, term used to describe a modification of an electronic consumer device through manipulating the hardware and replacing the original processor through a modchip. Different from *softmod*.

Homebrew software, describes software produced outside official production channels, often produced within communities for proprietary devices such as the Xbox, Playstation Portable, Nintendo DS, etc. Homebrew software is developed for many electronic consumer goods.

Honeypot, a server operated by contractors of movie and music industry associations for file sharing that is actually aimed at attracting users who are then persecuted for committing copyright infringement. It appears that the organizations providing these honeypots, often violate existing laws themselves.

Internet Relay Chat (IRC), an Internet application for real-time chat communication, either as one-to-one or as group communication.

Lik Sang, a Hong Kong-based company for modchips and accessories for gaming devices operated by Austrian citizen Alex Kampl. It was confronted with a series of lawsuits due to selling modchips and modded game consoles and had eventually to cease business in 2006 <http://liksang.com>.

MechInstaller, a software using an exploit of the game MechAssault (Microsoft Game Studios 2002). By using Mechinstaller, users could softmod their Xbox.

Metadata, or meta-information: information about information. The bibliographical information of a book can be seen as meta-information. In the Web 2.0, metadata are organized in tags, which are machine readable data added to a certain file, describing the contents of the file.

Mod, a modification of a game. The popular first-person-shooter game *Counter-Strike* is a mod of the commercial game *Half Life*.

Modchip, an electronic device for disabling built-in limitations in electronic consumer goods such as game consoles. The need for circumventing vendor limitations led to the emergence of a grey market. Their legal status is ambiguous; in the United States, modchips are prohibited due to the DMCA.

Mozilla, is the name of a foundation for the open-source development of the open-source Mozilla web browser, known as Firefox, and the e-mail client Thunderbird.

Napster, the first peer-to-peer application for sharing files, developed by university student Shawn Fanning in 1999. In 2001 Napster was shut down because of copyright infringement.

Netlabel, similar to a conventional record label, but music distribution takes place on the Internet. It mostly involves electronic music produced by musicians who often are not affiliated with the music industry and who generally distribute their music for free. An overview of the extensive catalogue of music is available at the Netlabel Catalogue

<http://www.netlabels.org>.

News groups, refers to Usenet mailing list accounts. News groups are discussions that can be organized and accessed through e-mail clients.

Open-source software, describes a practice in software development and distribution to provide the application together with the source code, which then can be reviewed and modified by other programmers.

Overclocking, describes manipulating the central processing unit of a computer or a game console for faster performance.

Participation, a term coined to describe the increasing productivity of consumers in weblogs, product modifications, and media productions.

Patch, a software module to change, improve, or revert functions of a software program.

Peer-to-Peer (P2P), describes ad hoc computer networks for file exchange. Peer-to-peer technologies are often used for file sharing. It is in fact a handy method for information retrieval and distribution.

Pirate Bay, a website providing indexing and searching of BitTorrent files.

Playstation 2, is Sony's very successful game console released in 2000 which sold over 120 million units worldwide.

Playstation 3, is the successor of the Playstation 2. It consists of sophisticated hardware and, as opposed to other game consoles, it is partially open source and runs a pre-installed Linux distribution.

Playstation Portable, a hand-held game console, famous for its large screen. The PSP was hacked within 24 hours after its release and developed a large homebrew scene.

Produsage, a term coined by Axel Bruns to describe a blurring of the producer user distinction in cultural production on the World Wide Web and in digital media in general.

Prosumer, a term coined by Alvin Toffler in his 1980 book *The Third Wave*.

Reverse Engineering, revealing technological design through step-by-step analysis of all components and principles.

RFC (Requests for Comments), created by the Internet Engineering Task Force, are available at <http://www.ietf.org/rfc.html>. RFCs represent not only a mode of collaboration but also reveal a certain engineering culture, its social codes, and its socio-political mindset, not to mention how it was implemented in the development of technologies.

Silent Modding, modifying a computer in order to reduce noise as much as possible.

Slashdot, an influential online platform for commenting on technology news and related socio-political aspects <www.slashdot.org>.

SmartXX, a team of modchip producers.

Softmodding, **softmod**, describes the modification of an electronic consumer device through a software application, often through exploiting security gaps in the design of the operating system or the executed software. When using a softmod, vendor limitations can be circumvented without using a modchip.

Software Development Kit (SDK), a collection of tools (either hardware or software or both) for software developers to develop applications for a certain device. Microsoft equipped third-party producers with an SDK for the Xbox.

Sourceforge, an online platform and repository for software developers to organize their work and communicate with their fellow colleagues, to present their project to users and to host the software for downloads. As of August 2010 Sourceforge counted over 240,000 registered projects and 2.6 million registered users <www.sourceforge.net>.

Tags, or **meta tags** are freely chosen keywords assigned by users to different objects stored online. Tags are used to improve information retrieval and navigation on websites.

User, initially used to describe a computer user, but used here to describe any user of software and computer technology. Companies and producers are as much users as the consumers of their productions. Users have to be differentiated according their involvement in power structures, technological skills, invested time, etc.

User-Generated Content (UGC) or **user-created content** (UCC) directly refers to the phenomenon of users producing media texts and describes foremost texts (either written text, photos, videos, or audio files) stored on websites. The Organisation for Economic Co-operation and Development (OECD) defines user-created content as "i) content made publicly available over the Internet, ii) which reflects a 'certain amount of creative effort', and iii) which is 'created outside of professional routines and practices'" (OECD paper, 2007).

Weblog, initially a website on which a user would report (log) websites she encountered while surfing. Weblog describes a website with a user interface for content management and a comment function for readers. Due to the easy-to-use interface these website systems became extremely popular as weblogs.

Wiki, the term originates from the Hawaiian word for fast, and describes a system of HTML documents on the Web that can be easily edited by any user. The most famous example for a wiki is Wikipedia.

WLAN, a wireless local area network refers to a wireless connected computer network.

Xbins, is the name of an ftp server hosting the largest collection of homebrew software for the Microsoft Xbox. To retrieve files from Xbins, users are required to request a one-time user name and password through IRC. The software collection can be browsed via the website <www.xbins.org>.

Xbox, the first Microsoft game console released in 2001. It consists largely of common personal computer components, but was limited to the functionality of a video game console. Despite the limitations, the console was hacked quickly, and a dynamic homebrew scene emerged.

Xbox 360, succeeding the Xbox in 2005 with considerable design changes, implementing many aspects developed in the homebrew scene and integrating the possibility for third-party software development through an integrated development kit aiming at game developers and homebrew scene.

Xbox-Linux-Project, a hacker project aiming at replacing the original operating system through installing Linux on the Xbox. With a Linux operating system the Xbox could be used for many different purposes unintended by the vendor. The project effectively provided the possibility to execute Linux without using a modchip.

Xbox Media Center (XBMC), the most successful homebrew application for the Xbox, turning the console into a media centre for playing music, movies, DVDs, and storing collections of media files. It even made the remote control dispensable that Microsoft required consumers to purchase in order to use the DVD function. The XBMC was awarded the Sourceforge award for Best Multimedia and Best Game Project in 2006 <www.xboxmediacenter.com>.

Xbox Scene, a major online platform for Xbox users <www.xbox-scene.com>.

Xbox Development Kit (XDK), a device for developing licensed software (e.g. games) for the Xbox. Intentionally aimed at official third party developers, the XDK 'leaked' and attracted many a dynamic scene to develop software that, however, was unlicensed, and is labelled homebrew software.

XNA, a software development kit integrated into the retail version of the Xbox 360.

Yahoo Pipes, a mash-up editor, a GUI for connecting different APIs together to create a data stream.

INDEX

BASTARD CULTURE!

Other titles in the MediaMatters series

Bay-Cheng, S., C. Kattenbelt, A. Lavender, R. Nelson (eds), *Mapping Intermediality in Performance*, 2010 (ISBN 978 90 8964 255 4)

Bleeker, M. (ed), *Anatomy Live. Performance and the Operating Theatre*, 2008 (ISBN 978 90 5356 516 2)

Boomen, M. van den, S. Lammes, A. Lehmann, J. Raessens, M.T. Schäfer (eds) *Digital Material. Tracing New Media in Everyday Life and Technology*, 2009 (ISBN 978 90 8964 068 0)

Lauwaert, M., *The Place of Play. Toys and Digital Cultures*, 2009 (ISBN 978 90 8964 080 2)

Sihvonen, T., *Players Unleashed! Modding The Sims and the Culture of Gaming*, 2011 (ISBN 978 90 8964 201 1)